Interpersonal Styles and

Group Development

Interpersonal Styles and Group Development

An Analysis of the Member-Leader Relationship

RICHARD D. MANN

in collaboration with

Graham S. Gibbard

and

John J. Hartman

University of Michigan

John Wiley & Sons, Inc.   New York   London   Sydney

To
Jean, Patricia, and Sheryl

Preface

By what route can we who spend so many of our waking hours in groups come to understand more sensitively what those around us are feeling?

How shall we develop the skills to diagnose why the groups in which we place so much hope often seem to stagnate or go off course?

How shall we act in order to be more effective in realizing the individual and collective potentials of the groups in which we are involved?

The three questions listed above spring from what we assume to be a common sense of bewilderment, frustration, and yet unquenchable optimism about group life. Our efforts in this book derive from just such a mixture of attitudes about groups, and we offer as a partial answer to these and the myriad of other questions an intensive analysis of four rather special but often revealing groups. The four classroom discussion groups we shall explore offer us a chance to look at both the individuals and the groups they create. The world of the group member radiates in several directions: backward in time to the significant and determinative experiences that have shaped his personality; inward to the levels of consciousness from which symbols and metaphors emerge to express unrecognized feelings; and outward to the set of persons, norms, and structures within which the member must maneuver and by which he will be deeply influenced. It is our task to develop an appreciation of how these perspectives can be merged into a composite picture of the member while at the same time seeking to understand how the various members come together to produce a group in action.

The primary focus of this investigation is upon the changing relationship between the members of the groups and their formal leader. Since only a small and often unrepresentative amount of what a member feels toward the leader is expressed directly, we were led to develop a scoring system that captured both the direct and the symbolic expressions of the member's feelings. Throughout the study, in the scoring system and in the interpretation of the results derived from it, we have tried to strike a balance between the rigorous, quantitative tradition of small group observation and the more holistic and naturalistic tradition of psychoanalysis and clinical psychology.

Chapter 1 presents an overview of the conceptual and methodological strategy adopted for this study. The next two chapters outline the kind of self-analytic group being studied and the observation system employed as the core of the research method. Chapter 4 sets up a conceptual framework for the analysis of an individual's performance, and here our emphasis is on the connections between the feelings expressed and the antecedent relationships that seem to be serving as models for the individual's experience. In Chapter 5 we turn to an analysis of the leader's role and to the influence he exerts upon the processes being observed. Chapter 6 treats the development of the group as a whole in terms of the shifting arrays of subgroups that seek to determine the course of the group. Chapter 7 returns to the individual level to explore the career of the group member, and our intent here is to see how the commonly observed member-leader relationships contribute to and are shaped by the development of the group. In the concluding chapter we develop a conceptual scheme for analyzing an individual's feelings and actions in groups.

It is humbling to call to mind the array of individuals who have inspired, encouraged, and assisted one over the years. The longest strands of continuous influence, if traced, would lead back more than a dozen years to my early association with Hugh Cabot, Robert F. Bales, Philip E. Slater, and Arthur S. Couch. It was Hugh Cabot, with his incessant curiosity and incisive questioning, who first showed me how fascinating the study of interpersonal relations might become. My years of working with Freed Bales convinced me that the task was manageable even though the number of paths worth following was nearly infinite; the importance of his generosity and example as a tutor and friend cannot be overstated. It is more difficult to put into words the impact of one's first relationships that include the possibility of personal and intellectual exchange, relationships in which insight and humor are intertwined and the integration of one's career with one's inner self seems more possible than before. I am indebted to Philip Slater and Arthur Couch for far more than their wisdom, although I have benefited greatly from their ideas and skills throughout this study.

My former colleagues on the staff of Social Relations 120 at Harvard who have included, in addition to Philip Slater and Freed Bales, Theodore Mills, Charles Whitlock, David Shapiro, Norman Zinberg, Walter Afield, Dexter Dunphy, and Stanley Milgram, have never failed to be a source of new perspectives, criticisms, and much appreciated support in carrying out this research. The one research assistant whose contribution to the scoring and the understanding of these data deserves my special appreciation is Mrs. Maxine Bernstein; but for the factor of geography she would have joined the three of us in preparing the final manuscript. William Joughin and Richard Cabot helped us over the immense task of processing the data by writing a whole series of programs for the IBM 7090 which even we could operate, and Walter Goldfrank, Anthony Tiano, and Charles Langley played an important role in the early stages of coming to grips with this material. More recently, we have been ably assisted by Douglas McClennen, Honor McClellan, and Barbara Ringwald as we moved toward the final analysis of the results and the groups from which they were obtained. The thoughtful criticisms of Leland Bradford, Charles Seashore, Walter Goldfrank, and Philip Slater were very helpful as we moved closer to a last draft, and Audrey Warren and Margaret Rahn deserve great credit for preparing the final manuscript under difficult conditions.

I have been most fortunate to have worked under two chairmen, Robert S. White and Wilbert J. McKeachie, whose encouragement and understanding of the latitude needed to strike out in new directions has been crucial to this effort. Their role in creating the general climate for work and in augmenting the desire of those around them to accomplish something of value has been an important one.

This study has been supported by the National Institute of Mental Health, the National Science Foundation, the Laboratory of Social Relations at Harvard, and an Office of Education grant under the direction of John E. Milholland, Wilbert J. McKeachie, and Robert L. Isaacson, but the crucial support in the first year of the study came from the Social Science Research Council. The cordiality and patience of Elbridge Sibley are hereby acknowledged with gratitude.

I wish to thank the students of Social Relations 120; the fruits of their energy and their creativity are much in evidence throughout this book, and we hope that our descriptions and interpretations do justice to the events in which they invested so much. Fanlly, permit me to express my gratitude to my wife, Jean, for helping to sustain the vision and for sharing with me the rigors and the rewards of a life that combines commitment, reflection, and a belief in the capacity to grow.

Richard D. Mann

Ann Arbor, 1966

Contents

Chapter 1

Introduction

There are two equally compelling ways to introduce the content of this book to the reader: one way starts at the end of the journey and permits us the pleasant fantasy that we knew all along where we were headed and what questions we could hope to answer. It can now be stated that we shall have something to say about individuals, about how they act, learn, and change in a group setting, as well as something to say about groups, the role of the leader, and the importance of group norms. It can also be stated that our concern with growth and development is accompanied by an equal concern with the myriad impediments to growth and with instances of personal and collective inability to change.

But it was not always thus. In the beginning, there was "the group," the course known to its local friends and detractors alike as "Soc Rel 120." This course, whose formal title is Social Relations 120: Analysis of Interpersonal Behavior, and whose origins are traceable to the case method of teaching developed at the Harvard Business School, is designed to teach students something about interpersonal relations and about the difficult process of making adequate inferences from the events of everyday life. To this end, the students are encouraged to consider not only assigned readings and cases as relevant material for the course, but also to view the group itself as its own primary case. The groups meet over an extended period of time, with twenty or so members per group, and they become engaged in the dual processes of creating and analyzing the data of human interaction. The result of this process is a group in which the degree of personal involvement, the range of topics discussed, and the variety of interpersonal styles exhibited are far greater than in the usual classroom.

At various times the authors of this book have been students in this course, have sat to one side and observed the groups, and have played

1

the role of group leader in these or similar groups. As group members we were intrigued and involved, but often unclear about the import of those inner and interpersonal experiences that unfolded over time; as observers, our occasional moments of illumination seemed more than counterbalanced by our chronic sense of being overwhelmed by the complexity of what was going on in the group; and, as group leaders, we operated under the additional pressure to respond effectively to events whose meaning seemed constantly to be in flux, if not totally beyond our immediate grasp. In short, all three experiences served not only to begin the process of accumulating a sense of perspective on group phenomena but, even more acutely, to heighten the frustration of being so close to meaningful events and yet so far from understanding them.

Looked at in terms of its origins, this study is a narrative account of three naturalists who found themselves immersed in a torrent of impressions, reactions, and hunches. Some naturalists solve this problem in one way and some in another. The specific heritage that determined much of our effort is the tradition of systematic observation of group phenomena and, specifically, the work of Robert F. Bales (1950). Many people seem to be distracted by the fact that Bales' work resulted in a tidy and widely used category system, and they tend to overlook the distance that was traveled in reaching that point. A more relevant model for this study than the final product of Bales' work was the set of decisions he made while sitting in the back of an Alchoholics Anonymous meeting, trying to devise some means of recording the complexity of that group's interaction process. Although we have developed, not surprisingly, a certain involvement in the concepts and propositions that occupy our thinking toward the end of this study, we would be more than satisfied if this book could serve as one model for the many teachers, healers, and other "front-line" professionals who would like to bring some order out of the rich but chaotic data with which they grapple daily.

It would be possible to overstate the extent to which the naturalist's effort to describe events and feelings is a discrete process. The task of describing a series of events does not end abruptly when one moves on to analysis and interpretation. Rather, it is a process that shapes subsequent analysis no less than the emergent analysis molds the forms that come to be useful in apprehending the world. Thus quite early in this study our interest in the feelings of the individual member and in his capacity to grow influenced increasingly the kinds of description that seemed appropriate. In fact, it might be more appropriate to say that our initial concern was not with learning and change but with their opposites, i.e., the endless set of detours, irrelevancies, blocks, and other eruptions that often seem far more visible than any sign of individual progress in groups. We were gradually forced to concede that change of a rather desirable sort seemed to accompany, even to be caused by, this interpersonal carnival. Not only were individuals learning something, but the group as a whole seemed to move forward over time, to be capable of greater insight and complexity of thought. The observational framework slowly took a form that some of our colleagues have deemed excessively oriented toward the pathological. Undoubtedly this was the result of quite a long period during which the mature, thoughtful, or brilliant comment seemed to be a member of a rare and residual category. Of far greater interest and diversity were the ways individuals had of saying that they would not or could not learn and change. Perhaps someday we shall find a group in which so much of the time is devoted to an orderly ascent to higher levels of knowledge or awareness that the balance of our attention will shift. For the present, our interest must span not only the vitally important issues of learning but the additional issues raised by the intrapsychic and interpersonal obstacles that deflect and subvert the learning process.

A second way to structure this investigation was to limit ourselves to less than the total set of interrelationships which develop in these groups. The primary focus of this book is upon the relationship between the member of the group and its leader. As in similar groups, the major agent for change, at least initially, is the group leader. It is usually he who has called the group together or permitted members to enroll in its ranks, and it is he who is the carrier of the subcultural values that legitimize the kind of group it sets out to be. The leader is by no means central to all the changes that occur in such groups, but the member-leader relationship does appear to be at least one very important context in which the group member tests the nature of the change process. From the leader's point of view, and this is not irrelevant to understanding the inception of this study itself, it is of particular importance to understand his developing relationship with each member of the group. Just as the study of growth must inevitably lead us to the study of stagnation and resistance, the study of the member-leader relationship must lead us in many directions. We must be prepared to recognize that the leader is hardly an unqualified blessing for the members of the group, and the members often seem to grow despite the leader's blunders and irrelevancies. Lest this focus upon the member-leader relationship seem excessively narrow, it should be pointed out that we plan to examine all of a member's behavior with an eye to its relevance for his relationship with the leader, not simply those moments of direct contact between the member and the leader.

It is our contention that all the underlying aspects of a group are simultaneously active, although in varying degrees. The extent to which the member's feelings about the leader determine his actions is not postulated, a priori, to be greater than other issues, such as striving for individual dominance or intimacy within the group. All that is maintained here is that each act can be examined for its possible relevance to the member-leader relationship, and from this examination may come some sense of how this relationship develops and how it bears upon the central issue of personal growth.

Up to this point it has been convenient to speak of the member-leader relationship, thus emphasizing the individual group member and his unique efforts to grow in this context. Although much of this study is devoted to the analysis of the individual group member's feelings, needs, and interpersonal strategies, we cannot overlook the group context in which the individual functions. Any analysis of individual growth in this setting must deal with not only the individual member's own striving to learn and the group leader's pressures for change, but it must recognize as well the important part that is played by the emergence of group norms. Some of these norms convey the gradually sharpening sense of how progress shall be defined in this group. Still others legitimize and encourage the individual's private efforts to grow. But there are group norms, just as there are aspects of an individual's personality, that impede group development and justify this impediment in the name of some other shared value. The overall effect of the group upon individual growth is certainly a mixed one. One need only think of the pressures upon an individual to behave consistently or to "stay in role" to recognize the complexity of the final picture. In studying the emergent group norms, the construction of commonly recognized roles, and the widespread sharing of affective states we will inquire into the two-way process by which the individual contributes to the group and is at the same time influenced by it.

The one word which, in an admittedly cryptic manner, best summarizes our concern in this study is "work." It is an interesting phenomenon in itself that such a term should gain currency among so many group leaders, whether their setting be group therapy, sensitivity training groups, or the classroom. In groups of these kinds, where many of the usual pressures to produce at a maximum rate of efficiency are removed, it is interesting that this term so clearly connotes the opposite of self-indulgence. In groups where the focus of attention turns inward upon the group itself, both the members and the leader of the group seem to feel some need to indicate that their activity has a purpose and is not "merely for enjoyment." On the contrary, the frequent invocation of such words as "hard," "rough," and "productive" to describe a group meeting suggests not only the underlying seriousness of the situation but also the need to bring into this situation the legitimacy usually associated with "the real world outside."

Whatever the reason the members and leaders of these groups may have for their constant use of work metaphors, our choice of this term is guided, in addition, by the pleasure it gives to connect this study with the masterful observations of W. R. Bion (1961). His way of viewing the "work group" conveys the importance, in groups such as these, of the goals of rationality, progress, and cooperation without making them sound as though they were taken from the *Boy Scout Handbook*. And yet many who read Bion seem to notice only his analysis of the obstacles to individual growth and group development, thus creating a one-sided image of him as someone content to reflect endlessly on the regressive aspects of group life. We will be content if, in the end, our use of the term "work" clarifies Bion's complex and rather utopian view of the goal of learning from group experience.

Thus far, we have discussed the substantive interests which led us part way out of the murky confusion known well to members, observers, and leaders of these groups. But one aspect of this study, its use of systematic observation techniques, stems directly from several aspects of the confusion which need to be described more fully. Consider the plight of the group leader, the observer, or the member as he sits in the middle of these groups trying to understand what is going on. Certainly one element of his experience is his inability to grasp the significance of events. But another element in his distractability, as each new day or each new minute compels him to think about one aspect of the group after another. Yesterday's insights, however brilliant and accurate they may have been, often have a way of seeming irrelevant on the new day. In large measure, this may be traced to a more fundamental problem, the seeming incomparability of two events, two groups, or two individual members. Mere recognition that people or events are different, without the ability to specify at least some of the dimensions along which these differences are revealed, is not sufficient.

How can one help the observer to become less distractable without condemning him to a worse fate, the distortion and boredom that accompany an excessively mechanical or superficial approach? The option chosen for this study is basically a scheme for recording and tabulating the observer's inferences about what the members are feeling toward the leader. Each single inference is highly clinical in nature, in Meehl's (1954) sense of that term, with one important difference. The observer must record his inference within a structured set of categories. While it is true that the use of a consistent category system makes possible and even essential the statistical techniques with which this study abounds, it would be wrong to overlook the continuity between the clinical approach and the research methods employed in this study.

It is always a matter of strategy to decide how great the gap shall be between the research methodology and the level of inference one wishes to employ in summarizing and conceptualizing the results obtained. In the field of small group observation, the work of Elliot Chapple (1949) defines one end of a continuum along which the diverse scoring systems may be arrayed. Although his observational technique consisted simply of recording the fact that a man was speaking or silent, from the patterns of interruptions and activity he derived a whole panorama of subtle and suggestive inferences. Mills' (1964) sign process analysis might come next on the continuum, followed by Bales' (1950) interaction process analysis, Leary's (1957) circle technique, and, finally, the member-to-leader scoring system employed in this research. Near the opposite end of the continuum from Chapple would be Slater's (1966) research technique, the heart of which is the extensive recording of observations and inferences by the participant observer (the leader himself) after each group session. We justify our research strategy of placing the observational categories close to the inferences and concepts which we intend to utilize in our thinking about these groups in the following manner. We were aiming for a category system that would have satisfactory reliability, as any such system must, but one that would also speak the language of the teacher, the clinician, and the untrained member or observer of these groups. We wanted a category system that connected us directly with the clinical and theoretical literature on group process. If we had to lean in any direction, we preferred to have our categories correspond to the inferences that would be embedded in our final analysis rather than to settle for categories, however reliably they might be employed, whose connection with our final version of what we had found would be tenuous at best.

It may be that progress in such areas of study as interpersonal behavior has been impeded by a pernicious dichotomy, usually referred to as the clinical versus the statistical approach. Our experience in this study suggests that we could not have done without either approach.

The pitfalls of the clinical approach are well known, perhaps too well known. Every beginning researcher can reel off, in properly disapproving tones, such issues as low interjudge agreement, personal distortion, self-fulfilling predictions, and many more. Obviously these are issues which must be faced by anyone employing the clinical approach. But what about the quantitative approach? Perhaps the most serious charge that can be leveled against the practitioners of this style of research is that too often they simply do not know their data. Between them and the real events which they study they interpose various measures and scores which do not, and cannot in our present stage of development in this field, provide a satisfactory substitute for what the human observer can see. Frequently the research techniques which were developed as an aid to the observer absorb more and more of the observer's attention. And in the end one finds some researchers developing a mystique which implies that it is better, after all, that they have not developed that intimate familiarity with their data which many of them formerly had.

Ask a group therapist, a trainer, or a teacher what use he can make of the voluminous outpouring of empirical research on small groups. The unhappy fact is that many, if not most, of the potential consumers of such work feel that such research is constantly asking the wrong questions in the wrong ways and that it is at best irrelevant and at worst inaccurate and misleading. Just as any beginning teacher is reassured by the maxim that students always complain, so many researchers are reassured by the maxim that clinicians are always ungrateful. But we are not reassured in this way, perhaps because this research germinated out of the frustration we felt as clinicians in trying to understand the group processes in which we were immersed.

We are arguing that without a combination of clinical and quantitative techniques one loses too much. Without the clinical, one loses the capacity to test the meaningfulness of one's findings by simply thinking about what they purport to describe. The researcher who puts his group inside a black box and depends solely on the droppings and jottings that emerge from one end of the box is trapped by his own technique, although his free associations about what these jottings might mean are often an interesting reflection of the human wisdom he has already accumulated. Without the quantitative, there are too few surprises. It really does happen that the data sometimes force the researcher to ask the new question, to revise the old conceptualization, and, in short, to enter into a creative dialogue with his data prepared to be disproved and challenged.

Throughout this book we shall lean heavily upon the systematic observation system and upon the quantified statements about individuals and groups that this system yields. But in the beginning, at the moment when the observer recorded his inference, he was engaged in a process of clinical inference. Thirty thousand inferences later, we were in desperate need of some kind of statistical assistance. The process is a circular one in which the computer helps us summarize what we have found; we look at the results to see if they make sense; and often we are forced to ask the computer for more concise summaries or more sensitive descriptive statistics. As we see it, the quantitative summaries serve as arrows, pointing us in the right direction but providing only part of the final answer. Back from the computer comes word that these two people are polar opposites or that at this point in time the group shifted gears. These reports indicate some of the dimensions along which we might conceptualize such differences or group developments. But this approach can carry us only so far, and we must return to the transcripts and tape recordings, even to our memories and impressions to fill in the rest of the picture. The interplay of quantitative techniques and intensive clinical analysis seems to us to avoid many of the pitfalls which either approach alone contains, but only time will tell whether we have managed to ask some of the right questions and to provide a first approximation to some of the useful answers.

In Chapter 2 the reader is introduced to the groups under study first by a review of the diverse expectations which the leaders and members bring to the situations and then by a verbatim transcript of one session. At the end of the chapter we consider the similarity between the Harvard groups and other groups to which the results of this study might be applied.

Chapter 2

Soc Rel 120

This study examines four classroom groups conducted under the auspices of the Harvard Summer School in the years 1961–1963. For some of the students the initial point of contact with the course was the catalog description of Social Relations 120e: Analysis of Interpersonal Behavior. (Social Relations is the department that houses sociology and parts of psychology and anthropology at Harvard.) For others who enrolled in the course, especially if they attended Harvard or Radcliffe during the regular academic year, it was already "Soc Rel 120." For these students, it was not the course goals as found in the catalog description ("to improve the student's ability to observe, analyze, and understand behavior in interpersonal relations") that set this course apart from all others, but rather the unique structure and content of the classroom discussions. A perceptive student from some other college might have noticed something unusual about one sentence in the catalog description: "Topics for discussion include events in the group itself, readings, and cases." To discuss the events taking place in one's own group is not the usual practice in a college course. What is this "Soc Rel 120?" The answer to this question has many aspects, and yet little of what follows in this book will make much sense if we cannot be clear about the nature of the course, its group leaders and members, its usual mode of passing the time allotted to it, and its structural givens.

Soc Rel 120 is a course which attempts to teach the students about interpersonal relations not solely through readings, and never through formal lectures, but by assembling 20 to 30 students into a self-analytic group. The most general way to state the teaching strategy involved is that there is a heavy emphasis in this course upon case analysis. Some of the cases are mimeographed vignettes handed out to the students, but the major "case" for the group is the group itself, its individual members, the relations that develop among pairs or factions of the members, the developing relationship with the leader, and any other aspect of the group which seems relevant at the time. Soc Rel 120 is a close cousin of the other self-analytic groups found in the group therapy and sensitivity-training traditions. However, these are regular academic courses, with requirements, grades, and credit, and thus they are also related to the more conventional classroom discussion groups found in any college environment.

What goes on in such groups? What might a new member expect on the basis of the catalog description and the scuttlebutt around the college community? Former students in Soc Rel 120 resemble the members of most self-analytic groups in their tendency to be mysterious and retentive about what goes on, to be tantalizing about the "experience," then to retreat and declare that the uninitiated simply cannot grasp its essence without "getting into one" itself. Thus it is doubtful that any of the individuals who entered these groups had a very clear idea of what to expect, except that some were not unprepared for the minimal amount of direction provided by the leader. But we intend to do a better job for our readers. It is very much in our interest to convey the richness and complexity of the interactions we propose to analyze. These are not ordinary classroom discussions, and many of the interpretations about what the group members are feeling, and why, will seem utterly bizarre unless the reader understands how heterogeneous and how intense the members' reactions can become. Perhaps we can serve our purpose best by providing the reader with a brief glimpse of what transpires in these groups. A full transcript of one session from one of the four groups under study, while it is less than one percent of the raw data on which the study is based, may help to define what sort of groups these are. We have chosen a session midway through the history of one group, and we have chosen it because the various facets of member-leader relations may be seen rather clearly. There are, in each group, sessions which are more dramatic or more intensely focused on one issue, but we are impressed with the range of feelings and behavioral styles represented here.

Aside from the not immediately obvious fact that Alvin Breeley is an Episcopal minister, in clerical dress, little need be done to fill in the background events in this group. Suffice it to say that the group had only recently gone through a period of sustained and direct attack upon the leader and upon Harry, a group member many felt to be too scornful of them and too closely identified with the leader. Here, then, is the transcript of session fourteen from group one.

Harry: It occurred to me yesterday that a good point of departure would be to talk about some of the people that seem to feel especially threatened by the discussion and would rather not speak, even though they have something to say. To give an example, yesterday [during the discussion of a case] Mr. Breeley got started and in the middle of saying something said, "Oh, now, I better not say it," and everyone said, "Please, come on, say it, say it, say it." He didn't seem to want to, and I think it might be interesting to get out what's underneath the suppression of thought.

Alvin Breeley: I think yesterday, Harold [Harry], that one reason I didn't say anything about this—there were several reasons. One was that I hadn't read the case (laughter), and I didn't feel at all called upon to comment, and the second thing was that after I did more or less look over this case, I felt that it would be something where anything that I said would perhaps prejudice people, or I thought it was something that you would probably expect me to speak out on, so to speak. [The case involved a sexual relationship between two young adults.] I felt that probably it might inhibit the discussion.

Harry: What feelings do we have about you that would make us inhibited by anything you might say?

Alvin: You mean particularly related to this case or just generally?

Harry: This case *and* generally.

Alvin: Well, I think it's been pretty obvious that there are two different types of authority that are more or less represented. One is the authority of the professor, and that was particularly verbalized when Frank said this about the grades. It's more or less come up all the way through. And also there is the clergy of the church representing another factor of authority, and I think in all these things that that comes into it. It seems like we've been pretty much authority centered.

Frank: We have an authority [in this group] that stands for *no* authority.

Alvin: Yes.

Harry (to Alvin): You are not here in a position as a clergyman is with his troops.

Alvin: His flock, you mean.

Harry: I don't think any of us look at you as a particularly authoritarian person who is trying to guide us or influence us in any particular way. I was really interested in what your feelings were, being reduced to peer status and not being able to dictate or have the leading role in having your communications accepted.

Alvin: I haven't felt any particular inhibition about speaking about anything. I have more or less come here as in the peer situation, knowing that in a way, in a very real way, a clergyman never completely divorces himself from his position, and you have kind of said that you *can* do so, so to speak. In other words, here I'm not a clergyman in maybe your eyes or someone else's eyes, but actually in my own eyes I'm always a clergyman. And though I don't exert the same type of influence here, at least consciously, that I do in a leadership role, as I do in my parish or in my student work, I'm not really . . . here I'm not deordained or anything.

Harry: Are you afraid of assuming a leadership role here?

Alvin: I'm not exactly afraid, no. I don't think I am. In fact, it doesn't particularly threaten me to assume a kind of leadership role.

Janice (to Alvin): You and I have talked about this outside the room, and we have talked about the fact that there is a possibility of somehow disassociating yourself from your calling or profession. Underneath the clergyman raiment, there's an Alvin, you know, who was a little kid and came from a family, and had. . . . Why are you reversing your position now? Really, I thought we kind of agreed about this.

Alvin: You mean in not becoming—in not being a leader in this?

Janice: Yeah, or in—no, in feeling that you can't shed the clergical aspects of your life, that you can't react just as Alvin the man or Alvin the person.

Alvin: You know, I think I have pretty much done this in most of the discussions. I think yesterday was the only time that I didn't, and there I was distinctly handicapped by not having read the case. But there is a certain defensiveness which I do feel in things like this and it really pervades many reactions. I feel that if I make a pronouncement or a statement about this, if I just make a statement as myself, it would be interpreted as the voice of the church or the voice of the Episcopal church. I feel—in that way I am inhibited in this situation to be me. Does that answer your question?

Gino: I don't really think that's true in a way. I think that one person can feel more or less when another is speaking as a representative and when as himself. I know I can. When you are talking of the church, your voice raises as though you were expecting some response. And when talking of yourself, your voice does not expect a response, it just reports and makes a statement. I don't know whether you noticed that.

Marie: You also tend to repeat things when you are talking about the church and say them over and over again as if you expect us to question them and once—

Alvin: I have a reason to expect this (laughter). Frequently, the church is put on the spot and it does become very defensive. I guess this is a way of coming out of it.

Marie: I got you kind of mad the day I was shouting, and I remember that the very next remark you made was as if it came from you, not from your church.

Alvin: What was this remark?

Marie: I've forgotten what it was, but—I know what you said. You said, 'Well, I too have had doubts about whether our discussions are relevant at all,' and you said it as if you really meant it, as if it were you.

Alvin: Being a little bit introspective here—and I have felt that maybe I completely deceive myself—but I have felt that I have been pretty much a part of the group. In other words, not just retiring from the group or sitting in judgment of the group. I haven't felt that I've done this—and maybe I have.

Marie: No, I think you are part of the group, but I think when you talk about things that are relatively impersonal to us, such as your missionary work [in your home city], this has been very praiseworthy, but it doesn't have anything to do with this situation here. That tends to make me rather uncomfortable. But when you speak of what you really think, such as that time, I think that—

Frank (to Marie): I don't see—I don't understand how something about a person that's in here does or does not have anything to do with the situation.

Alvin: Yes, I think that the reason that I said that, and I'm sorry that I did bore people with that—I had the feeling from Harold one day that I had bored him with that, and he had the feeling that I was a very fixed person, which he said, indicating to me, maybe his terminology was different, indicating to me that I was more or less narrow in this little rut, that all I could do is Latin American work, and actually my work has included many other fields of human behavior, such as alcoholism and many other things.

Marie: Well, yes. I don't think you are narrow. It's just that when you were talking about that, that was at the time when our discussions were about society, and it didn't have anything to do with *you* reacting to them, really. You were sort of describing what they did, and you didn't tell us a thing about you, and there is a difference.

Alvin: Well, I think at that point that I was rather unacquainted with this group, and—I didn't want to be tiresome about it, but the reason that I did bring that in several times is because I think about it very much—I knowing the situation and you not—that's where I didn't take into consideration that you were not familiar with this— I see human relations in a very real way and to me it is.

Marie: Oh, I have no doubt you do. You just wouldn't express it in terms of *you*.

Gino: One thing that bothers me. You're constantly bothered by the fact that you may bore us. I think you're pretty interesting all the time, and the most boring thing is your saying that you might be boring. This is true when you just went along and said anything you wanted to. I think it's pretty interesting.

Frank: I think one thing at this point. One person said to me that when he was in this classroom he felt like he was in a school of barracudas, and I noticed this person has only said one or two things since this class started, and maybe this has some significance for why people act the way they do, why some people in the class aren't saying anything.

Marie: But you notice there's a trend to cooperation and helping one another. Yesterday I had the feeling that the reason people didn't make long speeches by themselves was, as they had been doing, it was more or less a contribution from one then from the other and building on that, which I thought was very praiseworthy, and the reason for it was that it would have been impossible to give a long speech, because it would have been—it was too threatening, I think, because you would reveal your own condition and that's not the thing to do, and so I was rather pleased at the way everyone felt.

Bob: But, as you're saying, you think they took this attitude because they were threatened?

Marie: Well, what, what, so what about being threatened? I don't think it's wise or possible to be expected that anyone should not be somewhat threatened by our discussions.

Frank: Well, I think everyone in here is threatened by something. If there is a person included here who is not threatened about something, I'd really like to see them.

Kamala: I'm not.

Frank: You're not threatened by anything?

Kamala: No.

Frank: I can't believe that. I think that you are threatened, but you don't realize it (laughter).

Kamala: Well, if you believe in the theory of the Ucs [unconscious]. I'm not convinced yet.

Janice: Are you suggesting, Marie, the kind of thing that was discussed in the article on anxiety caused in the group—the kind of manic denial, you know, 'Gee aren't we having fun, we're great people. Look how we can talk about our sex attitudes.'?

Marie: Well no, I thought that we weren't really. I think maybe we could have gotten there if we had tried a little harder, because we were *pretending* to be great. But, at the same time, I thought that we were saying a couple of worthwhile things.

Janice: There is a funny combination in that. Somehow, I had the feeling, gosh, everything is so intellectual. We really must not be doing what we ought to be doing and yet it seems so good.

Godfrey: We never got around to *one* point. Someone's always skirting the issue and going back to something else. I think it's lack of logic (laughter). I speak collectively. And we never do think how we're going to attack a person. We sort of crash in and say 'Wasn't such and such in the case interesting?' and then we jump off somewhere else. We never say, 'Well, let's see what was one person's attitude, what was the next person's attitude.' We never have any attack, and I think probably as a result we are suffering.

Dr. Allen: Perhaps we have as hard a time integrating the ideas about a case as we do integrating the people who have said them.

Harry: But, I think that, especially since we just got these paper topics and we are made aware of the fact that we all have to write papers, and they are going to be graded by you, everybody kind of regressed to the way things were going in the very beginning of the course when we talked pretty intellectually and *non sequitur* about topics that really we pretended we were interested in, but really weren't quite relevant to what was going on in the room. Everybody got the same birthday present, and I think the effect of the paper topics, the paper assignment, and the fact that people have to think about what they write in their papers, as well as the fact that everybody has to do the same thing, is an inhibitory force. It really interested me that the paper assignments were handed out so sloppily and that Dr. Allen didn't remember to hand them out for two days and tried to catch people as they went out the door and say, 'You forgot my gift.' I think that it's kind of indicative that to some extent he's been pushed out of things and that he's not quite, you know, ready to accept this.

Janice: Why place the emphasis on his accepting us? What you mean is you are not quite ready to accept him.

Gino: I think you make a very good statement.

Janice: Do you think you meant what you said?

Harry: Yes.

Janice: Because I don't know. You're talking in generalizations about the way everybody felt, and I don't think I felt that way. I really don't think that the assignment of the paper was at all on my mind. Because I think I got this thing on Thursday or Friday of last week, and I don't think that I ever thought in terms of whether Dr. Allen was accepting me or I was accepting him or not.

Harry: I'm not talking about individually. I'm talking about him and and his group. Why do you suppose it was that he forgot to hand out the paper assignment sheet?

Janice: Maybe he didn't forget. You know, I felt very seriously—

Bob: I would say that the reason, perhaps, that he forgot to hand out the papers is because he might feel a little bit paranoid about it. Frankly.

Kamala: Well, that was the day he was under attack, if I remember correctly (laughter).

Bob: Well, not only that, but he also showed a great deal of how he felt last Friday, I believe it was.

Alvin: I always react when people speak of Dr. Allen's group. To me that takes away the dignity which each of us has as a person, to be classified as *his* group. I react the same way, in fact, a little bit to church practice when you say some clergyman's church. To me, that is really an insult to the dignity of the individuals who make up the church.

Gino: If you carry that to an extreme, when you say 'God's people,' isn't that an insult too?

Alvin: No (laughter). I don't concede that point at all. I think it's an entirely different thing.

Janice: It's kind of interesting, Harold, that during the first couple of weeks of the group you consistently asserted your right as an in-dividual and, I assume therefore, the rights of everyone else in the group to be individuals, and now you're trying to put everybody into a collective mass, as the little sheep and the shepherds or something, and that seems terribly inconsistent with what you were thinking or attempting to do at the beginning of the group. I wonder why you've changed.

Harry: I don't think there has been any change along those lines. I think everybody should speak up, but I think people seem to be feeling the influence of the paper. We had kind of forgotten, a little bit, that this was a teacher-student thing. Then, when the paper topics came out, it seemed to be right at that time—a cohesiveness and a kind of mutual act of sorrow that was very interesting, and I don't see any contradiction in speaking of a group as a group and saying that an individual should assert his individuality.

Janice: But isn't it possible that each individual has an entirely different set of reactions to something like being handed a paper assignment?

Harry: That is possible. In which case all you can assume is that your feelings are valid for you. I'm not talking about my feelings.

Janice: Well, what *are* your feelings?

Harry: *My* feelings?

Janice: About getting the assignment.

Harry: I was very interested to see what it would be because I was hoping that I'd be able to use a paper written for another course, but it didn't work out.

Kamala: What led to the conclusion that it seems the group feels this way? What was the index that indicated it to you?

Harry: It would be better to say that the group acted this way, and I was looking—

Kamala: What was the indication of the actions?

Harry: The lack of infighting in the last couple of days.

Kamala: The lack of infighting.

Janice: It seems to me as the father becomes more apparent, the infighting would become more apparent because the sibling relationship would become more apparent and so we would each vie for that precious 'A' rather than to . . .

Harry: That's what we are doing in making little stabs in the dark about what we thought was happening in the case.

Janice: Really?

Frank: Whaddaya mean, really? You have to believe what he says?

Janice: No.

Bob (to Harry): How did the word 'sloppy' come into that?

Harry: The word sloppy?

Bob: Yes, the word sloppy that you used. It seems like a pretty personal decision on your part.

Harry: Well, most teachers pass out paper assignments in a rather orderly fashion.

Marie: It *was* sloppy.

Harry: They say, take one and pass the rest, and here this guy has been teaching for three or four years and he forgets to pass out.

Janice: Most teachers don't sit with their feet on the desk. I think that we've learned that Dr. Allen in this course isn't acting like most teachers.

Harry: I don't think he did it intentionally either. I think that it would be interesting to try to see what was going on in the group, in the discussion, that held his interest so much that he didn't want to perform this most routine function as in menstruating.

Janice: Did you forget to hand them out?

Dr. Allen: It wasn't intentional.

Janice: You mean twice in a row you forgot?

Dr. Allen: Twice in a row.

Janice: What's *your* relation to the group (laughter)?

Dr. Allen: (Groan)

Alvin: I had the same feeling that Janice has just been talking about in connection with Harold and his—the way he kind of sums things up and seems to speak for the group and I have felt this contradiction, too. My impression of you, Harold, is that you are, at least at first it was, that you almost epitomize liberty of thought and action, and whether this is just kind of something which you have just gotten across in this particular situation, I'm not sure, but that you kind of epitomize this complete freedom, almost libertinism, etc., and then I get the same feeling here, sometimes, I think I said this one time, that you had mentioned something about something Dr. Allen had done, and you kind of spoke for the whole group about something he had said, and I hadn't even heard what he had said, which I hadn't, *really*. There was some confusion or something out here, and I had the same feeling that you are a little bit authoritarian and inclined to just more or less lump everybody here into a kind of mass and speak for them, when actually your personality seems to be in many other ways, just exactly the opposite of that. You react against any kind of authority or any kind of organizational structure.

Kamala: I think everybody does.

Harry: I try to be relevant to what happens in the room here, and I try to assess or just start an investigation of a certain incident, and all of a sudden you say that I'm speaking for the group. I make it quite clear that I haven't the slightest idea what's going on in most of the heads around here, and sometimes I think it's pretty amusing what's going on in my own. If you remember, the other time was near the very end of class, and you said you were going to talk about the reading tomorrow, and we didn't talk about the reading the next day at all. I wasn't—was I speaking for the group when I said we hadn't talked about the reading?

Alvin: No, not in that type of comment. But on several occasions I have felt that way myself, that you just kind of roll up the group and speak for them.

Gino: The reason he does that—maybe I'm commenting in the dark

—is that he takes chances and brings about prophecies, whereas other people don't want to do so, and you're bound to be wrong sometimes.
Alvin: I think you're right, and I was just going to say—to add to my comments there—that I think Harold has been very constructive in the group in his insight and in the way he has tried to drop things into a discussion. I think that has been his good contribution, and, as I said before, I think there have been certainly many negative contributions, which all of us make, but I think that has been his contribution up to this point.
Harry: Here you go. You're trying to put everybody on an equal plane in a much more overt way, saying that there are good contributions and there are bad contributions, which everybody makes, and there are some people who make no contributions—I don't see how you can lump them together, people who make good contributions and bad contributions.
Alvin: But I think I qualify that a little bit by saying, 'I think.'
Dave: It's more of a value judgment on his part.
Alvin: I beg your pardon.
Dave: I think there's more value judgment on your part than his grouping together of all the people here.
Janice: I think, in a sense—I may be wrong, Harold,—but I think, in a sense, that what you're dealing with smacks to me of applying the reading, or a theory behind the reading, directly to what's happening in the group. Now theoretically this should work. In other words, in this paper on anxiety depression [depressive anxiety] there was the discussion about the authority position of the leader of the group becoming more apparent because he had to hand out assignments.
Harry: I haven't read it.
Janice: Yes he did, because he made mention of it the other day.
Harry: The one in the second week's reading or the first week's reading? I haven't read it.
Janice: Where did you get the notes?
Harry: I don't have notes from that. I was talking about another article that was later on in the reading. And I often thought, wouldn't it be nice if we could see if we could apply some of the theoretical things and I was having a very hard time although there seem to be some very interesting parallels in some of the reading to what's happening here. There hasn't been anything really to hang your hat on as far as a coherent theory that would explain everything that is going on in here.
Janice: But still I know in my case the intellectual things that I'm

learning are way ahead of the emotional experience I'm going through, so that what you say may be quite right, and it's possible that emotionally I can't accept this point. This may be what sometimes hangs it up.

Bob: It may also be the reason why we can't discuss the reading, even though it's been told to us that we *should* discuss the reading. But the group as a whole has not arrived at a state where we could really benefit from this discussion. Too many more feelings within the group have to be worked through before it can be discussed.

Dr. Allen: I have the feeling that, by your discussion of Alvin and also our discussion of Harold, what has happened is that two aspects of my position have been split apart and resentment toward each has been expressed in a displaced way. On the one hand, I represent an institution in much the same way that Alvin does, Harvard College, and I have certain hidden powers. Not the thunderbolt of God perhaps, but the thunderbolt of the grade sheet, and a great deal of concern was shown about whether or not the person with the thunderbolt should be an equal or should not be an equal or whether he should set himself apart or not set himself apart. Some of the resentment which was expressed toward Alvin I really think was a part—had resonance with—some of the resentment toward the formal status position which I hold, and the way I use it. But another part of my position really comes out in the attack on Harold, namely that I have a tendency, perhaps, to be mysterious or mystical or nondifferentiating in the interpretation I might make of what's going on in the group, and that in a way this creates a certain discomfort. What, in effect, it seems to me you're saying to Harold is don't lump me with other people, as if you were accurate—the group *this* or the group *that*—and I wonder if that isn't parallel with the sensation of being undercut or of being somehow not being spoken to directly, as if an interpretation, and mine tend to be diffuse, because I think there is a lot going on in the group as a whole, or obviously not in all the group but a large enough part of it, that needs to be expressed, so I'll speak out. But to make a diffuse interpretation or a diffuse comment causes a good deal of resentment. On the one hand, it makes you feel that you are not being seen as a person, that I don't go around the room and say, well now, that reminds me of what you, you, you, you have said in the last three weeks. And I tend to make some amorphous characterization of some people in the group or something like that. And then everyone feels uncertain. 'Is he referring to me or isn't he referring to me.' There's a good deal of uncertainty about what my referent is. In a way, I think the attack on Harold had some of that quality; this kind of interpretation produces resentment.

Anna (in a sarcastic tone): Well, the fact that you and Harold *dare* accuse me or him or her or any of us of saying anything other than the *exact* words that come out of our mouths is a threat, I think.

Merv: It's a threat because a lot of people don't like the idea that there's an unconscious part of themselves. They like to think that they are in control all the time and what they say is what they mean, and when someone says, 'No, you didn't mean that, these other forces are operating on you,' it sort of brings about a kind of shudder. It's something you don't like to face up to. That's why there have always been lots of people who won't accept the idea of forces operating in themselves of which they are not aware—or of which they don't like to have control.

Kamala (to Dr. Allen): I thought that your second feeling probably applies to us all, that individuals are always wondering whether the statement made is applicable to them or not, whether they want to be included in the way the group feels. That's probably the feeling that everybody might have.

Janice (to Dr. Allen): I think this is the fourth or fifth time that you've equated your attitude with Harold's attitudes, and I think this is interesting, because I really don't think I do. I see Harold as a peer. I see you as somebody who has something to teach me, regardless of the method that you use. And so far as I know, I keep the two separate and my attitude of resentment towards a peer who tries to be all-seeing is much greater than my attitude of resentment towards you.

Dr. Allen: I think that is a separate issue. Namely, once you find the common quality and then wonder who's expressing it, you may have differential feelings. I still think the element is in common. I think it may well be that there are not as parallel feelings towards me and Harold on your part as there are on other people's. I just don't know about that.

Lloyd: As I remember now, I can certainly recall several instances where Dr. Allen had said something that he thought applied to all of us which I didn't resent and on numerous occasions I heard Harold say things which he applied to all of us which I did resent. Whether it was the manner of saying, or the source, I don't know, but certainly there was a difference in them.

Godfrey: I don't think it's a conscious attack on Harold, though. I don't think anyone's consciously attacking him.

Janice: Yes, there has (laughter).

Dr. Allen: One man's consciousness is another man's unconsciousness (laughter).

Frank (to Dr. Allen): I was interested, before, when you were first speaking. You sat down over there, put both feet flat on the floor and leaned up on the desk like that before you first started talking, and then as you began to talk on you went back into this deal (imitates leaning back). I just wondered, it seemed like you need to have conscious control of the impression you tried to give the group, that you stand up like this and put both feet flat, and then as you kind of thought more about what you were saying—

Dr. Allen: That's a very persistent theme in this group, that somehow I have more conscious control over my gestures and my behavior etc. than anyone else in the room.

Frank: I—I don't think you had when you put your feet back up on the desk, but I think you were trying to get it when you sat up like this.

Jane: I think it was probably just the opposite.

Frank (to Dr. Allen): Nobody knows but you.

Harry: I think it's a quite conscious thing on his part and a very interesting observation. I think once before I think I said to him, 'Put your feet back up on the desk,' when he had somehow gotten interested and had taken his feet down and forgotten the indifferent idea he had been trying to convey consciously.

Merv: Do you think that when he has his feet up on the desk like that it makes him stand out from the rest of the group, or does it make him look—he never really will be to us like a peer. Do you want him to be like a part of the group and sit forward? How much difference does that make?

Harry: I think this is something that's going on with him, not with what we say about him.

Frank: I think so, a lot of times you find short men talking real loud, and I think many young men put their feet up on the desk (laughter).

Gino (to Merv): One comment I'd like to make is that when you talk about Dr. Allen, you always put a little capsule on your right shoulder so as to shut him out. I have that feeling every time. You put it very definitely, so, there, to break that line of vision.

Merv: That might be true.

Gino: Do you know any reason why you might be doing that?

Merv: You mean shutting him out from my view?

Gino: It's a very curious thing about sitting on the side, most of you sit so that you can see the leader and avoid this influence.

Frank: Do you observe this consistently, or are you just putting a couple of points in here?

Gino: I'm not trying to be disruptive.

Merv: Well, the reason, I have to be frank, is that I get the impression that he is sort of floating over me—I like to shut him off. Sometimes I, the idea that he's sitting there with sort of a smug attitude. It does bother me. I—

Gino: Smug attitude?

Merv: Not smug. I'm using that because I heard it used too many times, I suppose.

Gino: You're using that because you have a reason to. What I wanted to say was this, it's amazing, I see it sometimes, it's the blankest face I've ever seen at times. He won't take the smile off for ten minutes straight.

Frank: That's a Mona Lisa look (laughter).

Gino: I think that it's an attempt to be ambiguous, so that we won't have guidance from his expression. (To Merv): Are you disturbed by this factor? If you're not, just say so.

Merv: Would you repeat that?

Gino: I am disturbed by the fact that you find a very ambiguous matrix in the discussion, and you try to shut it out when you, when you want to make a statement, you shut out that matrix so as to keep away from the ambiguity.

Merv: Make it clear cut, you mean?

Gino: You said float. Something that floats is not very well defined, very ambiguous. How do you know it's there? How it got there, where it went?

Merv: I don't think being sort of ambiguous is exactly what I mean. I mean a sort of all-pervading type of thing. In other words, I feel sometimes uncomfortable talking about Dr. Allen because of the fact that I see him in a position of power over me.

Gino: Dr. Allen?

Merv: I see him sort of like the analyst, sort of looking through me. He has got this power. He has more knowledge than I do and really knows what's going on in this group and sometimes I can feel the way Frank does. Frank wants to prostrate himself. You'd like him to just sort of just get out there in the middle and say, 'OK, here's the whole thing and this is what's happening.'

Frank: I don't think he has the capability of doing that.

Harry: You would like him to.

Frank: I don't think he knows what is going on in this group.

Anna: Frank just said something about the Mona Lisa in reference to him. I think this is a rather leading—(laughter)

Frank: Yeah, I think that this smile—for one thing, ignore the sexual implications for a minute and just leave the smile. Now this smile is a kind of a half smile—like that right there (indicates Dr. Allen)—Well, it's a smile, yet you can't really tell whether that's a frown or a smile or what, because it doesn't say really what the face is thinking. There's just a face there and you can interpret it a million different ways.

Bob: It has a lot of uncertainty, like a lot of other things do, though.

Gino: It's serenity.

Frank: Kind of a serenity maybe, but you really can't say. Have you ever tried to interpret what the Mona Lisa is like by looking at it?

Gino: I have sometimes. About serenity, it's a most disturbing thing, in the turmoil, to see somebody sitting there very calmly and serene serenity, all balanced.

Janice: There is a kind of ambiguity, Gino, in some of this, but at least for me it's a more complicated kind of thing, because when it comes to talking about Dr. Allen, I don't know whether to talk *to* him or *about* him. I don't know whether he is all-knowing and all-seeing the way we assume most teachers are or whether most of what he does or part of what he does is unconscious.

Gino: Have you ever noticed how teachers, I've known some professors who were great figures, I go to their homes, I meet their families, their wives are nice, and their children. I mean, you see their personal lives, and you can't but get an impression that these—and it's a tribute to their great work—through great effort they develop a very confident professional personality, in spite of some of their family troubles.

Janice: But you are getting off the central issue, which is not Dr. Allen as a person, which I'm sure he is, and I'm sure, but *Dr. Allen.*

Gino: The central issue is that he *is* a person and that we—He sits there and really *is* an authority figure.

Janice: Wait a minute. There is *another* central issue. Just let me finish *mine.* For me, the point is, is he a group member or is he not a group member? Do we talk *to* him or do we talk *about* him in the third person, or do we talk away from him? This gives me a tremendously ambiguous feeling, particularly in a classroom situation. . . . This is important to me because I raised the point before about differentiating my feelings between someone who interprets me as the teacher or leader of the group and someone who interprets me as a peer. Well, in a sense, Dr. Allen is both. It's ambiguous.

Gino: You know what you sound like to me right now: a person who divides good and evil and decides which things are good and which things are evil. Why don't you just say that he's a leader, or you're a leader, or you're a group member, it's not too much of a conflict. It's just a matter of distance, of how much distance you are going to give when you are talking about a person, and indeed you *are* talking about a person. Usually when you meet a person on the street or any social occasion, you don't say, 'Now, I wonder what your dynamic is.' You say, 'How are you, how've you been?' It's a very artificial thing to discuss his dynamic while he's sitting there.

Frank: I think you *have* to discuss him in the third person, for one reason because he doesn't talk back to you like other people in the group do. So you feel like he's *trying* to distance himself and—

Harry: If you accuse him more directly, he'll answer, I'm sure.

Frank: A couple of times he hasn't answered.

Harry: Ask him a question about himself.

Frank: About what?

Harry: About himself.

Frank: I know a couple of times I've asked him a question, and he sat there and stared with this kind of look like 'I'm not in here.' And so then you have to talk about a person in the third person.

Harry: Maybe he's saying about that, 'I can't answer that question.'

Bob: Maybe he's saying, 'You're asking too much.'

Harry: It may be a question that it's better, perhaps, to talk it out among us.

Frank: Well, anyway, there's some different relationship there. I think most people in this group feel that they could talk to any other person, person to person; with him, you have to use the long-distance operator.

Janice: Maybe it's because we're sitting back here. But somehow, you're right, Harold, when I ask Dr. Allen a question, he usually answers, but I have the feeling that I have to shout, 'Hello, down there.' (laughter.) And I don't know whether it's purely distance, because I don't feel that, for instance, when I talk to Anna, but there's kind of a—I have to break through.

Jane: I don't think it's—that he's an authority figure. I think actually it's just that you can't talk to him as a person because anybody that you talk to will respond and do what you sort of expect of them, and you *trust* them and they'll be trustworthy, you know, and give back to you what you give to them, but he doesn't. It's not that he's a teacher, I think he's not reacting as a human being.

Gino: One comment. Every time, we have the most amount of

laughter when an authority is humbled, each time. It just happened about the long distance. As soon as you're turning to a long-distance operator or a phone set, you're talking to a thing rather than a person.

Frank: That's the funny part about it, the fact that *you* thought it was humiliating.

Janice: This is mentioned in Freud's essay, 'Wit and Its Relation to the Unconscious'; and he makes a big thing out of the fall of authority.

Gino: He makes a big thing about challenging it.

Janice: Oh, no.

Gino: I'm afraid we disagree.

Janice: If you know me, you know that I revere Freud very greatly, so when I say Freud wrote a big thing on it—

Gino: It's very common to have reverence and hate allied.

Frank: I'd like to hear some of these people talk who never say anything, I really would.

Harry: It's not because you think they have something to say, it's because you feel threatened by their silence.

Frank: Are you telling me what I think, Harry? I mean—

Harry: It seems to me when I have the experience of wanting very much to know what people who didn't say anything were thinking, that it was because I felt that, you know, maybe they were in on something—had some insights to contribute.

Dr. Allen: I think it is interesting that the silent people would come up at this point.

Frank: Yeah, because, especially outside of class, some of these people say some very interesting things to me. I think more interesting than a lot of people who talk.

Harry: Why don't you repeat some of them?

Frank: I told you today about the barracuda, the school of barracudas.

Joanne: Would you continue what you just said in relation to, about why it was interesting that this should come up now?

Dr. Allen: Well, I think that Frank was expressing a good deal of resentment about my noncomplimentary or nonresponsive role in the group, that I wasn't a human being, and then very quickly shifted off to attacking the other people who are unresponsive and inhuman and try to get them to speak up.

Jay: Are you trying to transfer your role to Harold? I remember one time you talked about him galloping off, and also I remember today

when you were talking you, I don't know what the reference was, but you said Harold and I, or Harold—But I remember one reference today to Harold and I. In other words, you were putting the cloak of authority on the shoulders of Harold, perhaps you felt—
Dr. Allen: This seems to be the way what I said was picked up, but it wasn't picked up that I'm trying to transfer it to Alvin.
Anna: Well, somebody just got off the subject of what you were saying again with going back to you and Harold when you were talking about the silent people, and I think that maybe some people like Frank think that the silent people might say what you *won't* say and maybe he's also afraid that the people who have been talking are going to say precisely what he doesn't want to hear.
Frank: What I *want* to hear?
Dr. Allen: There is something a little self-defeating about demanding that the silent people talk. In my experience, when silent people are put under pressure, it makes it *less* likely that they'll talk.
[End of session fourteen.]

At this point, we can connect several of the central questions of this book with the session just presented. First, how would one go about describing the feelings expressed toward the leader? It might be helpful if the reader himself tried to summarize, in whatever form he prefers, the feelings behind Frank's statement, "We have an authority which stands for no authority," or behind Janice's direct communication to the leader, "Hello, down there." How would the reader summarize the current state of the relationship between Harry and the leader? Would it suffice to note only the relatively rare instances when he spoke directly to the leader, or should one attend to such events as Harry's initial taunting of Alvin? The descriptive issue generates two questions: how to describe the smallest unit, the act, and how to describe the larger and more complex segment defined by a person's contribution on a day such as the one presented above. We propose to describe acts in terms of a category system, presented in Chapter 3, and our analysis of an individual's contribution on a particular day leads us into a factor analytic study of performances in Chapter 4. If the transcript served one of its purposes, the reader can now see for himself that there is both diversity and passion in what members have to say about the leader, and it may also be clear that individuals, Harry and Frank, for example, differ considerably in the ways they conceive of and respond to the entire situation. One major assignment before us in this study, then, is the descriptive task of capturing the affect and the intent of individual acts and performances of a single day. Closely connected is the task of developing a conceptual scheme that will further a general understanding of the particular events observed in these groups.

The second question raised by this transcript concerns the leader. What do we learn about him by examining this and the other 120 group sessions? The leader initiates ten of the 200 or so speeches found in this transcript. One of these speeches, however, is the longest of the day. What was the leader trying to accomplish by this long intervention? Did it have any effect? How much might we agree with Jay, on the basis of even this brief observation, that the leader was setting up Harry to be the leader of the group? And how did the leader take this accusation? He seems rather defensive. What does that tell us about his role, or about his conception of his role? To a large extent, we intend to focus upon the professional role of the leader. One can see in this session that the leader is interpretative, but is that all? Who is he rewarding? By what kinds of feelings is he threatened or irritated? Above all, we want to inquire what his activities have to do with work. Can one infer from the transcript above how the leader defines work and what he sees as relevant or useful activity on the part of the members? Can one describe how he moves the group toward some goal even if he avoids spelling out this goal to the members or to himself? These are some of the questions we shall ask about the leader in Chapter 5.

For some readers, the transcript may raise questions about how the group arrived at this point and about where it is headed. In what terms and with what results might one trace the development of a self-analytic group? There were allusions to past events, to the day when the leader was under attack, for example, but what were the earliest days like? One senses that Jane is feeling quite apprehensive; the unresponsive leader bothers some of the members; and the whole question of structure is obviously still unsettled in more than one member's mind. One might conclude that Harry had been a central figure in the group thus far. Is there always a person like Harry in these groups? How much do the four groups suggest a common cast of characters with similar roles to be played in each group? It is particularly apparent that schism is more the mark of this session than homogeneity and consensus. What, then, do we mean when we say, "the group"? Is this simply a shorthand way of referring to some of the active members, to the most vivid members perhaps? Chapter 6 picks up some of these questions as we attempt to follow the changes in the group over time in terms of the shifting dominance of important sub-groups and cleavages.

The transcript raises still another series of questions, ones having more specifically to do with individual dynamics. Some of the references to the leader seem quite straightforward: the leader may be seen as distant, as the authority figure, as inhuman or unapproachable, etc. But what about Frank's reference to him as Mona Lisa; what about Harry's equating of the leader's passing out assignments with menstruating? We are edging toward the point where the personal and unique factors must be considered. We must approach these data with an awareness that the members have pregroup histories, that there is a transference component in their reaction to the leader and to the entire group situation. A central question in our examination of both the individuals and the group as a whole revolves around the notion of work: how do the needs, expectations, and characteristic styles of these members relate to their capacity and willingness to work in this kind of situation? What frustrates a member like Alvin so severely that he will never be able to get beyond his sense of outrage; what must a member like Frank test or resolve before he can get to work; or what must quite a different member like Gino add to his conception of work in order to avoid a partially successful but in some sense rigidly fixated mode of interaction? These kinds of questions concern us in Chapter 7.

Finally, we must return to the original question: What is this Soc Rel 120? For us it is the kind of research site at which we can attempt to answer some of the questions listed above. But what is it for the member? To answer this question we must go beyond the answer provided by the transcript. Not only is Soc Rel 120 a course in which discussions such as these may take place, but it is also a course with a certain structure. For the remainder of this chapter we will attempt to clarify the outlines of this structure. Only then will we set down a few thoughts on why these groups merit study and to what other group settings we feel our results might be applicable.

Social Relations 120, as developed by a staff that has included R. Freed Bales, Philip Slater, Theodore Mills, Charles Whitlock, and others, is a two-term course during the academic year. The four groups under study here were conducted in the summer sessions, and they met for 32 sessions, five days a week, from nine to ten o-clock in the morning, for slightly over six weeks. The present course is a direct descendant of a general education course, Social Sciences 112: Human Relations, which Hugh Cabot, Joseph Kahl, and others (cf. Cabot and Kahl, 1953) started at the College, following the pattern of teaching by the case method that Elton Mayo and his colleagues at the Harvard Business School had developed. From the start, the intellectual task of the course was composed of assigned readings, the discussion of cases drawn from real life, and some analysis of the group processes found in the here-and-now situation. The readings span psychoanalytic theory, studies of group interaction, and sociological or anthropological analysis of larger social processes.

In addition to the assigned readings and the six cases which were usually discussed on the first day of each week, the students were required to write a term paper describing and analyzing an incident or relationship within their own group. These papers and the final essay examination on the readings and their application to the students' own group were graded by the instructor, except in group two, which was provided with a graduate student teaching assistant. As we shall soon see, the fact that the group leader was also the grader aroused and/or crystallized a considerable amount of mistrust and uneasiness on the part of the members. The ambiguity of the leader's role so characteristic of all self-analytic groups is compounded by his dual function in and out of the group. One might, for some purposes, design the situation differently, but for these groups this was reality.

The students in these groups were drawn from many scholastic and occupational backgrounds. In each group of 20 to 25 there were four to nine Harvard or Radcliffe students and a dozen or so undergraduates from other colleges; those remaining were somewhat older students doing graduate work in education, business, or social work and a few already employed as secretaries, ministers, and so forth. In each group the male–female ratio was nearly even. The final set of members was selected out of a larger group of summer school students who wished to take the course. An effort to balance the number of each sex and to maximize the heterogeneity of the group on other criteria such as age and status determined most of the selections, although a few people whose experience and evident sophistication seemed to offer the group some particular resource were deliberately included. As we noted previously, one important difference between the members was their initial set toward the new group. For most students, even after the orientation session that preceded their application and selection for inclusion in the groups, the probable nature of their own learning and the probable structure of the class remained very hazy; but from others one could hear expectations such as, "the instructor says nothing at all," or everyone "spills his guts all over the table," or gets "cut to ribbons." As is usual in most self-analytic groups, the members arrived with a diversity of initial sets that ranged from no clear expectations to the distorted and fearful expectations that marked this course as special and somewhat threatening.

The four groups were led by three different men, two of whom were social psychologists, and the other a psychiatrist. All three were in their late twenties or early thirties at that point, and each had been the leader for at least several other such groups prior to the ones under study here. Three of the groups also contained an observer who would later score the sessions. Two of the observers were located off to the side of the U-shaped table around which sat all but a few group members, the other members being arrayed in an outer circle of separate chairs with a desk-type arm; the other observer sat at the side and in back of the leader whose chair was behind a desk that closed off the circle.

If, on the basis of the transcript plus these details of organization, personnel, and ecology, the reader can be assumed to have some idea of what these groups are like, we can turn to the question of why one might wish to study such groups. Relative to the panorama of groups to which attention has been or might be directed, these groups are natural, as opposed to *ad hoc*, groups of intermediate duration. Hopefully, the transcript and the chapters to follow will convey our sense that, for the members, the situation is genuine and that happenings in this setting bear upon a number of enduring and pervasive aspects of all human interactions.

If asked directly whether we would suggest that the findings obtained here can be transferred directly to other settings, we would have to answer in the negative. We have found certain methods and concepts to be useful; these, we would assert, are worth testing again in other kinds of groups. But we will also suggest that certain developments take place in these four groups and that certain types of members emerge with regularity. It is these latter findings which we cannot be sure will apply to even quite similar groups, let alone groups whose task does not include the analysis of their own processes. As anyone who has been in more than one self-analytic group knows, the odds are rather low that any generalization will fit all such groups. It may be that if one looks at certain aspects of the groups and their development, one's awareness of uniformity will increase. Such has been our experience in analyzing these four groups. It would be sufficient to begin accumulating not a model for all groups, but, more modestly, a way to know what differences do occur and the conceptual equipment to understand why these differences have occurred. It would be enough, in this view, to specify as clearly as possible how these four groups operate. Only in that way will our awareness of the determinants and the complex interactions among the determinants that underlie the member-leader relationship begin to expand to handle both the uniformities and discrepancies found in these and similar groups.

Our notion of what other kinds of situations we would call similar depends upon our mood at any given moment. In a conservative mood, we would see these findings as relevant, on the one hand, to the study of self-analytic groups and, on the other hand, to the study of classroom interaction in more traditionally organized courses. In relation to the former, it should be recognized that the grades and formal requirements set these groups apart, as do the ages and orientations of the members, from many therapy and sensitivity-training groups. In young adulthood certain issues, the authority issue among them, are particularly salient, and one might well find that other groups of older members either moved more adroitly through and beyond the authority issue or else successfully feigned that these issues were not of any great moment to them. It must also be recognized that these groups are more volatile, more self-absorbed, and more directly expressive than the normal classroom discussion groups. We do suspect, however, that many if not all of the feelings voiced in these groups are both active and expressed, if more symbolically, in the more typical classroom.

In our less conservative moods, we are struck with the relevance of the issues and the dynamics found in these groups to quite diverse settings. Since much of what happens in these groups seems to us to reflect familial and other prior experiences with authority, what emerges is in large part a commentary upon these earlier experiences as well as upon the groups themselves. In some settings one could not easily detect the feelings that exist between members and leaders or between the child and the parent by watching their interaction, but if one could listen in on the peer group exchanging grievances or have access to the private musings of all concerned, we suspect that many similar themes and alternative responses would be found. At the most abstract level, then, we are engaged in a study of the affective relationship between persons of different levels of power, expertise, and responsibility. How this relationship develops, what forms it takes, how fellow members combine and clash over the appropriate strategy to employ—these are some of the ways in which we define our concerns, and it remains to be seen whether the events within these Soc Rel 120 groups will yield useful information with which to pursue both our particular and our more general concerns.

Some Relevant Literature on Self-Analytic Groups

Our purpose in the concluding section of this chapter and each of the next five chapters is to indicate the context of this study more fully than is possible while presenting our procedures and findings. In this section, for example, we wish to suggest to the interested reader where he might look for additional descriptions of the diverse goals and processes found in self-analytic groups. The reader who is unacquainted with the sensitivity-training group (T-group) may find it useful to know of two relevant volumes of essays, one edited by Bradford, Gibb, and Benne (1964) and the other by Schein and Bennis (1965). The contributions by Benne (1964), Gibb (1964), Whitman (1964), and Blake (1964) develop particularly interesting perspectives on the purpose of the T-group. An earlier empirical study of many facets of the T-group by Stock and Thelen (1958) conveys very clearly the complexity of factors which play upon the member of a developing group. Other accounts of the T-group which are more in the reportorial genre may be found in the work of Wechsler and Reisel (1959), Barron and Krulee (1948), and Schein and Bennis (1965, Chapter 2).

The second variety of self-analytic groups which these resemble is the therapy group, although many of the factors by which Frank (1964), Kelman and Lerner (1952), and L. Horwitz (1964) differentiate between therapy groups and T-groups would apply to the differences between therapy groups and the Soc Rel 120 classes as well. Three excellent volumes on group psychotherapy (Whitaker and Lieberman, 1964; Bach, 1954; and Foulkes and Anthony, 1957) not only describe the proceedings in such groups but manage to master, in the process, the delicate art of interweaving individual and group level perspectives.

The third variety of self-analytic groups, groups in which educators, psychiatric residents, or other professionals come to learn about group processes through understanding the dynamics of their own interaction, are quite similar to these Soc Rel 120 groups. In contrast to both the T-group and the therapy group, where the goal of behavior modification is more important, this third variety of self-analytic group shares with Soc Rel 120 a heavy emphasis upon the member's development of greater insight and understanding as a result of his experience. These goals are not mutually exclusive, of course, but the trainer and the therapist tend to be far more concerned about the transfer of new behaviors and feelings to the "back home" situation than Bion (1961) seems to be, for example. Self-analytic groups in educational or professional training setting have been discussed by Jones (1960), Zinberg and Shapiro (1963), Semrad and Arsenian (1951), and Bion (1961), as well as by the authors who have studied other Soc Rel 120 groups: Mills (1964), Dunphy (1964), Slater (1966), and Friedman and Zinberg (1964). The rapidly accumulating literature on self-analytic groups extends far beyond the work cited here, but these references may serve as a useful starting point for the reader who would explore more fully the continuities and discontinuities to be found among groups of this general character and purpose.

Chapter 3

The Member-to-Leader Scoring System

The task of transforming the rich and subtle flow of group interaction into a sequence of categorized acts should be put in its proper context, namely, the familiar human task of trying to understand what people mean when they speak to one another. It seems important, before we describe one rather stylized method of observation and inference, to establish the continuities between our observation techniques and the techniques employed by both the trained clinician and the "untrained" participant.

The scoring system to be presented in this chapter makes extensive use of two commonplace insights into all efforts to understand what another human being is saying. These are: (1) that a person may express his feelings symbolically as well as directly; and (2) that the feelings expressed by a person will be "understood" or recognized within the particular conceptual framework of the listener.

If the listener is a therapist and the speaker-patient is going on and on about how cold it feels in the room that day, one hunch the therapist might entertain would be that certain symbolic equivalences exist, for the speaker, between the room and the therapist. Or, to take another example, if the listener is the oldest member of a group and the speaker is railing against the stifling influence such old men as DeGaulle and Adenauer had upon their nations, the listener may wonder if he should take the words as an indirect attack, or he may simply act as if he had been attacked and rise to the defense of DeGaulle, Adenauer, and the practice of venerating wise old men. The extent to which the speaker and the listener are consciously aware of the symbolization may vary, of course, but what is relevant here is that in the process of expressing feelings a person may establish symbolic equivalents for himself and for the target of the feelings. The challenge in attempting to make systematic observations of group process is, in part, the challenge of making valid connections between the subject and object of the content on the manifest level and, for our purposes, the feelings of the member toward the leader at a more latent level of meaning and awareness.

The second insight into any communication of feelings, the fact that the listener must conceptualize the feelings within a given framework, is reflected in the scientist's effort to build a category system for coding and recording the flow of interaction. Although it would be foolish to pretend that any set of four, 12, 16, or even the 85 categories with which Bales (1950) started his work is a match for the intricacies of a human being's conceptual framework, it is vital that the very act of categorizing be seen as a process common to both scientist and participant. The decision to settle for a limited set of categories is connected to the scientist's desires: (1) to reduce the redundancy and imprecision of his own private conceptual framework before, rather than after, making his observations; (2) to make it possible for two descriptive statements to be more comparable than a pair of prose paragraphs can be; (3) to work in terms of concepts which have yielded and will continue to yield the most useful results and theories; and (4) to invite other researchers to consider his concepts as one possible set on which to converge in their own future efforts.

There is no sense in dodging the issue that any category system is a wrench for those who are not familiar with it. We saw our task as one of not only maximizing the anticipated gains within the context of empirical research, but also of minimizing the discrepancy between this scheme and the already comfortable conceptual framework of those in our intended audience who are more interested in understanding our results than in applying our particular research methods. The resultant compromise is a category system which draws heavily upon the conceptual schemes embedded in the literary, clinical, and theoretical analyses of group process.

The member-to-leader scoring system is a product of our effort to capture both the process of expressing feelings, in direct or symbolic form, and the nature of the feelings expressed. The two coordinates of an act are the level and the category (or categories) in which it is placed. The level refers to the process of symbolization, each level representing a distinct kind of decoding which enables the scorer to match the manifest and latent content and to specify which symbols stand for the leader and which for the member who initiates the act. The categories constitute a highly restricted language within which the scorer records his inferences about the feelings being expressed by the member.

How does the scorer actually operate? What enables him to translate the flow of manifest content, which may be totally devoid of references to the leader, or even to the member himself, into a running record of the member-leader relationship? Two answers to these questions seem relevant at this point, one addressing the issue of the scorer's general set toward the impact of the leader upon the member's acts, a second addressing itself to the kinds of cues he tends to employ.

Our basic notion about the influence of the member-leader relationship upon the member's feelings and behavior takes the form of an operating assumption, to wit: the member-leader relationship is always influencing the member's feelings and behavior to some extent. To what extent is not a constant, and perhaps a metaphor might help here. Hopefully, most readers can recall a tall and narrow chart of world civilizations from their schoolroom walls. It showed in bands of varying widths, horizontally, the waxing and waning of the major civilizations of the world. If there was a band, perhaps the yellow one for China, which never was completely extinguished, and which sometimes swelled to suggest a period of great power, this might convey our feeling about the relevance of the leader. Other civilizations were far more powerful at times, and other determinants are far more powerful than the leader at times. A member's feelings about the leader never completely determine the member's manifest behavior, but they are always a component of the total set of determinants of any public act in the group setting.

Certainly there are moments when the member is preoccupied with the leader. His mind appears to be filled with feelings about the leader, and he may express some of these, perhaps even overestimating the extent to which the leader is influencing his state of mind at that moment. We also observe other moments when feelings toward the leader are expressed by employing a symbolic equivalent for the leader, perhaps his favorite in the group or a father in one of the cases. We do not discount the validity or importance of the member's feelings toward the leader's favorite or the case father; we simply focus upon what the member is telling us, simultaneously, about his feelings toward the leader.

What our experience of looking hard for that component of group life which bears upon member-leader situations has taught us is that members not only develop viable symbols for the leader, but that they can carry on whole conversations with the leader in mind without ever referring to him explicitly. We have also learned that the members know that the leader knows; the members learn that the leader is as likely as anyone else to pick up the undercover themes and imagery which refer to him. Thus it seems reasonable to conclude that one usually unconscious process in groups is that members pre-screen their remarks to make sure the feelings about to be expressed toward a case figure or toward another group member who generally stands for the leader are not too incongruent with the feelings they would care to convey to the leader.

We know we make mistakes in our inferences. We do not, of course, know which ones the mistakes are, but we are sure they are there somewhere. The scorer's task is to get his accuracy as high as possible. Later events, and even the final results of the study, may confirm his hunches for the most part. But as he scores, his major reassurance must come from the number of already known facts about the speaker and the context of the act which reinforce the interpretation he chooses to make of the given act.

The cues which initiate the process of scoring a symbolic act are varied. Imagine that the scorer is confronted with a long expression of feelings about the figures in a movie the member has just seen. What, he asks, has all this to do with the member's feelings toward the leader? For some acts, the first clue comes from the member's description of the relationship between the two people in the movie: father-son, sorcerer-victim, hero-admirer, etc. The scorer reviews in his mind the others times this member has spoken, to see what kinds of relationships the member tends to use for expressing his feelings in a disguised form. We do not necessarily assume that every father equals the leader. Sometimes the equivalence makes sense in terms of the member's prior behavior, sometimes not. For other acts, the first clue comes from the feelings expressed, perhaps anger or depression. If these feelings seem to make sense in terms of the member's history up to that point, or in terms of the feelings being expressed by other members, then the scorer is at least under way in his effort to understand the act.

The act is not scored, however, until both the symbolic equivalents for leader and member, on the one hand, and the feelings being expressed, on the other hand, are determined. Thus the scorer may start with the idea that the father being talked about stands for the leader, but when he moves on to assess the feelings, they might not square at all with the member's prior set of feelings toward the leader. Of course, the member's feelings may have shifted, and one would hope that the scorer could adjust to this as quickly as possible. But it also could be that the scorer's equation of leader and father was wrong, that in a moment of rigidity or low energy the easy path has been followed, without success. It is equally possible that when a member mentions anger, the scorer might find this so familiar a feeling on the part of this member that he might almost score the act that way, until he had to face the fact that the fictitious person expressing the anger was someone who the member would probably not use as his mouthpiece. In both these cases, the search must begin again. If, however, both the symbolic equivalents and the feelings make sense, given the member, the leader, and the context, both historically and at that moment, the act is scored.

The Levels of Inference

We return now to the levels, to specify precisely how we define each of the four kinds of inference which the scorer makes. There are basically two steps involved: locating the leader and locating the member in the manifest content of the act. The four levels record where the scorer had to look to find them.

The simplest case involves a direct expression of feeling toward the leader (e.g., "I feel irritated at the leader for just sitting there.") The member clearly identifies himself as the possessor of the feeling being expressed and the leader as the object of the feeling, and all such acts are scored on *Level one*. Unfortunately for the scorer, only a modest fraction of the total acts to be scored can be scored without some degree of inference about the relevance of the act for the member-leader relationship.

Levels two and three refer to those acts in which the leader is not clearly identified as the object. *Level two* is scored either when the feeling is expressed without any mention of an object ("I feel irritated today.") or when the object mentioned is the group as a whole or some member who serves as the symbolic equivalent of the leader for that particular member. For example, a member might say, "I feel irritated at Peter for constantly interpreting what is going on in here," or, "Why don't you silent members speak up?" If (and only if) the scorer infers that Peter or the silent members are serving as objects on which the member is displacing his feelings toward the leader, then he will score the relevant content categories at Level two. No assumption is made in scoring such acts that the member is not really irritated at Peter at all but simply that one component of his multiply-determined irritation is his feelings toward the leader, which find expression in an act directed towards some symbolic equivalent within the group. By the same logic, an act with no object specified would not be scored at all unless one could infer that one source of the member's irritation, anxiety, or whatever, was his feelings about the leader.

When the symbolic object is outside the group, the kind of inference made by the scorer seems sufficiently different from the inference made for Level two acts to warrant a separate scoring level: *Level three.* The scorer cannot, as he can with most of the Level two acts, determine the member's habitual way of relating to the symbolic equivalent, nor can he make use of the leader's habitual response to the member or clique to which the speaker refers. Here the speaker may refer to a figure in one of the assigned cases, to some author in the leader's field, or to a university or government official to express, among other things, his feeling toward the leader. Acts on Level three are thus one notch less direct, and the member who initiates them is one important notch less exposed for having expressed a given feeling.

As distinguished from acts on Levels one, two, or three, acts on *Level four* disguise or symbolize the member, but not necessarily the leader. The Level four acts involve mainly the dynamic mechanism of projection since the member expresses his feelings toward the leader by disowning them and treating them as if they belonged to some other agent, real or fictitious. The member may say to another member, "You look anxious," and if the scorer feels that a partial determinant of that observation was the speaker's own anxiety in relation to the leader, then the act would be scored on Level four. More commonly, the member will identify himself with a figure in one of the cases or in a movie. As Slater (1961a) has noted, in highly symbolic discussions the member may symbolize both himself, via projection, and the leader, via displacement. These acts would also be scored on Level four.

Recapitulating, the four levels of inferences recorded by the scorer represent four ways that a member can express his feelings toward the leader. The four levels, with their defining characteristics, are the following:

Level One. Both members and leader referred to directly.

Level Two. Member referred to directly, but leader symbolized by equivalent within the group.

Level Three. Member referred to directly, but leader symbolized by equivalent outside the group.

Level Four. Member symbolized by equivalent inside or outside the group, leader referred to either directly or symbolically.

Before turning to the content categories, one additional matter related to the scorer's inferences needs to be discussed. In scoring symbolic material, some of the objects referred to are not directly symbolic of the leader but represent, to the member, the symbolic antithesis of the leader. For example, when a member says, "Freud would never have badgered a patient with his interpretations; he would have waited until it made sense to the patient himself," it may, in the context, occur to the scorer that Freud is related somehow to the leader. But there are two different possible connections: (1) the member is defending the leader's passivity and cryptic style by equating him with "the master"; or (2) the member is indirectly attacking the leader for being too assertive in plugging for his own interpretations. It makes quite a difference whether the member is involved in indirect praise and defense of the leader or in invidious comparison. Only the context, the tone of voice, and the previous history of that member's relation to the leader can aid the scorer. The task of the scorer is thus complicated by the necessity of deciding not only what object symbolizes the leader or the member himself, but also whether the symbolic object is being equated with or opposed to the referent.[1]

Scoring the Member's Feelings

The content categories of the member-to-leader scoring system, as shown in Table 3-1, can be looked at as three separate systems, here used simultaneously. Eight of the 16 categories describe the affective response a member may have to the leader; three of the categories describe feelings which are activated by the leader's status in an (apperceived) authority structure; and five of the categories describe how the member feels about himself in relation to the leader. These three approaches to the member's feelings are reflected in what we shall refer to as the three *areas*: (1) the impulse area; (2) the authority relations area; and (3) the ego state area.

The impulse area is divided into two subareas, hostility and affection, and the ego state area is also divided into the subareas of anxiety and depression. The authority relations area is considered one of the five subareas. The reason for spelling this out now is that an important scoring convention rests on the division of the 16 categories into five

---

[1] It is worth noting that it is precisely at this point that Mills' (1964) sign process analysis and Stone et al.'s (1962) general inquirer system for analyzing content must be seen as permitting a major source of error, since they combine all references to authority figures regardless of whether the figure is serving as the equivalent or the antithesis of the leader.

subareas; the convention is that an act may be scored in as many subareas as seems appropriate, but no more than one category within a subarea may be used. Since self-esteem is never double-scored with an anxiety or depression category, Expressing Self-Esteem is considered a category, but not a subarea within the ego state area.

Some of the resistance one encounters in presenting a category scheme is of the form: "But can't an act be both hostile and seductive, or both anxious and depressed?" We feel it can and that our scoring system should accommodate this fact. Where we draw the line is that we feel the scorer should be forced (and we realize there is some violence to reality done even here) to decide upon which kind of hostility or affection, what kind of response to the authority, or whether the anxiety or depression is mainly expressed or denied.

In presenting each category, we shall attempt to outline the primary defining characteristics of the category. Each category inevitably con-

Table 3–1
The Member-to-Leader Scoring System Categories

Area	Subarea	Category
Impulse	Hostility	1. Moving Against
		2. Resisting
		3. Withdrawing
		4. Guilt Inducing
	Affection	5. Making Reparation
		6. Identifying
		7. Accepting
		8. Moving Toward
Authority Relations		9. Showing Dependency
		10. Showing Independence
		11. Showing Counterdependency
Ego State	Anxiety	12. Expressing Anxiety
		13. Denying Anxiety
		14. Expressing Self-Esteem
	Depression	15. Expressing Depression
		16. Denying Depression

tains somewhat disparate elements, but the common elements should be stated as clearly as possible. Examples of the various meanings and forms taken by each category will be included. We will also consider the boundaries between one category and another. Only within each subarea, however, need we establish mutually exclusive categories.

The Content Categories

1. *Moving Against.* The major characteristics of acts scored in this category are that: (1) the hostility is aroused by and/or directed to the person of leader, as opposed to his "in-role" behavior; (2) the expression of feeling has an active, self-initiated quality, rather than being mainly passive or reactive; and (3) the hostility expressed is couched in the personal terms of anger, criticism, and mistrust rather than in the moralistic terms of someone invoking a higher value as a weapon against the leader.

It is rare to find such clear and unmistakable instances as the following, but they do help to define one kind of Moving Against.

(1) "It would probably be lots of fun if some day he [the leader] got sick or got run over by a car. I would secretly feel pretty happy about it."

(2) "Yes, I am being hostile. I am tired of all this crap . . . this generalizing."

One aspect of Moving Against, then, involves the expression of personal animus. Less dramatic, but more common, are the instances in which the member mocks or belittles the leader, trying not so much to destroy him as to deflate him. One rather successful effort along this line comes to mind:

Female: Why did we identify with Jane in the last case?
Leader: Maybe there are many reasons.
Male: (in properly mysterious tones) The Shadow knows.

Beyond the most strikingly personal devices of attack and mockery one finds the acts of personal criticism, aimed more at the person behind the role than at the role itself. Members may announce, for example, that for the leader to teach them in such a passive and frustrating way can only mean he is weak, incompetent, voyeuristic, rigid, devious, or some other odious sort. All such publicly announced inferences and perceptions are scored as Moving Against. The desire to hurt the leader, to offend him, or to retaliate against him runs through all these forms of Moving Against. Some, but not all, of the acts which express mistrust and suspicion have this quality as well, and they are scored here with the more direct expressions of hostility. When a member equates the leader with Shaw's ("despicable") Henry Higgins, or when a member calls the leader's initial permissiveness "phony," the mistrust expressed is an integral part of his rejection of the leader.

2. *Resisting.* The essential ingredients of acts scored as Resisting are that: (1) the hostility is directed at the role or the performance of the leader; and (2) the hostility is largely responsive, occurring on the occasion of explicit pressures from the leader, or, at the very least, in response to the felt pressures generated by the entire learning situation.

The first ingredient, that the hostility is relatively impersonal and role-oriented, defines most clearly the boundary between this category and the person-oriented acts of Moving Against. In this distinction we were much guided by Bales' (1950) distinction, in his Interaction Process Analysis scheme, between Disagrees and Shows Antagonism. The process of disagreeing with, quarreling with, or in some way negating the leader's task contributions is one which conveys hostility, to be sure, but without the destructive overtones implicit in Moving Against.

Resisting occurs in numerous guises, but the clearest cases follow some intervention by the leader, for example:

(1) "I may have missed something, but why should we be mad? Who says we are?"
(2) "A lot of things you say are pretty far-fetched."

Closely akin to these rejections of an interpretation are the innumerable forms of contradiction. It seems unnecessary to elaborate on the ways in which people can say: "I don't agree."

More subtle, however, are the negative responses to the structure and pacing of the course provided by the leader. Some members blame the unsystematic flow of conversation on the leader's style, and their criticism of "aimless talk" would be scored as Resisting. So would the boy's impatient response in the following example, which occurred in the first session of the group:

Female: How long do we discuss each case?
Leader: A couple of days, in this instance.

Male: I think we've just about come to all the conclusions that can be drawn from it.

In thinking about this category, we tend to use some analogies from fencing. The thrust, or even the jab, is the analogue of Moving Against; blocking and parrying are the analogues of Resisting; and walking off the mat is the analogue of the next category to be discussed, Withdrawing. The correspondences are not exact, but they are perhaps close enough to suggest the basic differences between these three categories.

3. *Withdrawing*. We turn from hostility against the person and hostility against the role performance of the leader to a form of hostility aimed at loosening the bond between the member and the leader. Any act which expresses primarily the desire to decrease the intensity of the relationship, or to prevent it from becoming intense, belongs in the category of Withdrawing.

Two acts in the final session of one group show the process of withdrawing in its clearest form:

(1) "I have the feeling that we're retreating."
(2) "Or else maybe we're just sneaking away."

Some acts, at earlier stages in the group, also reveal clearly the wish to leave the group entirely. Similar to such feelings are the efforts to ignore the leader, exemplified by one girl in the first session of a group, speaking immediately after the leader's first intervention:

"I thought we were doing a pretty good job of forgetting you were in the room. We were looking around for a leader."

The acts above imply an effort to have no bond at all with the leader, but this is not the major form of withdrawal. More frequently the member, through acts which seem bland, disinterested, or distant, expresses his desire to keep the leader out of his inner world and to weaken the bond between them. Prior to the following interaction, the boy in the exchange had established himself as one of the more committed and introspective members, whereas the girl had oscillated widely between high involvement and the withdrawal expressed especially in her last statement:

Male: Aren't you looking for support?
Female: Well, I suppose so.

Male: Are you as uncertain about it as that?
Female: Well, I don't know if I care. I never thought about that.

A second form of detachment is reflected in the effort to isolate the classroom experience from one's "real self." In this connection, we should mention those feelings of reserve and shyness which make a member hold back for fear of being hurt or rejected. Sometimes these feelings are verbalized, and they belong with this set of acts and, usually, with the expressions of anxiety as well.

Finally, we should note the acts of Withdrawing which are, manifestly, attempts at humor. The introjected pun or the wild and escapist free-associations to a threatening discussion are scored as Withdrawing, which does not preclude the scorer from registering the denial of distress in some other appropriate category.

4. *Guilt Inducing.* Some hostility expressed by members seems to encompass a larger frame of reference than simply the momentarily accentuated dyad of one member and the leader. Some hostility depends upon the invocation of a "third force": the set of values, morals, and unwritten rules of etiquette which the member asserts *should* be operative and binding upon the leader's behavior. In a sense, the interaction becomes a triad, with the supposedly proscriptive norms firmly allied with the member against the leader. We suggest that when the desired outcome of the member's acts seems to be not to hurt, block, or avoid the leader, but to make him feel guilty in the light of these higher values, then the member is expressing hostility in a sufficiently distinctive way to merit special tabulation of such maneuvers.

The three verbs which recur again and again as one attempts to summarize these acts of Guilt Inducing are accuse, blame, and complain. Consider the girl who, less in anger than in a tone of moral reproach, says:

"I think you're deliberating trying to get people mad at you, and I can't understand it. It's really making me very upset."

Underlying her hostility are several assumptions about how people in general or leaders in particular should behave, i.e., they should not make people mad, they should be understandable, and they should not upset people. Since this leader is violating these principles of good conduct, he should be reminded of the ethics of interpersonal life and should feel guilty about his transgressions.

To name but a few, we find the members berating the leader for being inconsistent, for playing favorites, for being too impartial, and for being retentive, ineffectual, or hypocritical. We hear the members blaming the leader for making the group self-conscious, for causing the collapse of efforts to work, and for not preventing the end of the group. And although the members find ground for disapproval and reproach in practically every area of the leader's behavior, one area which brings out a volley of Guilt Inducing is the leader's assignment of work and grades. The work load is too heavy, the assignments are too upsetting or preoccupying, or else they are simply impossible. The very effort of the leader to evaluate members is a betrayal of trust. While this discussion suggests the range of feelings involved, it is important to distinguish between the three main premises that generate most of these accusations and complaints.

One premise is that the leader, regardless of his formal role, is bound by the ethics of ordinary human interaction: be humane, be sensitive, be honest, etc. The second is that the leader is bound, by convention if not necessity, to fulfill the members' expectations regarding leaders in general: be strong, be universalistic, be helpful, etc. Finally, he is subject to a premise which is, in some sense, the price of any leadership position: the leader should either be the paragon of all virtues or else manage to conceal any flaws from the believing multitudes. Guilt Inducing of this sort amounts to an unmasking of the leader, a process of exposing his selfishness or whatever, and, given the member's simultaneous desire to have the leader conceal his clay feet, the result is often a paradox of considerable intensity. None of these premises are operative at all times, or in all people, but they are recurrent and powerful forces in the group, and it is the assumption that they are *legitimate* demands which enables this form of hostility to serve, often, as a shield preventing the member from apprehending his feelings as any form of hostility whatsoever.

5. *Making Reparation.* Although there might be some advantage in discussing the most personal form of affection first, it may be opportune to describe next the affection category most directly connected with the set of hostility categories just presented. Reparation, the process of countering or undoing the hostile impulses one feels toward another person, is a concept discussed in great detail by Melanie Klein (1937, 1957), and most observers in the psychoanalytic and clinical traditions find some way to describe and analyze this process. The chief reason for distinguishing between this and other forms of affection is that one can only comprehend Making Reparation by considering the hostile context in which it occurs. When a member says, "Now, I don't mean

this personally, because I have high regard for you, but . . .," the initial clause is not a simple act of affection. It is one of the forms of reparation we include in this category.

Making Reparation is observed mainly in the forms of: (1) backing off from, or apologizing for, some earlier hostility toward the leader; (2) denying or in some way neutralizing any current hostility; (3) disassociating oneself from the hostility of others; and (4) expanding the target of some hostile act toward the leader to include oneself, sometimes to the extent that the self replaces the leader as the legitimate target.

Two examples of the first type of reparation, the process of backing off from earlier hostility, may help: the first showing how the sequence may occur within one speech, the second showing an attempt to redress the damage from a previous session.

(1) "You [the leader] don't look much older than the rest of the people here (Moving Against). Maybe you look younger than you are." (Making Reparation)

(2) "Oh, what the heck, let's forget about cynicism [a quality previously attributed to the leader]. Somebody say something. I don't think we have any real cynics."

The denial of current hostility is illustrated by Alvin's two acts, which follow a discussion of whether anyone is feeling angry at the leader.

Alvin: I don't see why there should have been any feeling of hostility or resentment toward him [the leader].

Marie: I am sure mad as hell at him right now.

Alvin: Perhaps you're just saying that.

The explicit disassociation of oneself from the hostility that another person is expressing needs no illustration; the member making reparation simply indicates he does not want the leader to confuse his feelings with those of the hostile speaker. Finally, we may suggest some ways that members absorb or diffuse the current hostility by recalling the instances in which the charge against the leader is muffled by the device of noting that "Everyone in here does that." Or we may cite the times when a conflict with the leader is transformed into evidence of some inner conflict within each member. The common element in all these examples is that, in understanding their meaning and intent, the figure of affection is no more important than the ground of hostility with which the affection contrasts.

6. *Identifying.* When one member takes the role of the leader in re-lation to another member, when he responds to another member in a manner suggestive of the leader's style or usual message, there is sel-dom any visible evidence that the member has feelings of affection for the leader. Sometimes one can notice a sidelong glance, as if to estab-lish a silent partnership with the leader, but more often than not there is simply an exchange between two members. Yet we would argue that it is precisely at this point that one of the most important expressions of feelings between member and leader occurs. With some trepidation, given the widely divergent uses of the term, we call this form of affec-tion Identifying.

Although we are sure that through those acts scored as Identifying members do establish bonds and indicate existing bonds with the leader, and although we think that to ignore these communications would be to miss a vital part of the relationship, we confess that cer-tain difficulties do arise in keeping a close record of this process.

We find that there are at least three aspects of the leader with which the members can identify: (1) his tendency to make interpre-tive comments about the group process; (2) his values, his general outlook on life, or his particular philosophy about how to teach; and (3) his mannerisms, or other rather superficial aspects of his behavior. When a member interrupts the flow of conversation in the group to comment on the feelings being expressed or to speculate about their origin in prior events, we feel that a useful inference about his feelings may be that he has identified somewhat with the group leader. Simi-larly, we include in our scoring a similar assessment when a member counters others' criticisms of the course with a defense of unstructured-ness, looking at group process, or revealing honest feelings. And, finally, we find ourselves, as scorers, entertaining the notion that the member is identified with the leader when the member leans back in his chair, as the leader does, or prefaces his remarks with a leader-like phrase, such as, "Well, from where I sit . . . ," or, "It might be fruitful to con-sider. . . ."

Of these three, the first is by far the most important and the most frequent. We are primarily interested in noting when the member adopts the interpretive vantage-point of the leader. But now we run into the difficulty we alluded to earlier. Consider two acts initiated by Ralph and Jack at different moments in the group's history, acts iden-tical in word, if not in meaning. They both might say: "I think this group is hung up on whether there is ever going to be any directive-type leadership in here." For Jack this might be the closest he had come to voicing his deep resentment at the leader's passivity. In Ralph

it might be an observation of many members' feelings, but not his own
and the purpose of the act might be to get the issue out in the open
and the feelings resolved, i.e., eliminated, so that the whole group will
be as satisfied as he is with the leader's behavior in the group. But both
acts are interpretive in form. Are they both acts of Identifying?

In the system, as we use it, they would not both be scored as Identi
fying; only Ralph's act would be. We distinguish between acts which
are primarily expressive, and which every other category in the system
is designed to record, and acts which are primarily interpretive. Thus
far we have suggested that when the feelings contained in the interpre
tation are not those of the member, but are, rather, feelings he has
chosen to interpret, as might the leader, we score the act as Identifying.
But what about the feelings the member himself does feel? Cannot the
member interpret them?

He can, of course. But here we must introduce a further distinction.
The stance of the member, relative to the feelings, is crucial. When
we hear the member adopting the observer's stance, we are inclined to
score the Identifying component of the act. For example, contrast the
following three acts, all dealing with anger: (1) "I'm damn angry right
now;" (2) "My stomach is churning around so fast, I guess I just must
be angry;" and (3) "You know when you put together my remark of
last time about Herod with my tirade just now about Nazis and Jews
the theme that comes through loud and clear is hate for people in a
position to judge me." Only the second and third would be scored as
Identifying because only they combine the observer's stance with the
expressive component so clearly stated in the first example.

The implicit rule which we have arrived at is that the scorer
when in doubt, looks first for the expressive aspects of the manifest con
tent and only later for the leader-like stance the member may be taking
toward the objects in question. The result of this scoring convention is
particularly important when we try to score acts on level three, acts
in which the leader is symbolized by various case figures or other ob
jects outside the group. Despite the obvious fact that in analyzing a
case the member is doing to one kind of material what the leader does
with material from the group, we seldom score Identifying when a case
is being discussed. The major reason for this is that case figures are
used so extensively for the projection, externalization, and symbolic
expression of feelings that, in looking for the member's expressive be
havior first, we most often feel that we have grasped the major rele
vance of the act for the member-leader relationship. In this instance
the fact that the member is interpreting the case is of less importance
than the symbolic content of the member's analysis.

When a member attempts to interpret his own or other members' behavior, as might the leader, we feel we are on much safer ground to call the act Identifying. Unlike the person who comments on the case, which the leader seldom does, the member who comments on group process often encounters even more resistance than the leader and stands a very good chance of being linked with the leader in members' minds. That is, his interpretations may earn him the title of "teacher's pet" or "first lieutenant." Members for whom such titles would not be even a little bit gratifying tend to avoid these kinds of acts almost entirely.

7. *Accepting.* Much of what was said about the second category, Resisting, can be applied to the description of Accepting. Both categories are primarily reactive to the role performance of the leader. Whereas Resisting is differentiated from personal animus and mistrust, Accepting must be distinguished from the personal form of affection found in the next category, Moving Toward.

The major forms of affection included under Accepting are: (1) agreeing with the leader; (2) approving of his behavior or the structure of the course; and (3) testifying to the validity or appropriateness of the leader's interpretation.

The boundaries between Accepting and the other three categories of Affection probably give a scorer more difficulty than those of any other category. We have touched upon the Accepting versus Moving Toward issue: whether the positive response to the leader is directed primarily at the leader's role performance or at the leader as a person. The next question is whether the affection should be scored as Accepting or Making Reparation, and the answer depends on the scorer's inference regarding how ambivalent the member is. Making Reparation involves an effort by the member to counter or undo his own hostility, and this effort sometimes produces overt acts quite similar to the typical act of Accepting. Before scoring an act of Accepting, the scorer must rule out the possibility of the act being one of reparation by satisfying himself that the act is not primarily an attempt to stifle the negative side of the member's ambivalence.

Finally, the boundary between Accepting and Identifying must be considered. The crucial issue here is the temporal or, if it can be ascertained, causal connectedness of the leader's act and the member's act. If the leader has just finished implying that the group is avoiding some topic, for a member to express the same perception might well be scored as Accepting. But if the press from the leader is sufficiently removed from the member's act as to suggest that the member had absorbed the leader's message, then the member's expression of the same percept as his own idea would be scored as Identifying. The message to the leader, in these two cases, is quite different. The act of Accepting says, "See, I support you," whereas the act of Identifying says, "See, I am similar to you."

8. *Moving Toward.* The expression of personal affection for the leader, the crux of the Moving Toward category, takes several forms. In the most unmistakable acts one finds the member clearly enunciating his own feelings in the form of liking, trust, comfort, admiration, etc. Other acts merely contain the member's perception of the leader, a perception which is usually associated with a warm, positive response. Finally, there are acts which indicate that the member is interested in decreasing the distance between himself and the leader, that he would like to know the leader or become friendly with him.

The most vivid example of an act scored as Moving Toward is drawn from a female member's account of a dream about the leader.

"We headed to the ocean. We were out in the country, and there was a certain amount of my wanting to overcome our leader through seduction. I was very aware of him being next to me and this sort of thing."

A second example initiated by a male member contains more evident mutuality of feeling than the first.

"Well, we have been chosen by a father figure. And now we're so terribly grateful for having been chosen for the group that we're afraid to transgress."

Most acts scored in this category are more elliptical and guarded. Some convey a desire to become involved, to be open and personal with the leader. Others seem simply to portray the leader in positive terms.

(1) "I think he looks very relaxed, and this is nice."
"It's serenity."
"It's the Mona Lisa."
(2) "I consider him qualified. I wouldn't believe just *anyone*."

While these acts express the members' feelings rather directly, some acts seem more like efforts to establish a close relationship with the leader.

(1) "We're trying to make contact with you."

(2) "I want you to see me as unique, as a person different from all the rest."

These efforts to establish, strengthen, or express feelings of personal affection have already been contrasted with the more impersonal affection found in Accepting. The distinction between Moving Toward and Accepting mirrors quite closely the difference between two of Bales' (1950) positive social-emotional categories, Shows Solidarity and Agrees.

9. *Showing Dependency.* The authority relations area assesses the member's feelings toward the power of the leader. The feelings may emerge as perceptions of the relative dominance of the member and the leader, or they may appear as efforts to transform the power relations between them. The distinctions underlying the three categories in this area are found in the work of Bennis and Shepard (1956), and the notion of viewing dominance and submission as distinct from the affective domain is derived from the work of Leary (1957) and others.

Showing Dependency is the category designed to record those feelings in which: (1) the member perceives the leader to be more powerful and then responds in a submissive and deferential manner; or (2) the member wishes the leader were more powerful and attempts to maneuver him into that position by appropriate action. In either case, the leader's power may involve: (1) the power to provide members with the crucial gratifications, sometimes in the form of rewards and punishments; (2) the power which derives from control over the means, such as knowledge and experience, which are relevant to the attainment of group goals; and (3) the power to determine the destiny of the group, for good or ill.

The leader's control over the crucial rewards and the relevance of his yes-no, stop-go signals are illustrated by the following examples of Showing Dependency.

(1) *Female*: What is it you're supposed to do with the cases?

Leader: Well, we discuss them. There are many ways to discuss them.

Male: With what reference though? Are you looking for anything in particular?

(2) "I sometimes feel I do everything I do to get the approval of the leader."

(3) "Your power comes from the fact that you dish out grades."

The perception that the leader controls vital resources for the group may lead to feelings of dependency, as seen in the next two examples:

(1) "It might help if you would compare the progress of our group with the progress of other groups you've seen."

(2) "Let's face it, you're the expert here. We don't know this stuff."

Finally, the most subtle form of dependency involves those acts which presume, often without stating it explicitly, that the group is weak whereas the leader is strong or that the group is passive and the leader is (or should be) in full command of the situation. Take, for example, one member's angry outburst:

"There's twenty-five hundred dollars [in tuition charges] resting on what happens in here, and to me that's a lot of money. I want to see something done."

Taken in isolation, this act might have several meanings, but in conjunction with the member's later remark: "According to the school records, he's [the leader's] the one in charge," the act becomes clearly an effort to force the leader to assume his proper role of steering the group out of its doldrums. This example is also useful because it reveals how some acts of Showing Dependency arise in the context of hostility and others in the context of affection.

10. *Showing Independence.* In contrast to either Showing Dependency or Showing Counterdependency, those acts scored as Showing Independence express the member's feelings of autonomy and freedom from the constricting influence of the leader's power. There are three basic ways in which this feeling is expressed: (1) acts which emphasize the member's own responsibility for his fate; (2) acts which attempt to clarify the member's goals and values or to enunciate the member's criteria for evaluating his own and others' behavior; and (3) acts which convey a sense of colleagueship and equality between member and leader.

Perhaps the clearest example of Showing Independence of the sort described as clarifying one's own values and responsibility would be the following:

"OK, OK, I know he's [the leader's] there, too. The question still is, though, what do we really want out of this group? What's the point of all this talk if it isn't to learn something for us?"

The more direct form of Showing Independence, in which the member moves toward a partnership in learning, is seen in the next two examples:

(1) "I'll bring in an observation to break the depression, but first I wanted to give him [the leader] an opportunity to figure out why everybody won't speak."

(2) "I do want him [the leader] to be down here with us. I want everybody to be on the same level."

The second example could, in another context, have been an act of Showing Counterdependency, but in this case it occurred at precisely the moment when the member had decided that the leader was "human." For him, at that moment, the weight of the leader's authority had lifted somewhat, and he felt free to see the leader as a fellow human being.

11. *Showing Counterdependency.* The line between independence and rebellion, as any adolescent knows (or is soon told), is both important and exceedingly fine. On one side of the line is the person who is free of, or at least relatively free of, dependency. On the other side of the line is the person who attempts to counter dependency, either by denying his inner needs or by various assaults upon external manifestations of power and control. Acts scored as Showing Counterdependency are of two forms, one aimed at the denial of and the other aimed at destruction of the existing authority structure.

The denial of inner needs for support and guidance takes many forms. In one group, in the first session, a boy interrupted a series of dependent questions aimed at the leader with a vigorous attack upon a case figure, on the grounds that she was too dependent. In his differentiation of himself from the dependent members, and in attacking the "wishy-washy" case figure, the member was effectively denying his own needs to join in the initial dependent reaction to the leader. Much the same process seemed to be operating in the girl who turned to another group member and said, in a rather scornful voice: "Maybe you just want him [the leader] to say things you can hang onto."

The effort to undermine the leader's position of power, to compete with the leader or at least to neutralize his effectiveness is the second important form of Showing Counterdependency. In the following exchange, the male member first attacks the leader's right to have power and then complains about the leader's attempt to impose his views on the group.

Male: None of us really knows what's going on in here, and I wonder if you [the leader] do yourself.
Female: Why don't we play it by ear?
Male: Yeah, but whose ears are we playing by, ours or his?

Both acts by the male member qualify as Showing Counterdependency.

Any effort to decrease the leader's power for reasons of enhancing the member's own sense of power belongs in this category, and since many such efforts are also hostile attacks, it is not uncommon for acts to be scored in one of the hostility categories as well as Showing Counterdependency.

12. *Expressing Anxiety.* Our conception of all five categories in the ego state area has been greatly influenced by the work of Edward Bibring (1953) and his effort to understand anxiety and depression in terms of ego psychology. Anxiety is defined as the affective state which accompanies a person's recognition that he is approaching, or is already in, a dangerous situation. The magnitude of the danger may vary widely, but the common element is the sense of threat to one's own safety or self-regard. Observable indications that a person is experiencing anxiety are of the three major forms: (1) semivoluntary and nonverbal indications of inner tension; (2) public assessment of one's own inner state; and (3) the person's assessments of the environment, or of particular people, which seem congruent with the inner experience of anxiety.

The first form of anxiety includes such indicators as stuttering, disorganization of speech, and gestural expressions of inner tension. In the second, or verbalized, form of anxiety the individual is attempting to convey his apprehension and feeling of being threatened by attending to his inner feelings rather than to the external cause of the anxiety. Several examples might be helpful:

(1) "At this moment, I can feel my heart beating about five times too fast. I feel very uneasy."

(2) "We're like a bunch of mountain-climbers caught in a blizzard."

(3) "Yes, I feel threatened. I think we all feel threatened as hell in here."

More common than reflections upon inner feelings are those expressions of anxiety in which the object, or cause of the anxiety, is explicitly mentioned. Misgivings over where the leader is taking the group, uncertainty about what will anger him, fear of the leader's judgment—these forms of anxiety localize the danger and give it substance.

(1) "I have the crazy idea that he [the leader] has X-ray eyes, that he will see through me even if I say one word, or nothing."

(2) "He's [the leader] just sitting there. What's he thinking about us?"

(3) "What would happen if we had no rules and no structure to guide us?"

The ingredients of the complete act are a vulnerable, threatened self in relation to a judging and dangerous object, and many of the acts convey both sides of this relationship.

13. *Denying Anxiety.* It is one thing to sense that some expressions of feeling calm, at ease, and secure are defensive; it is another to separate the denials from the (relatively) genuine expressions of self-esteem. Our scoring of Denying Anxiety depends largely on the context of the act. When the act is cast primarily in negative terms, e.g., "I am not feeling tense," we tend to score it as Denying Anxiety. Similarly, when the act follows closely on the heels of an expression of anxiety, and the person seems primarily concerned with negating the import of that prior act, we tend to score Denying Anxiety.

It must be made clear that in doing so we are making a rather limited statement about the feelings of the member. When A says, "I am anxious," and member B says, "I am not anxious at all," we are not asserting, when we score member B as Denying Anxiety, that he really is just as anxious as member A. We are asserting that he feels like denying anxiety, like asserting his lack of kinship with someone protesting that he does feel anxious. Consider the following examples:

(1) "I don't see what everyone is so worked up about him [the leader] for. He's probably silent because he's half asleep."

(2) "I couldn't care less what he [the leader] thinks my motives are for saying things in here."

The element of negation is crucial, as is the context of others' expressed anxiety.

There are other acts which seem to belong in this class but are more difficult to define and score. They are the more truly counterphobic maneuvers by which the member expresses trust and confidence primarily in an effort to reassure himself that all is well. These acts sometimes seem based on the quasi-magical belief that if one says it is all right, it will turn out to be, even if it is not all right at the moment. Two examples from the group setting seem relevant:

(1) "Despite the fact that she nearly always sat with her hand cupped over her face, as if to shield herself from the leader's glances, one girl initiated a long speech to the effect that the group was being slowed down by its anxious members. The speech ended with: 'I think it's just silly to be afraid of him [the leader]. If we can't trust him, we can't trust anyone.'"

(2) "Actually, I have been rather amused by his [the leader's] little interpretations. They really are rather soothing."

Both of these acts would be scored as Denying Anxiety. The qualities of protesting against inner distress and of belittling what is threatening are crucial cues.

14. *Expressing Self-Esteem.* Those acts which belong in the Self-Esteem category are the expressions of self-satisfaction and contentment which seem motivated more by the need to express oneself than by the need to counter and deny feelings of distress. This distinction is not always easy to make, but the goal of the category is not hard to state. We intend to record the moments when the member "feels good" in relation to the leader.

The major ways in which a member expresses his self-esteem are: (1) through his sense of being relaxed or secure; and (2) through feeling capable of performing some important task and capable of being what he wishes to be (honest, warm, etc.). Some of the acts scored here are quite diffuse:

(1) "Well, finally, after all these weeks, I'm beginning to feel comfortable in this class."
(2) "Everyone has something to contribute to the group."

But other acts are addressed mainly to the leader and relate to a specific moment in their relationship:

"I felt proud to have you use my comment as an example."

The essential defining characteristic of these acts is that they convey a feeling of self-esteem which is credible, which leaves it to the scorer to separate the expressive from the defensive, the denial from the valid self-report. Despite the errors which will inevitably be made, this distinction is vital to any portrait of a person's feelings about himself and the leader.

15. *Expressing Depression.* Bibring (1953) identifies the feeling of helplessness as the essential ingredient of all depression, but he goes on to imply that this feeling has two main components: one when the person is helpless to effect desired changes in the external world, and the other when he is helpless to control inner forces which he wishes to restrain. These two themes, powerlessness and guilt, underlie most of the acts scored as Expressing Depression.

Powerlessness is expressed in terms of a sense of inadequacy. The members may portray themselves as weak, ineffectual, and insignificant and the leader as competent and powerful.

(1) "How am I supposed to analyze the case? I don't know anything about all this."

(2) "You [the leader] have seen groups like this before. It's all just one big blob to me."

A related issue is aroused by loss, which is sometimes experienced as proof that the person is either too inept to prevent the loss or too unworthy to deserve any other fate.

(1) "You sit there and sit there, and I wonder if we just bore you, or what?"

(2) "I can't believe the group is ending. Somebody has to do something, but I don't know what he should do."

The close connection between guilt and depression seems to stem from the fact that after doing something "bad," a person is forced to realize how unsteady the inner controls can be at times, how helpless the ego is in the face of massive arousal of unacceptable impulses of any variety. As the following examples suggest, the feeling of gloom which follows such reminders are reflections of a person's pessimism about ever being the master of his own fate.

(1) "It just got going, and we were all in it, or almost all, and things were said that I, at least, would have just as soon not have said, not so angrily anyway."

(2) "If we could have just stayed on the surface, and not showed you or ourselves how dependent we really were, I guess we would have saved ourselves all this agony."

(3) "I feel we let you down."

16. *Denying Depression.* Much of what was said regarding Denying Anxiety would apply to Denying Depression, except that what is being denied shifts from feeling threatened by a dangerous external force to feeling powerless and guilty. The efforts to deny depression range from the immediate contradiction of someone else's (or one's own) expression of depression to the manic defenses described by both Lewin (1950) and Klein (1950, 1957).

The content of the denials, when the issue is powerlessness, may involve strident assertions of potency and efforts to disparage any power differential between the members and the leader. When the issue is one of loss, the denial may involve plans to minimize the effect of separation, or it may simply involve unwillingness to share in the feeling of sadness. Denial of guilt feelings often proceeds down the familiar blame-avoidance path of defensiveness, deflection of blame, and self-justification.

The manic defenses against depression often involve more active modes such as euphoric denial of sadness, separation, and guilt. Many of the joking efforts to pass off the depressing implications of failure or impulsiveness belong to this class of feelings.

The Unit of Analysis

Now that we have finished the presentation of the category system, it may be useful to clarify our definition of the unit of analysis, the act. Other observers of social interaction, notably Bales (1950) and Mills (1964), have used the simple sentence as the prototypic act in an effort to isolate the most rudimentary element of interaction. In contrast, the member-to-leader scoring system requires a more global approach for several reasons.

We are attempting to infer the member's feelings from statements which range from the direct to the symbolic, and in many cases the scorer can only discern the latent, leader-relevant feelings by examining the recurrent shadings of many phrases and sentences. The meaning of any single sentence may be far more problematic than the cumulative import of a series of sentences. For this reason we define an act as a single speech or burst of sentences within which the expressed feelings are uniform. One of two events signals the end of an act: (1) the speaker is interrupted by another member or by the leader; or (2) the speaker shifts from expressing one set of feelings to expressing feelings which call for a different array of scored categories.

This procedure makes the scorer's job a good deal easier, since he can summate the impressions he receives about a series of simple sentences before registering his scoring decision. The length of an act, in this scoring system, varies from a single word to a speech extending over almost a page of double-spaced transcript. Whereas Bales typically records around 1000 acts per hour using the smallest unit which would be coherent, this scoring system averages 200 acts per hour.

The difficulties inherent in interpreting a simple sentence are not the sole determinant of our decision regarding the length of our act unit. It is also desirable to eliminate the redundancy within long speeches, in order not to let such long bursts overwhelm the shorter, perhaps equally intense, expressions of feeling. In effect, for a person to be recorded as expressing the same feeling twice in a row, he must yield the floor and then manage to regain it for a second time. We certainly have not solved the problem of how to weight long and short speeches in a way that corresponds to the subjective realities of all members, but this approach is based on the assumption that people adapt to, and eventually tune out, redundant speeches of great length. By the same argument, only if the speaker alters his expressed feelings will listeners record a significant addition to his earlier remark.

Scoring the Leader

The behavior of the group leader is recorded in terms of the 16 content categories, but, in this study at least, we do not ask what feeling he is expressing toward the members. Rather, we chose to record his reflection of members' feelings back to the group.

The first question we ask of an act by the leader is: "What feelings does he imply that the members are expressing toward him?" Thus if a member asks, "Where do we begin?" and the leader parries by saying, "You wish I could get things rolling for the group," we would note that the leader is calling attention to the member's expression of dependency. If he had replied by commenting, "You seem concerned that what you do be OK in my terms," we would note that he is moving in on the anxiety issue as well as the obvious dependency theme.

The first question the scorer asks in examining the leader's acts bears on the feelings he suggests might be active. The second question adds an evaluative dimension to the description by asking whether the leader seems to be approving, disapproving, or merely noting without judgment the member's feelings.

The leader may approve of a member's feelings by actively rewarding the member or by implying that such feelings are legitimate or even desirable. The following exchanges illustrate these two techniques:

(1) *Member*: I may be nuts, but I feel completely the opposite of all of you. I'm actually going to miss coming here every day.

Leader: I imagine it took some courage to say that in this session. I think you're right in sensing that most people are handling the end of the group in a more giddy fashion.

(2) *Member*: I feel mad that we have to have any grades at all.

Leader: Perhaps it *would* be useful to look at how you and others actually do feel about this rather difficult aspect of our relationship.

In both cases the feelings expressed, depression in one and Moving Against in the other, were not only attended to by the leader, they were encouraged and made legitimate by his responses.

Some group leaders may recoil at the thought that they are engaged in a process of encouraging certain feelings, or certain feelings from certain members. Still more may recoil at the thought that they depart from a neutral or blandly accepting stance in the negative direction, that they actively discourage and punish certain feelings. These negative responses include the unresponsive answers leaders are prone to make when assaulted by dependent questions in the first session. They include the rather impatient interventions aimed at uncovering denials. And they include those more personal barbs which do emerge from leaders, as in the following examples:

Member: I'm getting tired of you pulling the rug out from under this group. Is it our group or not?

Leader: You continually assume that your freedom is a substance I'm carrying around in my pocket, to dispense or not to dispense according to my own whim. That's just not the case.

One might characterize this leader's response to hostility as defensive in part, but it is also clear that he has told the member that his hostility is illigitimate, juvenile (or at best adolescent), and not to be encouraged.

The scoring of a leader's act proceeds along two dimensions, the content categories and a three-point evaluative scale, by which the scorer records the leader's attitude toward the feeling being reflected as: (1) positive and encouraging; (2) neutral; and (3) negative and discouraging. As with the member's act, more than one category can be used in describing the act, and the definition of what constitutes an act for the leader is identical to the definition of a member's act outlined above.

The Reliability of the Scoring System

Before turning to the various empirical outcomes of our study, it may be useful to discuss some evidence that the scoring process, although difficult and time-consuming, can be mastered in a way that produces reliable results. Typically, it takes two to three weeks for someone to learn to score, but it would be an error to assume that *anyone* could score reliably after that short a time. Probably the most important characteristic of a scorer is his prior experience with groups, with the world of feelings, and with the self-critical process of assessing the accuracy of his own hunches and observations. It should be clear that a person whose characteristic defense is to deny the subtleties and many-layered quality of interpersonal life would be totally at a loss in the role of the scorer. What we have to examine is the actual correspondence among scorers who were not only trained in a particular system but whose habitual response to the world within and beyond them is psychological in the sense that feelings constitute a relevant part of their concern.

This section summarizes four efforts to assess the reliability of the scoring system. Three of them compare two scorers working on the same material, and the fourth compares one scoring a session before and after a three year time interval. One way to describe the correspondence between scorers is to evaluate the extent to which they agree upon how to score a single act. Regarding the most fundamental issue, whether or not to score a given utterance as relevant to the member-leader relationship, there is very high agreement, ranging from 93% to 98%. The next issue, at what level of inference to score an act, is also one upon which the amount of agreement exceeds 90% in all four studies of interscorer reliability. The picture is more complex when one examines the content categories.

In a scoring system which permits double-scoring of a given act it is possible to have not only perfect agreement and total disagreement but partial agreement, as when two scorers agree on part of the scoring but only one of them goes on to add a second or third content category. The rate of perfect agreement between scorers ranges from 67% to 81%, with a rate of 73% as the average. However, more than half of the disagreements involve not a difference over which category in a given area to score but whether to double-score the act to include that area at all. Thus in the four estimates of the scoring system's reliability, the percentage of acts scored over which there was *substantive disagreement* between scorers regarding which category to score ranged from a low of 9% to a high of 13%. These figures compare rather favorably with the estimates of interscorer agreement for other scoring systems.

The second way to assess the extent of interscorer agreement is to ask whether a given pair of scorers end up, after scoring a whole session, agreeing on which of a pair of group members are higher on each of the 16 categories. In one set of data two-member groups run by T. M. Mills of Yale were used, and a second such comparison was made with the Harvard groups under study here. For the Harvard groups, the question asked was whether the scorers agreed when comparing the most active member with the second most active, the second with the third, and so on to the fifth against the sixth. The percentages of all comparisons made which were in agreement were 87% for the Yale data and 92% for the Harvard data. Since no statistical use is ever made in this study of any summary of over a shorter time span than one session, it would seem that a satisfactory degree of interscorer agreement has been reached.

Several thoughts suggest themselves at this point but they must be identified as speculations without a firm foundation in evidence. It may be that as the length of the scoring unit, or act, increases from the simple sentence to the short paragraph (typically), it is easier to obtain interscorer agreement. It may also be that scorers from quite different intellectual-interpretive traditions might experience greater difficulty in reaching agreement in using the 16 categories than did the scorers in the present study, most of whom had read the same rather unique set of theoretical and clinical studies. But our impression is that the crucial question is whether the particular set of categories used "feels comfortable" to the scorer. Awkward as it is to fall back upon such a vague phrase, it may convey the scorer's legitimate concern that the categories be neither too all-encompassing nor too narrow, neither too superficial nor too deep. Undoubtedly there exists a host of other category systems which would fit these and other criteria of "feeling comfortable." What we are driving at is that one need not abandon all claims to reliability simply because one goes a bit beneath the surface to record interpersonal behavior at the feeling level, and even at the level of symbolically expressed feelings. We would readily grant that at times the process of scoring these groups is anything but comfortable. But evidently, given the results of these reliability studies, two scorers can agree sufficiently often to compensate for the murky passages whose meanings are not apprehended in a similar fashion. It remains now to demonstrate the validity of the scorer's efforts in the only way available. We must determine whether the descriptions that derive from the scoring process aid in developing a coherent picture of individual and temporal differences in these groups.

Some Relevant Literature on Group Observation Techniques

Before concluding our presentation of the member-leader scoring system, we wish to indicate some alternative techniques that illustrate other strategies and other goals in the study of human interaction. We will not discuss the various techniques for recording nonverbal behavior, except to note that Weick's (1967) review article provides an excellent introduction to the literature. The first distinction to be made concerns the level of analysis. On the more sociological level, one finds Bales' (1950) interaction process analysis and Mills' (1964) sign process analysis. Bales' observation scheme begins with an interest in the functioning of small social systems and the process by which members move the group toward or away from the attainment of two fundamental goals, adaptation and integration. Mills' scheme begins with an interest in the process by which members of a collectivity assign value to the objects within and beyond the group's boundaries. Although these systems have been used with success to describe certain aspects of self-analytic groups, they were not designed to assess the feelings of individuals but the relevance of an individual's behavior to the problem-solving and culture-building processes of the superordinate system, the group. At a more psychological level of analysis, we find a number of scoring systems which describe the needs and feelings of the individual. Leary's (1957) two factor scheme for describing interpersonal mechanisms in terms of dominance versus submission and love versus hate dimensions has been used in the coding of interaction in therapy groups and extended by Couch (1960) into a system for observing initially leaderless groups. Schutz's (1958) analysis of interpersonal behavior in terms of need for inclusion, control, and affection has been translated into both an observer rating form and a more continuous observation system. Thelen et al. (1954) observed member behavior in self-analytic groups from the perspective of Bion's concept of work and the basic assumptions which interfere with work: dependency, fight-flight, and pairing.

As one's scoring system moves toward the analysis of inner needs and feelings, a most perplexing problem arises, one which we have ducked rather than solved. In observing initially leaderless groups or in the study of member-member interaction one must, it would seem, accept the fact that for member A to express a feeling to member B often entails a simultaneous expression of quite different feelings toward members C, D, E, etc. A large part of our decision to concentrate on the leader, who is one important but frequently not the most important object for the speaker, derived from our sense of how difficult it would have been to record even a major portion of the feelings which one act may express to its many listeners. To our knowledge, no scoring system has been used in this manner, although it seems a logical consequence of moving away from the system-referent level found in the work of Bales and Mills to the interpersonal and intrapersonal level needed in a more psychological study of human interaction. To score the communication of feelings within *each* dyad would have been a huge undertaking, and we have reduced the task to a manageable size by considering only the dyads which include the leader.

A second issue which differentiates among scoring systems is the matter of how deep one wishes to go in describing the feelings or other psychological states of the individual. Most researchers tend to associate greater depth with decreased reliability. Although this is probably the case, we would add that the problem of observer reliability can be attenuated if greater depth is associated with decreased speed of scoring, the use of multiple scorers, and the use of scorers who have actually observed the group whose tapes or transcripts they are coding. We would not have been able to score these self-analytic groups from the other side of a one-way mirror while they were in process. We would have benefited from Dorothy Whitaker's [1] technique of having scorers confer over the discrepancies between their coding. But one could imagine a degree of depth which could not be managed in an act-by-act scoring system since the relevant cues for the inference would come only from the most careful collation of widely separated acts. In effect, we are proposing that the depth to which one can go and the length

[1] Personal communication.

of the unit-act are positively related. One example of the use of an entire session as the unit is found in Slater's (1966) post-session logs which permit him, the observer-leader, to summate a whole series of impressions in their proper context. Other research techniques which span the entire session are the post-meeting rating, reminiscence, or Q-sort techniques found in the work of Blake and Mouton (1956), Watson (1952), Wechsler and Riesel (1959), and Stock and Thelen (1958). Aside from their greater ease of administration, post-meeting data collection techniques often have the additional merit of extracting comparable data from each participant, something we could not do except for the most highly vocal members. An interesting example of a content analysis system that involves the use of a high speed computer, the General Inquirer, and its application to post-meeting self-report data is found in Dunphy's (1964) study of two Social Relations 120 groups and their development.

Beyond these observations it remains simply to say that the differential usefulness of the various content analysis systems can only be assayed by the potential user of the given technique in terms of his interest and skills. The interested reader may find it helpful to consult the major review articles on observation techniques (Weick, 1967; Medley and Mitzel, 1963; and Heyns and Lippitt, 1954). Furthermore, although the content categories discussed in this section, together with the systems developed by Borgatta (1962, 1963), Carter (1954), and Glad and Glad (1963), offer the researcher a wide variety to choose from, it may be hoped that new observation systems will be developed to fit the particular needs of future research efforts.

Chapter 4

The Individual Performance

The usefulness of an act-by-act scoring system in describing the member-leader relationship can now be tested in three quite different ways: in Chapter 6 we shall consider all the acts initiated by group members within a single session to see how the group as a whole changes over time, and in Chapter 7 we shall consider the members singly in a search for the important individual differences. But prior to either of these analyses, a more elementary question can be raised regarding the feelings expressed by a single member in a single session. We can attempt to develop a meaningful description and conceptualization of what a person is up to on any given day. While this analysis presents us with some data more complex than a single act, it permits us to bear down on a unit of behavior that is considerably more homogenous than either the composite of all members during one session or the entire career of a single member. We shall refer to this one member, one session unit as a *performance*.

The homogeneity of an individual performance is a relative matter. Members do, of course, change tacks in the middle of a session, but a line must be drawn somewhere. What we must hope or assume is that the feelings expressed by most members within the fifty-minute time span of a session will form a coherent whole. The member may leave, feel dissatisfied with what he has said, and return in quite a different mood without disrupting the unity of the single performance. We begin our approach towards understanding the performance with two basic questions: "What is going on?" and "What does it mean?"

The first question is largely a matter of description, the second a matter of interpretation, and the task of interpreting these performances extends our assignment to include the development of a useful theoretical framework. Some of the descriptive process has been presented already in the previous chapters; the member's performance is at first simply a record of how he distributed his acts across the 16 categories and the four levels. We might well have stopped there, but for two reasons we did not. First, we were not entirely sure that we needed 20 dimensions (16 categories and four levels) to describe a performance. Perhaps there were some distinctions in the category system which made no difference, as one might suspect if one found categories that were very highly intercorrelated. If this were true, it would be helpful to reduce the dimensionality of the scoring system from 20 to some more manageable number. Second, and this turned out to be the more important reason for going beyond the single category, we found that all too often the single category could be interpreted meaningfully only by considering the values on one or more other categories. As we reviewed the various performances, it soon became apparent, for example, that for Moving Against and Showing Dependency to be high at the same time meant something quite different than for Moving Against and Showing Counterdependency both to be high. The former suggested disappointment and the latter rebellion. Important patterns of variables were cropping up all over, and it was increasingly difficult to be satisfied with knowing how high the performance was on one category without noting what other feelings were being expressed.

One statistical technique that can reduce the number of dimensions being considered by identifying the important clusters of variables is factor analysis (see Thurstone, 1947, or Harman, 1960). Our examination of the individual performance will be in terms of six bipolar factors which emerge from this statistical treatment of our data. Each factor will be described in terms of the cluster of categories and levels which define each end of the dimension. That is, at one pole of the factor we find a set of variables on which the performances are high and a set on which they are low; the variables defining the other pole are simply the same two sets with high and low reversed. For example, two of the variables that appear on the Rebellion end of one of the factors are Moving Against and Counterdependency; Moving Toward and Showing Dependency are high on the other end of the factor, the pole labeled Loyalty. Thus a full description of the Rebellion factor pattern would indicate not only the relative presence of Moving Against and Showing Counterdependency but the relative absence of Moving Toward and Showing Dependency also. The six factors or 12 factor patterns, which we will call the poles of these six factors, constitute both the basic descriptive scheme to be used in analyzing the individual performance and the basis for developing a conceptual framework for the analysis of individual performances.

The factors whose titles are listed below and which are the concern of the rest of this chapter are our estimates of the basic dimensions underlying the various categories and levels used in the scoring system. The 430 performances subjected to this factor analytic procedure represent the total set of performances in which there were the 20 acts needed to provide a stable base for the percentages used initially to describe each performance. The six factors and the titles given to the factor patterns at each end of the factors are the following:

Factor I: Relations with the leader as analyst

> I+: Enactment
> I−: Dependent Complaining

Factor II: Relations with the leader as authority figure

> II+: Rebellion
> II−: Loyalty

Factor III: Relations with the leader as manipulator

> III+: Counterdependent Flight
> III−: Resistant Complaining

Factor IV: Relations with the leader as audience

> IV+: Relating to the Leader as Colleague
> IV−: Concern with Inner Distress

Factor V: The effect of the leader on the ego state of the member

> V+: Anxiety
> V−: Depression

Factor VI: Commitment to the member-leader relationship

> VI+: Emotional Involvement
> VI−: Emotional Neutrality

One way to define the factors is in terms of the variables which are related to the positive or negative ends of the dimensions. To simplify matters we classified the relationship between a variable and a factor into three degrees of association: major, minor, and no association. Each end of each factor is thus described by a set of variables, some highly associated with (or having a major loading on) that factor pattern and others only moderately associated with (or having a minor loading on) it. Conversely, each variable may bear no relationship to a factor, or it may be positively or negatively related to the factor, to either a major or a minor extent. This information is summarized in Table 4-1.

Table 4-1
Idealized Factor Matrix for Individual Performances

			Factors			
Variables	I	II	III	IV	V	VI
Hostility						
1. Moving Against	−	− −				+
2. Resisting		− −	−	+		
3. Withdrawing						− −
4. Guilt Inducing	− −		− −			
Affection						
5. Making Reparation						− −
6. Identifying	+ +					+
7. Accepting	+	+ +		+		
8. Moving Toward		+ +				+
Authority Relations						
9. Showing Dependency	− −	+ +				
10. Showing Independence				+ +		
11. Showing Counter- dependency		− −	+ +			+
Ego State						
12. Expressing Anxiety		+		− −	+ +	
13. Denying Anxiety		−		−	+ +	− −
14. Expressing Self-Esteem				+		
15. Expressing Depression		+		− −	− −	
16. Denying Depression	+	−		−	− −	+
Levels						
17. Level one	−		− −	+ +		+
18. Level two	+ +		−			
19. Level three	−		+ +			
20. Level four				−		

Note: + + or − − indicates a major loading; + or − indicates minor loadings.

Factor Pattern Titles: I+, Enactment, I−, Dependent Complaining; II+, Loyalty, II−, Rebellion; III+, Counterdependent Flight, III−, Resistant Complaining; IV+, Colleague, IV−, Distress; V+, Anxiety, V−, Depression; VI+, Involvement, VI−, Neutrality.

The table reveals, for example, that four variables contribute to the definition of Factor I+, the Enactment factor pattern: two major variables, Identifying and Level two, and two minor variables, Accepting and Denying Depression. It also reveals a set of five variables that tend to be low when Enactment is high: namely, the set of variables that defines the Dependent Complaining factor pattern which turns out to be the opposite of Enactment. We may now avail ourselves of six factors which do what we intended them to do. They reduce the number of dimensions from 20 to six, and they suggest a series of factor patterns that isolate the important combinations of variables.

At this point most factor analytic studies come to a full stop, and all too often what results is that the researcher spins off a series of interpretations of the factors based upon the titles of the variables and what he surmises the various combinations might mean. This study goes one step further by taking the factor matrix and using it to identify those performances that were particularly good examples of each factor pattern. This procedure involves weighting the original 20 variables six different ways in order to derive six new "factor scores" for each performance. Consider, for example, a performance that was high on the four Enactment variables and low on the five Dependent Complaining variables; such a performance, especially if it was appropriately high or low on the major variables given double weight, would turn out to have a high factor score on factor one. Thus for each of the four groups we collected a list of performances that were high on each factor pattern and went back to the tapes or transcripts in an effort to assess more carefully what was going on and what meaning such performances might have.[1] What follows, for each factor, is an attempt not only to explicate the particular set of high and low variables but also to describe and analyze the best examples of each factor pattern.

Before turning to these performances, we shall set down briefly the conceptual framework that emerged from these clinical analyses. We found it useful to view the individual performance in two ways: first, as expressing or revealing various themes in interpersonal life and, second, as constituting for the member a particular strategy that is aimed at achieving certain outcomes and preventing others. The first or thematic approach serves as our way of tracing the enormous variety of responses to and feelings about the leader backward in time to what we consider to be some of the fundamental antecedent relationships. The four themes which seem to recur with considerable regularity are

---

[1] Most of the direct quotations in this chapter are drawn from group one, the only group for which a full, verbatim transcript was available.

the themes of nurturance, control, sexuality, and competence. To assert that a particular performance seems to connect, for example, with the nurturance theme is not unlike an interpretation that the member, as in the transference relationship, is reacting to the leader as he did his own mother in her capacity as feeder and provider. But there is no sense in getting tangled up over this, since we cannot hope to find adequate evidence to support such a conjecture. However, we may adopt a more conservative form of the statement, asserting simply that whether the response is habitual or new, it can be viewed in terms of its relevance to each of the four themes. Each theme points to a complex of issues, experiences, and residual needs which offer to the member a way of understanding the new group, a way that permits him to connect the member-leader relationship with important antecedent relationships at both the conscious and unconscious levels.

No useful purpose would be served by developing here an elaborate definition of each theme; much of what we intend to include within each theme will be clarified in the process of going through the six factors. Our understanding of the nurturance theme is much influenced by Erikson's (1950) and Klein's (1957; 1963) discussions of the early stages of life and the attendant struggle for safety and support. Unquestionably, the feeding situation is a fetching simile for certain later interactions, but the nurturance theme persists through bruised knees, moments of panic, and periods of high risk and uncertainty.

Similarly, the control theme should call up a more extensive set of familial vignettes than the poignant drama of toilet training. In its more general form, the control theme involves primarily the management of impulse, whether through subjugation, acquiescence, or the semiautonomous process of internalizing the appropriate moral and ethical standards. It is particularly important that the leader's relevance for the control issue be seen as a result of both the leader's authority and power and the member's tendency to project already internalized standards onto the leader. Out of these two aspects of control emerges the dual processes of control through the manipulation of rewards and punishments and control through the manipulation of guilt and shame.

Although the point could have been made earlier, it is particularly relevant, as we turn to the theme of sexuality, that we remember that we are primarily interested in understanding the feelings of group members toward a leader. As a result, some early sexualized relationships are relevant to our study, but many aspects of sexuality are not. At least as we apprehend the situation, the fact that the object of the member's feelings is the group leader makes the oedipal situation far more relevant than the individual's sexual experiences among peers. The oedipal triangularity suggests a set of relationships in which either parent can be a sexualized love object at one moment and a watchful, jealous, or vindictive rival at the next. It is small wonder that the adult who emerges from such a maelstrom finds that the sexual theme raises not only the issues of attractiveness and/or seductiveness but also the issue of potency, the threat of humiliation, and all the consequences of a deadly rivalry.

The unique quality of the competence theme is that the satisfactions involved are solitary and/or self-defined; in the interpersonal context, they depend primarily on the learner's sense of mastery, rather than the teacher's or model's approval. The pleasures of effecting changes in the physical or personal world and the growing sense that one can handle these worlds with knowledge and skill have been elaborated upon by White (1963) and Erikson (1959). Our thoughts on this theme are also much influenced by Bion's (1961) notion of the work group, by which he means the collaborative effort of individual group members to achieve a common goal through rational and explicit modes of interaction.

If the thematic analysis is to be maximally useful, it should connect with our other way of viewing an individual performance, the analysis of performances as strategies. In this view, the performance of any individual is a compromise between the seeking of goals and, as Ezriel (1952) suggests, the avoiding of disasters. Thus in addition to sketching some of the earlier, prototypic interactions which give a performance its thematic underpinning, we shall inquire into how the performance expresses certain latent needs and latent fears of the member and how it balances these forces in the observable behavior. This analysis of behavioral strategies has been employed with particular success by Whitaker and Lieberman (1964) in their study of therapy groups.

Recapitulating, our analysis of each factor pattern asks the following questions: (1) What categories and levels define the pattern? (2) What categories and levels define the opposite factor pattern? (3) Looked at more clinically, what is going on in the particularly high performances? (4) What themes seem to underlie these performances, what kinds of antecedent relationships are most suggested by them? (5) What latent hopes and fears combine to form the observable strategy adopted by the member? With these questions in mind, we may now proceed to the analysis of the six factors.

Factor I: Relations with the Leader as Analyst

I+: Enactment
I—: Dependent Complaining

Enactment I+ Variables	Dependent Complaining I— Variables
Major: Identifying Level two Minor: Accepting Showing Independence Denying Depression	Major: Guilt Inducing Showing Dependency Minor: Level three Moving Against Level one

The major issue reflected in the first factor is how the member reacts to a leader whose behavior is characterized by relative inactivity and by a marked tendency, when he does speak, either to interpret some aspect of the group interaction or to raise questions about it. The leader's professional role fails to provide the expected control, direction, and mildly nurturant behavior which many students anticipate on the part of a teacher.

The pattern of factor loadings on the positive and negative poles of this factor suggests that these two quite different reactions on the part of group members have in common the fact that they are both addressed to the analytic aspect of the leader's total role. A performance high on the Enactment factor pattern represents an attempt to take on and enact the leader's analytic role vis-à-vis other group members. Although the function of this enactment may and does vary greatly from one performance to another, the common elements include some satisfaction with the leader's contributions and acceptance of his implied injunction that the group members should attempt to carry on the analytic tasks of the group for themselves. A performance high on Dependent Complaining reflects the member's dissatisfaction and frustration with the leader's analytic role. These performances are characterized mainly by complaints which derive from a dependent orientation to the leader. The import of the complaints would seem to be that the leader has disappointed the member's legitimate expectations that he play a strong, supportive, and/or controlling leader role rather than the weak, indifferent, and overly permissive role they see him playing. To the extent, then, that the Dependent Complaining performance indicates a frustration of dependency needs and concern over the inadequate behavior of the group leader, it is not surprising that such performances are particularly lacking in evidence of internalization of the leader's role and a corresponding focus on the meaning of the group interaction.

Enactment. A more careful analysis of the ten performances in each group having the highest factor scores on Enactment suggests some important aspects of this way of relating to the leader *qua* analyst. The primary means by which members enact the leader's role are by questioning other members, by reflecting their words back to them and encouraging them to speak further, by arguing for a pragmatic, non-moralistic, and exploratory attitude as one attempts to analyze behavior, and, above all, by offering interpretations of some aspect of the group experience. When Gino reacted to the comments of another group member by saying: "If I was a psychoanalyst, I'd go to work on that and say . . .," or when Harry set himself the task of connecting one day's discussion with the underlying theme of a previous day ("I could offer an interpretation of what has been happening here today"), the attempt to take on the previously established role of the leader was clear and unmistakable, to the scorer, to the leader, and to the other group members.

In one of the more direct statements of the feelings underlying enactment, Peter, in the midst of a performance which was high on Enactment, said to the leader:

"We accept what your role is now. I stopped trying to call you by your first name. I stopped trying to fight it. We had that flurry over dirty words, but now you're Dr. Dawes. You sit up there and make interpretations. That's fine and good. You're a perfectly functional member of the group. . . . Now we're away from mothers and fathers."

A more subtle form of enactment is found when one member "takes on" another member whose complaints and value position have cast him in opposition to "the course" and, either implicitly or explicitly, the leader. When Alvin, an ordained minister in clerical garb, made a sustained attack on the group for ignoring the spiritual and ethical implications of a case, Harry, Marie, and Frank all counterattacked. Their response to Alvin soon took the form of a heresy trial with Alvin as the heretic and themselves as true believers. Alvin had "introduced morality into a group that is trying to understand things, not judge them." Furthermore, he had introduced a chilling note of conscience. As Marie put it: "I think this repression of more earthly things is very bad." In short, it is quite common for members to assert a "new and more relativistic ethic," opposed to "conventional" or traditional morality, by way of defending and representing the leader in the group.

The one remaining form of enactment which deserves mention is found when group members take on some characteristic behavior pattern of the leader. It may be a favorite introductory clause ("Well, what I hear you saying is . . .") or it may be a more global aspect of the leader's style, such as his tendency to be elliptical or mysterious in his comments.

In reviewing the performances which were high on the Enactment factor pattern, it is clear why Identifying and Level two have the two major loadings on this factor. Since this factor pattern picks out performances in which the member is enacting the leader's role, not only is Identifying the relevant category but nearly all of this behavior would be scored at Level two since the feelings are relevant to the leader but are not addressed to him personally. The member who is high on Enactment tends to focus, as does the leader, upon the various individual and group dynamics that he observes. The categories with minor loadings on the Enactment factor pattern, Accepting, Showing Independence, and Denying Depression, tend not to occur together; rather, each one, when it combines with the major defining categories, gives to Enactment its distinctive shading. The various shadings that are possible within this single factor pattern can be most clearly explicated by turning now to the four themes described earlier: nurturance, control, sexuality, and competence.

Of these four themes the one most relevant to Enactment seems to be competence. The leader, like teachers and parents before him, serves as a useful model for the member. One senses in such performances, and these tend to be the ones which are also high on Showing Independence, the delicate process found also in the latency period boy working alongside his father in the workshop. Some of the boy's productions may be imitative, but they must be treated as independent creations or the precarious sense of autonomy will evaporate; at some level the boy wants approval, but if it is given in other than an offhand and indirect fashion, the boy's pride in his own accomplishment may wither. What we are describing here is the often difficult process of increasing one's own private sense of competence while at the same time using one's elders both as models and as sources of support and reward.

Viewed as strategy, this form of enactment seems best characterized as an effort on the member's part to move parallel with the leader, neither toward him nor away from him. One often senses that the member harbors positive feelings toward the leader and perceives that the leader reciprocates these feelings, but neither the member's feelings nor his perceptions about the leader tend to be verbalized in the context of the Enactment performance. The latent goal of the Enactment performance, to the extent that it reflects the competence theme, may well be a situation in which the leader expresses his regard and respect for the member. But several latent fears restrain the member from moving too abruptly toward such a goal. Perhaps the leader would be alienated by a direct bid for positive evaluation in the member's contributions, or perhaps, on the contrary, the leader might become directly rewarding and thereby destroy the member's slowly increasing sense of autonomy and intrinsic motivation. Perhaps the leader only appears to esteem the member. Or, to look at quite a different issue, what would the other members think if the leader did become more rewarding toward the member? The fear of being seen as the teacher's pet, the fear of being treated with jealousy and contempt, and the fear of being absorbed with the leader to the exclusion of the potential gratifications that are possible with other members all restrain the member and give Enactment its highly indirect, even furtive quality.

A second theme that sometimes seems to underlie the Enactment performance is nurturance. Here the whole process of taking on the leader's role seems to be less in the service of autonomy strivings than the service of quite a different goal: fusion with the leader. Such performances often have a rather manic quality, with Denying Depression replacing Showing Independence as the characteristic minor variable. The latent desire of such performances seems to be to break down the boundary between member and leader and to achieve the kind of primary identification with the leader that forms the basis of many Eucharistic and cannibalistic rituals. Enactment in the service of fusion is not only characterized by high levels of Identifying and Denying Depression, but also by an absence of complaints and expressions of dependency. To express dependency is, in effect, to call attention to the member's separation from the leader, which is precisely what this magical or mystical version of an Enactment performance is intended to deny.

Two other aspects of Enactment should be mentioned. It is not uncommon to find such performances reflecting the control theme, to find the member behaving like the leader because he feels it is the appropriate thing to do. In place of the concern over one's own self-directedness, a concern that was central to the competence version of

Enactment, one finds concern over the leader's approval. As reflected in the high level of Accepting which is characteristic of these performances, the member seems to be like the child who imitates and anticipates his parents' behavior and underlying standards in order to be rewarded and praised.

The sexual implications of Enactment vary according to whether the leader (or parent) is seen as a rival or a love object. Taking over the role of the rival suggests the interpersonal process of replacement and the intrapsychic process of identification with the aggressor. The function of what Slater (1961b) calls positional identification is to achieve the status and benefits which accrue to the envied rival. On the other hand, the familiar consequences of dyadic involvement, i.e., that some aspects of each person's behavior are taken over by the other person, should not be ignored as one possible basis for enacting the leader's role. We are speaking here not of regressive fusion nor of imitation, but of those testaments to the paradox of separateness and intimacy which both express and further cement a sexualized relationship.

In summary, a pattern of categories that center around instances of identification and an avoidance of categories that imply some objection to the leader's role has led us to consider a number of interpretations of such behavior. Looked at in one light, Enactment is a way to learn, but it is also a way to fuse with the leader, to comply with his standards, to replace him, or to express one's affection. It may be of some help to remind ourselves that most Enactment performances seem to be influenced predominantly by the competence theme, but we are also reminded that the member-leader relationship is no place to look for simple and unequivocal connections between the overt behavior and the underlying motivation of the individual. On the manifest level, the Enactment performance is relatively devoid of direct contact between member and leader; the member's eye-contact with the leader is clandestine and sidelong, and we are left with little more than the evident similarity between the member's and the leader's interpretive, analytic role. And yet the thematic analysis of the Enactment performance suggests that the latent goal varies from a moment of recognition and esteem by the leader to rather primitive fantasies of identity and fusion. Only when one considers the various fears, fears that range from unreciprocated affection to loss of autonomy to isolation from the group of peers, can one understand the member's overt strategy as a compromise betwen what is desired and what is feared if the desires are pursued too directly.

Dependent Complaining. If we turn to the factor pattern that is both statistically and conceptually the opposite of Enactment, we find quite a different reaction to the leader's silence, interpretations, and analytic role. Far from being an appropriate model for identification, to some the leader who insists upon behaving in such an unexpected and unhelpful manner becomes the object of considerable reproach.

Many, but by no means all, of the Dependent Complaining performances are highly symbolic. In the first few sessions case figures and outside authorities are the prime targets for group members' feelings that they are abandoned and deprived of love or that they have had the misfortune to be stuck with a weak and inept group leader. Later in the group's development the same feelings are heard again, and a number of Dependent Complaining performances are direct expressions of the members' disappointment and exasperation with the leader.

The content of the symbolic and displaced performances vary somewhat. Eunice, in the first group meeting, viewed almost every case figure as needing support, and since the other case figures had failed to provide it, there was a tone of reproach and pleading throughout the comments. From other cases emerged other figures who became the focus of these feelings: a mother who didn't understand, a dead father who would have, a coldly superior young man whose interest in a girl was more to remodel than to love her, a weak father who had no control over the family, a distant mother who was not involved enough in the children, and another who only went through the motions of warmth and love.

The more direct performances express quite similar themes. One member reacted negatively to the leader's silence at a point when an encouraging or guiding comment would have been a relief. Other members agreed that the leader was like "an impenetrable fortress." In another session Frank said, with considerable emotion: "There's 2500 dollars [in tuition payments] in this classroom resting on what happens here, and to me that's a lot of money. I want to see something done." The implication would seem to be that by his inactivity the leader is causing the group to be a failure, and this should not be permitted to continue. Two sessions later Frank said bitterly, "We have an authority that stands for no authority." In another group, Paul put his reaction to the leader's inactivity in somewhat similar terms: "Aren't we important here? Doesn't anyone care that we may fail miserably? We need direction and control to salvage anything at all from the group." Not only should the leader provide the control and eadership; he should share his secrets, the hidden insights which members feel are "what we're supposed to find out here."

One complaint against the leader which is frequently used to express both the hopes and the disappointments embedded in this performance is that the leader, in talking about "the group," is guilty of "over-generalizing," by which is conveyed the desire to be distinguished as a unique member. We must ignore here, but not by way of discounting, the probability that the leader has, in fact, misrepresented some members' feelings in his comments. All we can say at this point is that when the member is feeling unseen by the leader, he is not likely to enact the leader's role in relation to other group members.

Thus the content of the performances high on Dependent Complaining reveals two major complaints about the group leader as analyst, one that he is weak and another that he is cold. Underlying both these complaints is an assumption that this situation was to have been an appropriate context for the expression and gratification of dependency needs. But the desired strength and support were not found, and at least for that session, the member appears snagged on the dependency issue and unable to perform the various analytic tasks of the group.

The two main themes underlying Dependent Complaining performances seem to be nurturance and control, but there are important connections with the issue of competence as well. In Melanie Klein's stark vocabulary, the leader as analyst becomes, for some members, "the bad breast": deliberately depriving, teasing, and remote. For others, this frustration is compounded by the leader's failure ("at the very least," one can almost hear them say) to provide structure and direction for the group. Not only are the fantasies of unconditional love destroyed, but efforts to determine the leader's conditions for approval are frustrated when the leader vacates the familiar position of the active, dominant authority. And out of this frustration come the various accusations that the leader is too weak and passive to save the group from floundering in chaos.

The competence theme is activated by all of the considerations discussed above in that the member may feel that the leader is an altogether inappropriate model from whom to learn. For some the fact that he is "doing nothing" disqualifies him; for others, the fact that his interpretations are either inaccurate or too devoid of compassion disqualifies him. In either case, the leader stands in the way of the member's expcted gain in personal competence.

Out of these responses to the leader as analyst comes a particular strategy, one designed to arouse the guilt of the leader, to remind him of his proper function, and to achieve a radically different state of affairs. The goal of all this complaining would seem to be a relationship in which it is the member and not the leader who is the passive one. One senses that any activity on the leader's part would be better than none, but there is obviously a preference for a leader who provides support, direction, and wisdom. The question of why this goal is not pursued in a more straightforward manner is answered in part by a look at some of the member's latent fears. The worst imaginable outcome would seem to be one in which the member moved toward the leader, in the guise of a trusting and vulnerable neophyte, only to have the leader move away with disgust or utter indifference. Thus the member's goals are couched not in terms of personal needs but in terms of moral imperatives appropriate to anyone who would dare set himself up as a leader: be strong, be warm, be the model of all that is wise and good. If the leader still refuses to obey these imperatives, it is not the member he is rejecting; it is common decency and the moral order.

The contrast between Enactment and Dependent Complaining can be cast in terms of the relevant themes and strategies. One difference between the two responses to the leader as analyst is that in the Enactment performances the member sees the leader's relevance primarily in competence terms, as opposed to the primacy of nurturance and control issues in Dependent Complaining. But even within themes there are differences. To the extent that nurturance themes affect the factor Enactment implies an effort at fusion and primary indentification whereas Dependent Complaining implies both a sense of loss or disappointment and an effort to force the leader to become more protective. Similarly, within the competence theme the issue is whether or not the leader provides an adequate model from which the member can learn. At another level, the contrast can be seen as a divergence in latent goals and fears, with Enactment implying a goal in which the member is active but fears a loss of autonomy and Dependent Complaining implying a more passive goal state and fears of rejection.

Factor Two

The second factor isolates two quite divergent reactions to the leader in his capacity as authority figure. The positive end is characterized by the two most direct forms of affection; the negative end by the two most direct forms of hostility. Accompanying the two hostility categories on the Rebellion end of the factor are efforts to counter and deny feelings of dependency, anxiety, and depression, whereas these three feelings are revealed directly on the Loyalty end of the factor.

Factor II: Relations with the Leader as Authority Figure

II+: Loyalty
II−: Rebellion

Loyalty	Rebellion
II+ Variables	II− Variables
Major: Showing Dependency	Major: Moving Against
Moving Toward	Resisting
Accepting	Showing Counter-
	dependency
Minor: Expressing Anxiety	Minor: Denying Anxiety
Expressing Depression	Denying Depression

The main issue indicated by this polarity is one of how shall the group member respond to the authority and power of the leader. One option open to a member is to oppose the leader, to challenge his authority and combine overt hostility with efforts to conceal or minimize any inner distress brought on by the confrontation. Another option, an opposite reaction in most respects, is to accept the leader's authority. The pattern of Loyalty categories suggest that, despite some inner trepidation on the member's part, the leader is seen as a dependable and valued figure who will protect the members from undue stress. The shadings and variations in the reactions to the leader as authority figures can be made clearer by referring to the particularly high and low performances.

Loyalty. The ten performances which emerge as best representatives of the II+ or loyal response to the leader reveal not only an absence of hostility and rebellion but the presence of dependency and affection. Perhaps the best examples to start with would be the reactions of Marie and Jane after an attack on the leader. Jane announced her loyalty with some embarrassment over how willing she is to believe others, but still, as she put it: "He's an assistant professor, I mean, he knows so much more than I do—and I think, 'He must be right'—because he's sitting there for a long time and really thinking about it, you know? Not getting involved—I don't know, it's very upsetting." Marie, in the same session, made Jane look like a doubting Thomas by comparison. She followed Jane's declaration with: "You see, I believe—I believe every word he says, and I don't justify it. I believe people in similar positions. I believe just about every word a therapist would say to me." And then a moment later, "I feel everything he says to be true, I mean, some of the things, I don't know if I agree with some of the things intellectually. I probably do; but not only that, I believe them." It is not entirely relevant to the present discussion, but perhaps it should be pointed out that Marie and Jane were soon to express quite different feelings than these toward the leader. What matters more at this point is the clear equation of the leader with the image of professor and therapist and the positive, dependent, and trusting response to such a figure.

Some of the Loyalty performances were primarily dependent, for example when Merv directed a series of course-related questions to the leader and then justified them by saying, "This was set up as a course, and he *is* the authority figure, and he's the one who's going to dispense the grades." Other such performances reveal the affection more clearly, as when one female member reminisced about "stealing pennies from Daddy" or when another female member interpreted a boy-girl relationship in one of the cases in father-daughter terms. She said: "She's lacking a father and I think his being older . . . and being a male would make Russ [the case figure] the kind of father she probably always wanted, the father incorporating all the good points of the mother but still being a male. What could be nicer than having a nice seductive father so far as she's concerned, having been rejected by her father when she was young? I don't know."

One example of the sexual aspect of Loyalty, which still preserves the dependency theme, is Lili's report of her dream in the last week. The figures in the dream were the group leader, a male member of the group, and Lili herself. The content involved these three leaving the total group, driving fast in an open convertible, and ignoring a policeman, and ended with the leader and Lili walking off together, hand in hand, into the woods. The sexuality is obvious, but the importance of the status difference between Lili and the leader was also evident. As she put it, "There was a certain amount of wanting to overcome our leader through seduction." After some probing by some other group members, particularly the boys, she went on to connect driving at 85 miles an hour with the speed at which her father often drove.

A second example of the fusion of submissiveness and sexuality on the part of a female member would be Dolores' responses when the group's most dominant male (Peter) suggested that everyone free associate on the topic of sexuality. Dolores' were: "dominance, need, unhappy, cry, dirty whore, floor, Peter, Dr. Dawes," in that order. Dolores then teased the priest in the group for being celibate, entered into a brief discussion about incest, and then grew visibly anxious and withdrew. In another session, Dolores' performance was notably high on Loyalty, and it featured one exchange about the leader in which she said, "I put my complete faith and trust in him, like a daughter puts in her father, because I feel that when the group needs some direction he'll be there." When a male member asked, "Are fathers perfect?" her answer was, "My father is."

It would be difficult to draw precise boundaries between the themes of nurturance, control, and sexuality within a given performance that is high on the Loyalty factor pattern. To be sure, the nurturance theme seems particularly relevant when the imagery dwells upon oral gratification or the quasi-religious constructions of the beneficent leader, but these manifestations of Loyalty are often blended with a form of sexualized submissiveness, particularly among the females. No single factor differentiates among males and females, as they interact with a male leader, more than this one. Females initiate nearly two-thirds of the Loyalty performances but only one-third of the performances high on Rebellion.

It is altogether possible that females are more likely to experience dependent feelings, at least toward a male authority, but it is also likely that for females such behavior is more consonant with the sex role definition of the appropriate way to be seductive and close. Evidently, the image of the loving and compliant daughter can be transferred to the classroom interaction without great difficulty. But, again, it would be unwise to draw too heavy a line between the various themes. The not infrequently pregenital quality of the member's sexualized fantasies yields an image of the "nice seductive father" who is gentle, benevolent, and infinitely reassuring; to wit, an image that condenses nurturance, control, and sexuality themes rather neatly.

One of the rare performances by a male group member that was high on Loyalty was totally symbolic. It involved a projection of feelings into the case of a girl who had lost her father and who was searching for a way to preserve "some connection with him." As such, it fits the above picture quite well. Another such performance by a male ocurred in the final session, and it followed by one session this boy's report of a dream in which he was strapped down and had his tonsils removed by a doctor who "bore a resemblance" to the leader. In the final session, this member was particularly dependent, referring to the session as the Last Judgment and the Day of Atonement. He wondered aloud whether the tape recorder would be on during the exams, "to record the sighs." Finally, a third Loyalty performance by a male contained a rather clear statement of filial submission: "The world is filled with authorities; they're all around you; you can't fight them; you have to give in to them." This statement jarred considerably with the rebellious tone of the session in which it occurred. From these details, it may be suspected that the Loyalty pattern in boys resembles primarily the defeated son vis-à-vis the potent arbiter of a father.

The thematic analysis of Loyalty performances thus yields a composite of passivity, trust, submissiveness to authority, and either a variant on sexual thralldom for the females or post-oedipal capitulation for the males. But what do the expressions of anxiety and depression signify? They may simply be testaments to the degree of trust placed on the leader. But one wonders if there is not inevitably a persistent uneasiness that derives from the very circumstances of dealing with someone in a position of formal authority. Things are not always what they seem in such relationships. There is always the possibility that the authority is concealing his true feelings out of genuine consideration or out of a sense of professional good form. "Perhaps, behind the facade, he is really scornful or impatient or disinterested." "Perhaps I am only being patronized or praised beyond my true merit." These thoughts are the basis of the members' apprehensions, and they underlie both the pleasures and perils of many dependent relationships. Young adults are particularly prone to differentiate between the rewards possible within a formal, hierarchial relationship and the rewards possible when two people of equal status are honest with one another. To the extent that the Loyalty performance is restrained by the latent fear of presuming too much upon a formal relationship, the expressions of affection and trust will tend to be counterbalanced by indications of the member's inability to feel entirely relaxed or self-assured.

Rebellion. In contrast to the positive and dependent response to the leader as authority, the Rebellion performances emphasize the oppressive and autocratic aspects of the leader's role. Frank's attack on the leader, about a third of the way through group one, is a good example of what rebellion sounds like in this context.

"A lot of things you said yesterday were really farfetched. This could be described as the revolt against authority, you see, and all that. You can weave all kinds of theories out of it. I'll let you have some fun today. Yesterday you said something about him [another group member] galloping off into the hills with the women and something like this, and I conducted a little private poll out at the Yard punch yesterday, and I found that you are all washed up."

He went on to berate the leader for his "authoritarian attitude," referring mainly to his power to intimidate people into believing his far-fetched interpretations. The issue veered off onto another track and returned only when one member referred to the leader as a father figure; this rekindled Frank's anger. "All right, maybe Dr. Allen is supposed to be a father figure, but *I* don't see where he's a father figure. To tell you the truth, I think *my* opinion's as good as *his.*"

The other high Rebellion performances reflect this opposition to the leader's authority in one way or another. Gino challenged one interpretation with the reply: "Stuff like that may very well be true and then again I say: So what?" Others opposed the leader more by mocking and ridiculing his interpretations than by expressing anger. But one implication is clear: the members who are being rebellious feel that the leader, by virtue of his power and the repetition of his own viewpoint, has had an undesirable effect, particularly upon the more docile and gullible members of the group. Since the leader will eventually grade the group members' papers and exams, the fear that he will attempt to establish and then insist upon adherence to a "party line," prompts increasingly direct challenges to his position of perceived power.

Beyond the direct challenge to the leader's authority, one finds that the issue of sexual rivalry is frequently fused with the issue of power. Harry, in the first session of the group, mocked the case figures for their "rational sitting around and working out their little problems" and then went on to eulogize those who are "strong, clever, and wily" enough to get married as early as possible. Gino, in another early session, expressed his admiration for "showmen . . . and that is one of my great ideals—a performance, vaudeville." Following a session in which the leader alluded to the operation of a group norm that sexuality was a taboo topic, two members reacted angrily. One implied that the leader had been taking unfair advantage of information the member thought the leader had received outside the group context from a girl the member had been dating. The other member said, "I get a little angry when you say this is unsexual. I consider myself sexual. When you say this, I get pretty angry. This is a positive threat where I have to come out and prove myself." In all of this, the leader emerges as both a threat and a rival in the area of sexuality and as a major hindrance to any heterosexual pairing among the members.

As in the case of the Loyalty performances, there is a mixture of nurturance, control, and sexuality themes in almost all of the Rebellion performances. The control theme seems most central, however, and the fundamental issue throughout these performances is, "Who's the boss?" The answer varies; some members assert only that members and leaders should share the power equally ("One man, one vote."), whereas others imply that an inversion of the power structure, to the exclusion or total replacement of the leader, would be desirable.

If the various nuances embedded in the nurturance and/or sexuality themes are added to these goals, which are stated here simply in terms of power, the picture is more complicated. In nurturance terms, the resentment can be expressed as bitterness over who controls the satisfactions in the group: whose smile of recognition means the most to people or who "dispenses" the grades. The rebellion performance, in this light, is an attack upon the source of supply, a form of robbing and spoiling that Klein (1957) describes so vividly.

More common than Rebellion which focuses on nurturance issues is the rebellion in which control and sexuality themes are combined. The classical oedipal pattern in which the boy resents and seeks to end the father's domination in the sexual sphere is reflected in this factor pattern. The fact that males are more commonly found at the Rebellion end of the factor than at the Loyalty end is an indication of the extent to which the male members tend to see the male authority as blocking them from developing their own autonomy, sexual relationships, and sense of competence.

Beneath the surface appearance of hostility and counterdependency one finds some evidence of distress, although this tends to be denied by the member. The denials of anxiety and depression that accompany Rebellion seem designed to hold in check the fear of retaliation and the exposure of one's own self-doubts and weaknesses. Without the member's own fear, guilt, and lack of self-esteem as part of the picture, the rebellion would lose much of its strident tone. Another way to put this is that the latent fear of the leader's retaliation takes the edge off the attack, as does the member's latent fear of succeeding in the revolt only to be found lacking in whatever qualities of strength or maturity it takes to manage the job of being the leader.

Contrasting the two responses to the leader as authority, the main difference between Loyalty and Rebellion seems to be over whether the leader will provide the desired satisfactions and license and whether, even if he did, one would want these benefits as a gift from a well-meaning and generous authority rather than as a victory prize for challenging and defeating the authority. Loyalty seems to imply somewhat more involvement with nurturance than Rebellion, but the latter is not without its antecedents in early oral phenomena. The latent goal of the Loyalty performance seems to be security and reciprocal affection with the leader; the goal of Rebellion suggests more the aim of independence from the leader and freedom to pursue private or peer-group satisfactions. For a member high on Loyalty the gravest disaster would be rejection; for the member high on Rebellion it would be defeat and loss of power.

Factor III: Relations with the Leader as Manipulator

III+: Counterdependent Flight
III−: Resistant Complaining

Counterdependent Flight III+ Variables	Resistant Complaining III− Variables
Major: Counterdependency Level three	Major: Guilt inducing Level one Minor: Resisting Level two

The performances at either extreme of factor three call attention to the fact that some members respond to the leader not primarily in terms of his interpretive-analytic role or his formal status and power, but in terms of his capacity to influence the members. Not all modes of influence are relevant here; factor one and factor two suggest that the leader can attempt to influence the member by example or by coercion. In factor three the attempted influence process is seen as personal, devious, and manipulative. Here we find the image of a leader who, for highly suspect motives of his own, is trying to control the members through trickery, through raising the member's guilt— the list of artful ruses is endless. In short, the members are here responding in a vigilant and mistrustful manner to a leader who is seen as clever but basically narcissistic.

The two poles of the factor, although they are responsive to the same percept of the leader, differ markedly in that Counterdependent Flight amounts to a heroic rejection of the leader and his snares, whereas Resistant Complaining suggests that the member feels caught by the leader but is doing his best to escape or to prevent further entrapment. The fact that three of the levels help to define this factor indicates that the strident Counterdepndent Flight reaction is more likely to be expressed toward symbolic objects outside the group; the leader and the group as a whole tend to be railed against more for having already succeeded in manipulating the member.

The Counterdependent Flight performance is not directed against the structurally determined power of the leader but against his capacity to influence and even stifle the group members by being overly intrusive or protective. This flight reaction is an attempt to preserve one's autonomy despite the presence of such a figure. These performances are usually found as one-half of a dialogue, especially in discussing the case material; the issue may be joined, for example, over whether the case son is in dire need of someone to love and direct him (a performance we have already described as Dependent Complaining) or whether, as the Counterdependent Flight performance suggests, the son needs to leave home and live his own life. The covert message for the leader in such case analysis seems to be that the leader should recognize the member is a fully self-reliant person who would resent any attempt on the leader's part to encroach upon his freedom.

The Resistant Complaining performance also succeeds in conjuring up the manipulative leader, but whereas Counterdependent Flight implies a rejection of the leader's control, Resistant Complaining has a more pleading and suspicious quality. The member's perception that the leader has already had a great influence upon the group, without the member's being quite aware of how this came about, leads to a hypersensitive and mistrustful response to his slightest gesture or remark. The complaining tone stems almost entirely from the unhappy awareness of having been manipulated by the devious leader. The subjective loss of freedom impels the member to plead with the leader either to leave him completely alone or to make every act fully explicit in order that he may more deliberately accept or reject the leader's influence attempt.

Counterdependent Flight. The best examples of Counterdependent Flight tend to occur early in the group's development, when cases and more general topics hold the group's attention. In one such discussion the group's attention was focused on the "teen generation" and its tendency to play it cool. Harry voiced the theme of Counterdependent Flight by defending those who "question many, many things" and approved of playing it cool as "a conscious attempt to disassociate yourself from society." In some examples the flight takes the form of "getting out on your own" and "learning not to need all this security." But in others the resolution involves "staying within the family or society." As Merv put it, "I think nothing at all about telling an outright lie to my parents." This was in relation to his being free to go where he wants with friends, since the truth would upset or "hurt" his mother. Whereas Merv was reacting against the potentially suffocating mother, Marie stressed the need to gain freedom within the family in another way. Her notion was that, "If you're diplomatic and good at handling parents, you make everything all right." The son in the case under discussion should have been a better "parent-handler," a phrase which portrays nicely the countering of dependency needs and the emphasis upon maintaining a free hand in relation to pressures from above.

Perhaps the epitome of the Counterdependent Flight which retains some vestige of the old dependency relationship is Harry's insistence that, "It's fun to milk your parents for as much money as you can," provided that you thereupon clear out of the family and get married. Particularly salient in all these performances is the scorn directed at those who are "submissive," who accept rules as "crutches," or who feel that they have "to be mothered by this great institution called society." The contempt for those who have "sold out" and the emphasis on self-assertion and autonomy reveal how touchy the member feels about being influenced or being viewed by the leader as a passive conformist.

When we yielded to the temptation to discuss the previous factor, Loyalty and Rebellion, in terms of the father image, the reader might have wondered whether we were not being deceived by the fact that all the leaders in this particular study were males. Perhaps some of this wondering can be removed if we underscore the extent to which the present factor lends itself to discussion in terms of one aspect of the mother imago. That is, we would prefer to conclude that a leader of either sex will be reacted to both as a father and as a mother than to ignore the common images of mothers and fathers that emerge in groups and in the society at large. We can grant that a particular member might have had a stern, terrifying mother and a sentimental, overpersonal father while at the same time invoking the prototypic or archetypal images in terms of which the members tend to communicate with each other.

The basic theme underlying the Counterdependent Flight performance is that the member must avoid being suffocated. In nurturance terms, this may come through as an aversion to someone, prototypically the mother, who seems bent upon endlessly feeding and babying the child who has, unbeknownst to the mother, outgrown such needs or pleasures. Or is it that simple? The theme is often complicated by a frank admission of the member's longing for nurturance, plus an admission of weakness to temptation, and both the longing and the weakness are seen as the individual's greatest enemies. If there were a group called Oral Dependents Anonymous, it might appeal to a person in this mood. The smothering mother is like the wife of an alcoholic whose ambivalence about her husband being on the wagon leads her to offer him a drink "as a reward for being so good." And therein lies the anger; the mother is accused, throughout the Counterdependent Flight performances, of continuing to stir up the child's dependency needs not as an act of generosity but out of her own selfish need to be important. This factor pattern suggests a solution: Get far, far away ("And don't even send your laundry home every week, either.").

The control theme is inextricably bound to the nurturance theme in these performances. Other accusations against the overcontrolling parent include the charge that the parent cannot stop running the child's life, which usually implies a continuing imposition of the parent's standards upon the child. The preferred solution is either to "get out on one's own" or to learn how to "handle" one's parents so that their demands and judgments seem to them to be having a greater influence than they are, in fact, having. One aspect of the Counterdependent Flight performance is sufficiently common to deserve particular attention: their morally superior tone. If this superiority were maintained merely over the submissive peer, it could be integrated into the general description attemped above. But this is not so. The parents or authority figures referred to in these performances are often tarred with the same "sell-out" brush as the dependent and docile sibling-figures. This may be expressed, as in the case of Merv, by an effort to be more honest about his sexual adventures than his parents, who "did the same in their day anyway" and now had covered it all up with conventional morality. It may be found in earnest efforts to reconcile one's actions with higher principles, to keep one's word, or to maintain one's "human dignity," even if one's parents were already in a seriously compromised position.

At least one chain of associations leads from these performances to the interaction between Hamlet, the pure, and Gertrude, who had "sold out" more than once. As one finds in Erikson's (1959, 1962) view of Hamlet in particular and adolescent fidelity in general, the struggle to forge one's own identity often involves an extended period of disparaging the compromises made by those who would dare offer themselves as models. And, further, this disparagement can connect with earlier disillusionment over the willingness of the oedipal mother to submit to the father.

In terms of sexuality, there seems to be a dual effort: to cast some doubt on the parents' right to be judgmental and to construe one's own sexuality as pure and innocent. Thus many of these performances suggest a kind of teasing of the parent by recounting various sexual adventures; this provokes the parent into a moralistic spasm to which the child responds either by attacking the judge's credentials or by adopting an air of offended innocence. In competence terms, these performances suggest most strongly the prolonged process of testing the potential model to make sure he is worthy of one's fidelity, a testing process in which the model must be proven to be both perfect and completely disinterested in attracting followers. The import of these performances is that the potential model is not only imperfect; he is also far too involved in molding the learner in his own image to be a satisfactory model.

The Counterdependent Flight performance, viewed as a strategy, serves two important latent goals: avoidance of the leader's pressures and intrusions and, on the other hand, the heroic mastery of one's own regressive inclinations to succumb. Viewed in this light, and in the light of the member's fears of being swallowed up or magically controlled, the flight strategy seems like a reasonable choice for an individual to make. But there are other goals and other fears. One additional hope is that the dramatic display of self-assertion will cure the leader of any interest he might have had in manipulating the member, with the result that the member and leader can continue their relationship, but on a mature and mutually respecting basis. One additional fear is that the leader, or parent, who is subjected to this barrage of counterdependent behavior will simply disappear altogether. There appears to be considerable ambivalence over whether to terminate the member-leader, or member-parent, relationship entirely. Thus the Counterdependent Flight performance strikes a delicate balance, leaving the person in the situation but presenting him as an advocate of a more distant, more mutual member-leader relationship.

Resistant Complaining. Particularly in the later stages of the group's development, one finds in the Resistant Complaining performances not only more direct communication with the leader but more and more protests that the leader has, by his devious means, made the members feel passive and out of control. Frank, in a session midway through the group, stated these feelings with clarity. After expressing some concern over why the leader puts his feet up on the desk, and what purpose of his that might serve, Frank wondered aloud about the look on the leader's face, which another member had just described as "smug." "That's a Mona Lisa look. I think this smile—ignore the sexual implication for a minute—it's a half-smile. You can't tell whether that's a frown or a smile or what, because it doesn't say what the face is thinking. There's just a face there, and you can interpret it in a million different ways." The elusive but threatening quality of the group situation is expressed at another point in that session through Frank's simile: the group is "like a school of barracudas." In the Resistant Complaining perform- ance the core of the passivity, or the fear of being passive, is found in the recurrent charge that the group is all one big experiment, with the group members as the subjects and the leader as the deceptive experi- menter who has betrayed them and now controls everything that is happening in the group.

The dangerous consequences of the group were expressed by Frank in several ways. Early in the group, he voiced his apprehensions mainly on behalf of other members who might suffer from the group. ("Some- one might have an identity crisis.") Later in the group, however, he revealed the impact of the course on his own sense of identity in a way which fits the Resistant Complaining pattern very well. He described how his efforts to write the assigned paper made him wonder whether trying to please the leader was equivalent to "selling out." In discuss- ing the paper, he also said, "I have the strange feeling, which is prob- ably paranoid, or will be jumped on as such, that when we turn in these papers, the secretary will make a copy of them, and I don't want her to have mine." Finally, he said, "I feel like this course kind of drained me of creativity, like pulling out the stopper."

Through all of these performances the member's perceptions of self and leader center closely on the leader's threat to the member's iden- tity. Alvin, a minister, complained to Marie, and his feelings toward the leader ran quite parallel to this: "You're trying to deny what I am by rejecting me. . . . This attempt to defrock me means that you would deny what I am." A sense of being persecuted, or experimented upon, and a sense of the leader's underlying malevolence, run through most of the Resistant Complaining performances, producing both a guilt- inducing display of the damage already done and a plea for the leader to change his ways. In addition, these performances are characterized by a very high rate of disagreeing with, or haggling over, the leader's interpretations. The member seems to take enormous pleasure in point- ing out that an interpretation could not possibly apply to this or that group member, that it does not square with some previous interpreta- tion, or that the interpretation can be viewed as another attempt on the leader's part to manipulate the group.

Of all the various developmental crises that might serve as a starting point for a thematic analysis of Resistant Complaining, the most apt analogy seems to be "the feeding problem," especially if this is seen as a continuing problem and not simply a phenomenon of early infancy. Some or all of the following components of the feeding problem tend to be present: a perception that what is offered is either no good or too much; a belief that continuing to accept it passively is in conflict with inner needs to be autonomous; a suspicion that the feeder is more preoccupied with having a certain quota of the offering ingested than in responding to the needs of the child; and a passive aggressive response that amounts to disparaging or rejecting outright both the offering and the motives that seem to lie behind it. In contrast to the response of fleeing from the narcissistic parent, these performances often suggest a masterful capacity to block and parry the parent's influence, combined with a pitiful display of the damage already done, a display designed to convince the parent that things could go no worse if the child were permitted, say, to choose his own diet or friends or career plans.

The control theme is best illustrated by the fantasy that the leader is not conducting a group in which individuals can become more autonomous but rather is conducting a sinister experiment in which all of the members' responses were either preordained or subtly influenced by the leader's behavior. Without denying the partial validity of Slater's (1966) observation that such fantasies are efforts on the members' part to reassure themselves that at least someone is clear about the group's ultimate direction, we would note that "the experimenter myth" is also highly disquieting to the members. It drives them into a frenzied search for the hidden manipulations so they can resist and undo them.

As control issues shade into sexuality issues, it becomes clear how grave a threat can be posed to the child's sense of sexual potency and attractiveness not only by the castrating father but by the castrating mother. The child has suffered not only as a result of punishment or prohibition but as a result of being patronized, teased, or alternately aroused and ridiculed as well. We may turn again to the image of the leader as experimenter, himself so unaroused although others around him are agitated and exposed. Or we may reflect upon the minister's dismay at having his very identity denied by various attempts to "defrock" him. In sexual terms, what these performances say is that the member feels enervated, toyed with, and maneuvered into a position in which he seems immature to everyone, including himself.

There is one final indignity in store for the member, and Frank's concerns express it well. Evidently it is altogether possible to decrease a person's sense of competence by getting him thoroughly confused about where learning for its own sake ends and "sucking around for a grade" begins. Frank's wail that all his creativity had drained out of him was in part a reflection of how much the course had intruded into his private domain, how much wanting to do well in the leader's estimation was accompanied by an increasing alienation from his own standards of excellence. The hazard that students will feel diminished by an educational experience, despite all their newly acquired knowledge, is surely one of the givens in all teaching and learning. The Resistant Complaining performance is not unlike the nationalistic or anticolonial move to end all foreign influence on the theory that even the innovations that seem the most innocent turn out to warp and erode the traditional and still preferable value structure.

In summary, the Resistant Complaining performance may have, as Frank defiantly tagged his own behavior, a "paranoid" quality in its preoccupation with insidious influences and manipulations. The pathos of this solution is that while the goal is to be free, the member does not dare take his eyes off the leader for fear that he will execute some new and more devious plan to trap the member. The basic mistrust, the fear of being intruded upon or humiliated, is, of course, predicated on an assumption of the member's own extreme vulnerability and weakness. The only hope for redressing this imbalance lies in blocking all further attempts at manipulation and in causing the leader to recoil from taking further advantage of the member. In contrast to the Dependent Complaining performance, which asserts that the leader has not done enough, the Resistant Complaining performance emphasizes the woeful effects which the leader has already had upon the member's autonomy, self-esteem, and sense of confidence.

Taken as a whole, factor three is a reminder of the fact that narcissim in one quarter tends to breed narcissism everywhere. Or, to be more precise, the perception that someone else is self-absorbed or self-seeking tends to provoke and justify a parallel development on the part of the perceiver. Both the Counterdependent Flight and the Resistant Complaining performances are self-centered in the extreme, but both would seem to be rationalized as vital to the survival of the member in the face of such a leader. The image of the narcissistic or manipulative leader conjures up malignant witches, possessive and smothering parents, and deflating, emasculating love objects. All told, it is a most uncomplimentary picture, and, as we shall see in Chapter 5, the leaders are somewhat ruffled by these performances. Nonetheless, this factor calls attention to an aspect of the member-leader relationship which is every bit as dramatic and complex as the rebellion against the leader's use of his formal status to dominate and inhibit the group members.

Factor IV: Relations with the Leader as Audience

IV+: Relating to the Leader as Colleague
IV−: Concern with Inner Distress

Colleague IV+ Variables	Distress IV− Variables
Major: Showing Independence Level one	Major: Expressing Anxiety Expressing Depression
Minor: Resisting Accepting Expressing Self-Esteem	Minor: Denying Anxiety Denying Depression Level four

The leader, as one audience for the members' expression of their own self-concepts, hears members express feelings which are relevant to him primarily because he is an important part of the audience for, rather than because he is the major cause of, the feelings. Factor four isolates two of these self-perceptions, one emphasizing the members' inner capacities and assets, the other emphasizing the members' distress.

The Colleague pattern brings together three of the most impersonal categories and reveals, in addition, a relative absence of comments referring to the member's inner tensions. It should be recalled that for an act to be scored as Showing Independence the scorer must be satisfied that the member is not primarily interested in countering dependency, and these rare acts denote at least one person's assessment that the member was feeling free of the authority issue vis-à-vis the leader. The Colleague performance is best characterized as an effort to state, in the leader's presence, but not for his benefit exclusively, some important aspect of the member's own values, goals, and strengths. To the extent that the member does respond to the leader, there tends to be a balance between accepting and resisting, but little arousal of either the more personal forms of affection and hostility or the feelings of distress tapped by the ego state categories.

Conversely, the Distress performance is filled with signs of personal discomfort, mainly in the expression but also in the denial of anxiety and depression. What distinguishes these manifestations of inner disruption from the ones found in the first three factors is their isolation from the entire range of impulse expression and authority relations. The member's concern over his own distress is manifest, but it is evidently not part of a larger effort to alter directly the affective or dependency bonds between himself and the leader. The possibility arises, then, that these performances are primarily a display, in part for the leader's benefit.

Colleague. The best single example of the Colleague performance is Leroy's discussion of morality and maturity. Leroy, a social worker and civil rights leader, was the oldest and probably the most respected member of the group. The one day he spoke more than a few times came after several sessions in which the group had split into those who were interested in evaluating behavior in moral terms and those who resented any effort to pass moral judgment. The crux of his argument was that one should examine not only whether an impulse is expressed through an overt act but how, when, and in response to what stresses and inner tensions. He went on to describe the inner conflict he was then "having to wrestle with," which amounted to a searching of himself regarding the basis of his own decisions. "Is it a course I have chosen out of maturity? Is it one that I feel is effective? Is it a compromise, as an attempt to be respectable? I'm not at all certain." Throughout Leroy's performance the relevance of the leader is primarily as an audience, as a separate individual with whom one could talk, but not someone who is used to avoid the personal responsibility of decision-making.

The Colleague performances are of this general order. For example, Anna entered a discussion of morality by saying, "There is nothing right or wrong in the sexual situation, no matter what it is, and anything right or wrong is projected into it from the person rather than drawn out of whatever the situation is." Thus she maintained that the individual is left to find his own "human dignity" and to learn to "trust oneself." In this and in several other such performances the emphasis is on the member's own inner capacity to tolerate ambiguity and to accept partial solutions to difficult situations.

Within the performances which bear directly on the leader one finds an absorption in the issue of whether the leader is "a member of the group." Janice's comments are indicative: "There is an ambiguity when it comes to talking about him [the leader]. I don't know whether to talk to him or about him. I don't know if he is all-knowing and all-seeing the way we assume, or whether most of what he does and says is unconscious . . . I am sure he is a person . . . It is hard to break through him. (To the leader): Hello, down there."

The ambiguity of the leader's position in the group, as someone in or out of the group, as above it or on the same level, is embedded in these performances. The resolution which characterizes them is that the leader *is* both in and out, above in some ways and equal in others, and the group members will just have to accept the ambiguity of it all without veering off to one partial solution or another. As one index of the member's own ability to handle this issue, it is appropriate that one finds that the Colleague performance is often addressed to the leader directly, as if to demonstrate the member's capacity to speak to him, person to person, without either complaining or expressing personal distress.

The major theme underlying the Colleague performance seems usually to be the competence theme. The search for one's own standards is a prolonged process for most people, and the relevance of formal authorities, or of one's parents, throughout the transition from dependence to independence is variable. The Colleague performance suggests a point midway in the transition at which the child, or more properly the adolescent, makes an effort to relate to the authority as a peer but hedges a bit by keeping the conversation as impersonal as possible. Perhaps the adolescent is a bit unsure of what might happen if the conversation were too intense or mutually threatening, so a compromise strategy is employed.

The discussion is not only impersonal but tends to focus on those value dilemmas over which two people may agree to disagree. Without implying that maturity is evidenced first or most easily in the value domain, it is nonetheless true that it is toward matters of opinion, and not matters of fact or strategy, that discussions between adolescents and parents tend to gravitate. The adolescent can converse with his parents over such matters more easily in part because they are often matters of more intense preoccupation to him than they are to his more pragmatic or routinized parents. But the parent plays a role in this as well, in his longing to have said his last ". . . because I say it's right, that's why." Discussions of values more often cause the parent to relax and slide into a relativistic mood than do discussions of fact or strategy, matters over which he still maintains some assurance of knowing better. What all this suggests is that for some members a sense of personal competence is developed more easily in areas where it is particularly difficult to be proven right or wrong. The role of the leader in such discussions is that of audience, or sounding-board perhaps, but little more than that is requested or desired.

It may be superfluous to note that the Colleague performance is a variant on the control theme, a particularly independent and autonomous variant. It would be unfair to underestimate the extent to which some performances reflect an already established independence; the case of Leroy is but one example. But it is also true that for some members this is the preferred path of gaining independence or preventing an attempt on the part of some authority to encroach upon their still tenuous sense of autonomy.

Distress. Quite another use of the leader as audience emerges when we turn to the Distress performances. In nearly every case, the leader is not held to be directly to blame for the distress which the member feels. Indeed, if we interpret the communications correctly, the member has failed or suffered not at the hands of the leader but at the hands of the group, when all the time the member was trying to carry out the leader's injunctions to work.

More than any one session, the group's discussion of the Biblical story of Joseph revealed this theme of the suffering, favorite son. Harry saw Joseph as an extension of the father: "These people viewed their sons as newborn phalluses." The brothers' hostility toward Joseph was seen as a symbolic attack on the father, in these terms: "Because Joseph was their father's favorite, it made him a readily identifiable target, easier to attack than the father." Joseph was not even old enough to have joined his brothers in their phallic adventures outside the family unit. In group terms, a member may feel that others have attacked him merely as the convenient surrogate for the leader.

While this was, in fact, Harry's fate a number of times in the group, it was not until he could perceive this role in Frank that he clearly enunciated, two day after the discussion of Joseph, this complicated relationship with the group and the leader. Frank had been the butt of much teasing in the group for his insistent expressions of anxiety over grades and apprehension about the leader's feelings toward him. Suddenly, in quite a reversal of form, Harry sided with Frank, defending his suspicious orientation as being at least more honest and probably more appropriate than all the denials which underlay the attacks on Frank. It would not be stretching a point to equate honesty, as opposed to denial, with Harry's conception of what the leader was urging upon group members. Thus by supporting Frank and by listing a few suspicions of his own, Harry placed himself in a position strikingly similar to his image of Joseph, the favorite son.

Harry was not the only group member to identify with Joseph in some way or other. The performances of Marie and Joanne, who also identified with Joseph as the innocent victim, emerge as particularly good examples of Distress. One way in which they use the Joseph figure points up another part of the total relationship with the leader. Both identified themselves with the abused father-surrogate, and both would wish, despite the abuse given them by "jealous brothers," to be the favorite child. One element they add gives a clearer sense of how one attains this; the path of glory is through suffering and magical intervention from above. Marie conjured up Joseph sitting in jail, pretending to be omniscient, when what he really needs is a "spell," presumably a divine intervention on his behalf. The purpose of the magic is twofold, in part to give him the superior powers and in part to overcome "this terrible, terrible guilt," caused by the very act of replacing the leader and his magic. Joanne also traced Joseph's experience in terms of being "killed or banished and then deified."

At one level, then, the Distress performance concerns the fate of the "teacher's pet," how he suffers in the group while advancing the cause of the leader, and how he is finally rewarded for all his efforts. However, not all the distress is caused by others; in Merv's case, it results from a sense of failure when he tried to be honest with his mother, or, in Gino's case, from his chagrin over misreading a crucial passage in a case under discussion. We find a similar depression being experienced by someone who feels unable to enact the leader's role with sufficient skill or self-control.

It seems appropriate to view the Distress end of factor four as no less relevant to the competence theme than the Colleague end of the factor, except here the effort has collapsed. In the case of Distress, the effort to be competent is heavily loaded with extrinsic motivation: a desire to serve as the parent's agent in the world. In part the uneasiness of the member derives from the stress of being the favorite son and coming under attack from the peer group, but it also derives from the guilt and shame of replacing the leader and then feeling unable to do the job.

The message to the parent at this point is condensed with particular clarity in various religious services, particularly the litany. Here one finds the distant God, the faithful who are tormented by all their jealous enemies, and repeated references to the human failings which have contributed to the disaster. In control terms, then, the litany is a plea for the all-powerful to work a miracle and save the day; failing that, the next best thing would be to be forgiven for the innumerable consequences of human frailties and sin. In nurturance terms, the litany expresses the latent hope of many Distress performances: to be rescued, to regress and be rewarded, at least for one's efforts, by the compassionate God "from whom all blessings flow."

In a manner not unlike a litany, the Distress performance has a certain edge to it; pleading shades into insisting, supplication into demand. The fact that the leader "just sits there like old stone-face" is reacted to in a way that suggests the latent irritation and impatience which breaks through the surface of the manifestly abject entreaty. The distant but loving god is replaced by the forgetful or malicious god who has to be reminded of his basic responsibility to his people. So too the leader is urged to call off the experiment, to reveal all, to take over the group.

To the extent that distress signals have failed in the past to bring help, the current signal will be either of increased intensity or highly guarded and offhand, since no one wants to appear foolish enough to cry in vain beyond a certain point. Thus the fear that the leader will remain unresponsive and leave the member stranded with nothing but the echoes of his pleas for help affects the net result. The member may oscillate back and forth from expressing to denying the distress, or he may swing from emphasizing his peril to brooding about his deficiencies. In whatever form the distress emerges, the stance of the leader as distant audience is not one which the member would care to have continued. The plea is for the leader to return, to rescue, or perhaps simply to wake up and pay attention to what is becoming of the group he brought into being.

This factor reveals, as do factors one and two, a basic split among performances: one-half suggesting satisfaction with some aspect of the leader's total behavior, the other half suggesting dissatisfaction. In factor four, the relevant aspect of what the leader is doing is listening, not interpreting as in factor one and not exercising his power as in factor two. The Colleague performance portrays the leader as a "good listener" to whom one can communicate one's search for a personal set of values and goals. The Distress performance portrays the leader as too distant, and the various expressions of anxiety and depression are efforts to bring the leader back into the picture not so much to gratify dependency needs, as in the Dependent Complaining performance, as to offer some relief to the faithful who display themselves as bruised and discouraged.

Factor V: The Effect of the Leader on the Ego State of the Member

V+: Anxiety

V−: Depression

Anxiety	Depression
V+ Variables	V− Variables

Major: Expressing Anxiety	Major: Expressing Depression
Denying Anxiety	Denying Depression

The simplicity of this factor pattern is refreshing. The issue isolated by factor five was built into the scoring system explicitly, following Edward Bibring's (1953) conceptualization of the ego states. He views anxiety as an ego response to internal and external danger, serving as a mobilizing signal. Depression, on the other hand, results from a sense of helplessness, from a perceived inability to control either the outside world or the inner psychic forces. Although Bibring implies that both anxiety and depression may occur simultaneously, as indeed they do in two of the factor patterns already discussed (Loyalty and Distress), he conceptualizes them primarily as antithetical ego reactions.

Anxiety. Most of the Anxiety performances occur in the first third of the group's development. Jane, in the first session, revealed one persistent anxiety theme when she questioned the leader about the purpose of having a tape recorder. The diffusely vigilant and apprehensive quality of her response was given some focus by Merv, two sessions later. His first remarks were to the effect that although he was nervous the first day, "Now the class is the most comfortable hour I find I spend in the day. I mean it's so comfortable that I'm actually very much relaxed. And I wonder if most people here feel comfortable in this group, discussing these things, or feel they're not comfortable." Three rather different pieces of evidence contributed to our conclusion that Merv was denying anxiety in this speech. One was that his voice was tremulous and his body not at all relaxed; a second was that, when he was reminded of his remarks several days later, he confessed to being amazed that he could have ever said he felt at ease in the group; and the third piece of evidence was his discussion, within five minutes of saying he felt comfortable, of his fear of revealing himself. As he put it, "It's a fear that I have of really exposing myself to some other person. Sort of, you might say, a fear of rejection," a fear of feeling "that my whole personality had been rejected."

Many of the Anxiety performances emphasize the member's sensitivity, but some also express a concern for what will become of them in the group. Marie, who gave evidence of knowing full well how lovely she was, announced one day that the course discussions would probably make her "very wise and very ugly." The recurrent discussions of who is and who is not threatened or whether people should "get personal" conform closely to our view of anxiety. The whole situation and the leader in particular mobilize that signal of impending danger which gives the early sessions their cautious, testing quality.

Later sessions contain anxiety-related performances, but the early anticipation of what might happen if one revealed oneself tends to give way to suspicions about what might happen since so much has already been revealed. The dangers are more diabolical and better organized. Lloyd's argument that castrating females exist solely in Freud's mind followed other concerns of his about the John Birch Society and Hitler. Throughout, Lloyd seemed to reveal that a coalition between the leader and his lieutenants or the leader and the girls would constitute a serious threat to him. Other members found the theme of Hitler and Southern racists could express some important feeling aroused by the total group situation. Harry's suspicion was that, in wearing a suit one day, the leader was allying himself with a group member who wore a suit regularly. ("Has my buddy turned his back on me? Is he joining sides with Lloyd?")

To the extent that anxiety and depression represent opposing states of mind, the difference between these ego states might be found in the characteristic imbalance between the member's view of himself and his view of the significant other. Anxiety implies an imbalance between the malevolent, threatening other ("the bad object") and a self which is seen as good or at least worth preserving. On the other hand, depression tips the balance the other way, opposing the good but perhaps lost object to the impulsive, helpless, and bad self. As Klein (1963) points out, the mechanisms of introjection and projection often serve to heighten these contrasts, turning self and object into mirror images of each other. The pressure toward disequilibrium with respect to the relative goodness or badness of self versus object, which in turn is related to the difficulty in managing an ambivalent attitude toward either self or object, underlies the see-saw quality which sometimes characterizes an individual's shift in ego state.

If one looks for the way in which the object can appear menacing to the individual, one soon covers the whole range from nurturance to competence themes. Therefore, since we must proceed in a rather systematic manner through each of the four themes, we propose to deviate from our usual procedure and will wait to discuss both the anxiety and the depression variants of each theme together.

Depression. Most of the performances which serve as examples of Depression are found in the last third of the group sessions. The early examples of Depression seem primarily concerned with guilt and responsibility, the later ones with the approaching end of the group.

Merv's discussion of the unpleasant consequences of trying to be honest with his mother and his defense of lying as preferable to hurting someone are examples of early depression. The same issue is reflected in Anna's intropunitive refusal to blame society for any of her misfortunes and in Harry's denials of personal responsibility. He responded to various intimations by others that he had been crude, insulting, and deliberately provocative with a series of ingenuous denials which implied that honesty, not personal venom, compelled him to act as he did.

A distinctly different aspect of depression emerges in the final week or two of the group. Marie broke a long silence by saying, "Tears, idle tears, I know not what they mean," and then proceeded with an account of how hard it seemed to find the right words to express herself in writing the assigned papers. Two sessions later, she implied that the fast-approaching end of the group would be a welcome relief from "this hateful marriage," and she went on to share in a "silly" barrage of nursery rhyme associations.

The end of the group had other effects on members. Gino, hiding his own depression in one session, was busy interpreting and probing into other members' depression, e.g., "What makes you say funeral?" or "Did you mean to say reincarnation?" In the same session Harry more directly expressed his own sadness over the loss of the group: ". . . some part of me will be left out, will be taken away."

The final session was alternately heavy and exhilarated, filled with long silences and excited discussions of reunions and rebirth. Several Depression performances in the last session deal with the lasting impact of the group and with a final review of the members' own failures to accomplish all that once seemed possible.

✻   ✻   ✻   ✻   ✻

In turning to the thematic analysis of both poles of this factor, it may be useful to emphasize the generality of Bibring's (1953) conceptualization of the ego states. In describing anxiety and depression as ego reactions appropriate to a wide range of intrapsychic and interpersonal situations, Bibring permits one to look hard, for example, at competence-related depression without needing to find the hidden link to orality, the psychosexual stage which has most often been connected with depression in the clinical literature. Similarily, there is enough difficulty in understanding anxiety without fixating on castration fears as the prototype of all anxiety. The goal of our discussion of Anxiety and Depression performances is to illustrate how each theme can give these two factor patterns a distinctive thematic shading.

The first theme to discuss is nurturance, and here our view of the early feeding situation, its terrors and its uncertainties, is much influenced by the work of Klein (1932, 1957) and her colleagues. Whatever the accuracy of their reconstruction of infancy, their analysis is particularly helpful in understanding the nurturance-related eruptions of anxiety and depression in childhood and beyond. On the anxiety side, we must consider the infant's fear of either being abandoned or attacked by a depriving and malevolent mother; on the depression side, we must consider the issues of loss, emptiness, and the hazily conceived notion that one's own greed is somehow to blame for one's misfortunes.

Given the habitual set of many members that to learn is to get, and given the inactive and unrewarding stance of the leader, it is not surprising that the new group stirs up feelings not at all unlike those experienced by the abandoned and terrified infant. Bion's (1961, p. 29–30) description of a first session is a particularly good account of this situation. The new group seems hardly to be a place where unconditional love can be found. As in the case of the newborn's effort to discern regularity and purpose amidst chaos, group members often find the first question is, "Can the leader be trusted?" For some members the answer is negative, thereby triggering off the anxiety alarm signal, and for others who find the negative answer unsatisfactory the anxiety gives way to a valiant effort to deny various aspects of inner and outer reality. Many of the high Anxiety performances suggest an oscillation between the two answers to the question. Whatever the answer, the Anxiety performance, to the extent that it touches upon the nurturance theme, entails many aspects of what Klein describes as persecutory anxiety. In particular, one finds evidence, especially in performances where Expressing Anxiety is high, that the leader is invested not only with the frustrating attributes that set off the mistrust reaction but with all the aggressive feelings that develop within the frustrated member. Thus it becomes the leader who would drag information out of the member, not the member who would gladly drag something, anything out of the retentive leader. In this situation, the member construes the leader as not only annoying and disappointing but as terribly strong, diabolical, and dangerous.

In contrast, the leader in the nurturance-related Depression performance is as likely to be all good as he was to be all bad in Anxiety performance. The self, meanwhile, has changed from the victimized self described above into a tragic figure, fated to drive away any potential source of affection and support. In this intropunitive solution to the new situation and all its uncertainties the member resembles the lost child who blames not the parent but himself for some not easily discerned failing. Sometimes the blame falls on one's inability to be appealing: "Others receive love, what's the matter with me?" At other times, the blame falls on one's inability to control one's needs, one's greediness. In this view, the parent appears wholly justified for refusing to be tormented by such an insatiable child, and abandonment seems like a just but nonetheless devastating fate. The emptiness or loneliness that characterize the nurturance-related depression is one reaction to the various issues of separation and helplessness; another way to respond to precisely the same issue is elation. As Lewin (1950), Klein (1950), Bibring (1953), and Balint (1959) point out, the denial of separation, guilt, and even hunger forms the basis of the manic reaction. Magical fusion with the lost object is one solution to the potentially depressive situation.

In summary, then, the basic contrasts between anxiety and depression cleave the nurturance theme into two quite distinct parts. The Anxiety performance is more vigilant and exteroceptive, more preoccupied with whether the leader is dangerous, and more directed toward self-preservation. The Depression performance is more self-absorbed, more preoccupied with whether the self is dangerous to the leader, and more directed toward the preservation or restoration of the leader.

The control theme raises quite different issues, but the distinction between anxiety and depression runs along lines quite similar to those discussed above. The control-related Depression performances shift from an emphasis on loss to an emphasis on impulsivity and guilt. In addition, the central issues in the control theme, power and morality, give a distinctive coloring to the kind of threatening object or the kind of bad self which is imagined.

The vigilance so characteristic of the Anxiety performance is directed toward avoiding punishment or censure, and the members frequently interpret the leader's silence as disapproval. The image of the leader as the wrathful, distant god, ready to hurl thunderbolts, is but one manifestation of the member's intense effort to discern what the leader values and what he will sanction. In addition to the clear expressions of concern, the Anxiety performance often contains elements of the counterphobic solution to the basic fear, a solution that taunts the authority with progressively more defiant behavior, all the while asserting that the authority is either asleep or endlessly tolerant of such behavior.

In contrast, when the control theme joins with the depressive reactions, the verdict seems already to have been handed down. The sense of guilt that underlies the depressive performances within this theme seems usually to be predicated upon some betrayal of trust placed in the member by the leader. Such performances resemble the guilt of the child who cannot resist the allure of some forbidden object or the pressure of some forbidden impulse, and the transgression is felt as doubly shameful since the watchful eye of the parent had been removed as an act of confidence. When the group is "silly," at least within what it sees as the leader's definition of silliness, or when a member goes beyond some invisible boundary of legitimate anger, the ensuing depression is compounded by the awareness of how much self-control was expected in the situation. Just as one finds counterphobic solutions to the anxiety raised by the control issue, so too one finds various manic denials of guilt. What some may shamefully see as impulsivity, others see as the legitimate activities of a buoyant, liberated soul. By equating all efforts to control or judge them with an authoritarian constriction of freedom these individuals manage, often for quite long periods, to escape the depressing awareness of their own insensitivity and their inability to regulate the expression of their own impulses.

In turning to the sexuality theme, it may be useful to clarify what issues need to be added to the control theme in order to understand, for example, the oedipal triangle. One view might be that the control theme centers on behaviors and impulses which the parent and/or child feels are bad. The relevant behaviors and impulses within the sexuality theme, on the other hand, are a peculiar mixture of good and bad: good when the parent-rival expresses them, bad when the child does; good when they do not succeed in attracing the love object, bad when they do succeed; good for later, bad for now, and so on. Sexual anxiety is thus as much a fear of winning as a fear of losing, although both fears are present. Sexuality-related depression is likewise a mixture of hopelessness over ever winning and guilt over fantasied successes.

In terms of the member-leader relationship, this leads, as we shall see in a later chapter, to a rise in sexual anxiety among members at precisely the moment when the members are becoming most able to be intimate with each other. To the extent, for example, that male members see the leader as the sexual rival, increasing success in the sexual sphere triggers not only vigilance regarding the leader's reaction but also aspects of the member's own superego system: the internalized prohibitions previously hooked in with sexual arousal. The fear of retaliation and the fear of being rejected or humiliated combine to give sexuality-related Anxiety performances the dual quality found first in the oedipal situation, where both parents are simultaneously rival and love object. This unstable arrangement of three sets of needs and perceptions is mirrored in group life by the fact that the leader is also both rival and object, and the anxiety that might be generated by either possibility is compounded by their conjunction. Sexual depression in a group setting is reminiscent of the self-deprecation found in the post-oedipal phase. Oedipal defeat, with its recognition that one is still too young or hopelessly outclassed in the competition for the love object, leads to resignation, and resignation is seen most clearly in the presentation of self as impotent and unattractive. As Slater (1966) has observed in other groups as well, some male members tend to retreat from competition with the leader over the females, while others display quite similar concern over their own adequacy not by resigning but by hurling themselves into the fray full of strutting and exhibitionism.

The fourth theme, competence, connects with still another set of anxious and depressive reactions to the leader. The leader's knowledge and experience may seem to some members like his most threatening weapon, and their fear of his criticisms points to an area of vulnerability that is particularly sensitive in the educational setting. Much of the competence-related anxiety crystallizes around exams or other evaluations of intellectual capacity and achievement. The member's concerns here are less often a fear that they will forget some fact or other than that they will be shown to be incompetent in a larger or deeper sense. And the leader's intentions are crucial as well, since much of the tension derives from the perception of the leader as eager to show up the members. Presumably all the members have had teachers who took pleasure in catching their students' mistakes or in belittling the students' contributions, but perhaps of equal relevance are the antecedent experiences in which the parent comments critically on each fumbling effort of the child to master some vital skill like counting or tying his shoes. The inner tension, the need to do it all perfectly and avoid still another exasperated look, has a most inhibiting effect upon the performance itself. The willingness to take risks is reduced, and the various tentative efforts at mastery dissolve into efforts to avoid failure and disgrace.

On the other side of the factor, in the Depression performances, the leader is less a menace than a hopelessly out of range model of excellence. The sense of failure or stupidity is already part of the picture, whether it is expressed through apologies for one's own ineptness or denied through an implicit overestimation of one's contributions. In the group situation the competence issues are often exacerbated by the fact that the leader can and does sit back and watch, while the members tend to be more engrossed in their own immediate reactions and goals. Thus it sometimes happens that the leader can pull together events or symbolic meanings with greater clarity than can the members who are more absorbed in the situation. One effect of this may be to induce in the members a feeling of incompetence, a feeling that their experience does not lead to insight and understanding. Since one purpose in joining the group was to gain some understanding of group interaction, this disparity between member and leader is often doubly important to the member.

The range of antecedent situations that connect with the Anxiety and Depression performances is only approximated by this review of the four themes, but, hopefully, even this limited summary conveys both the diversity and the common elements of the two different performances. Both performances represent, at the simplest level, the member's effort to define and express his feelings about himself and to communicate these feelings to the leader. Beyond this, it is sometimes apparent that one function of raising issues pertinent to the Anxiety performance is to stifle issues more appropriate to the Depression performance, and vice versa. This may be especially true when either anxiety or depression are becoming excessively burdensome to the member; to shift from one to the other at least relieves the sense of stagnation.

Finally, we may look at the Anxiety and Depression performances as strategies that not only reveal various expressive and defensive needs but even more basic goals as well. The Anxiety performance is a compromise between the wish to destroy the threatening other and the fear of being destroyed by him; the performance that results from these two forces usually manages to obscure the hostility by focusing attention upon the member's ego state, but these performances are often as effective in mobilizing the other members' hostility toward the leader as a militant call to arms. By the same token, the Depression performance expresses the member's latent desire for affection together with his feeling of being unworthy of such affection; the net result is a rather passive performance which implies that the leader can, if he wishes, absolve the member's guilt or contradict the member's self-deprecations.

Factor VI: Commitment to the Member-Leader Relationship

VI+: Emotional Involvement
VI−: Emotional Neutrality

Involvement VI+ Variables	Neutrality VI− Variables
Major: None	Major: Withdrawing Denying Anxiety Making Reparation
Minor: Moving Against Identifying Moving Toward Showing Counterdependency Expressing Self-Esteem Level one	Minor: Level three

Factor six distinguishes between a large set of categories, all of which indicate some form of involvement with the leader, and a smaller set which constitutes the major ways group members can keep their relations with the leader on a neutral plane. The Emotional Involvement factor pattern combines the two most personally directed impulse area categories, Moving Toward and Moving Against, with Identifying and the three most "heroic" categories, Showing Counterdependency, Expressing Self-Esteem, and Denying Depression. Few members are simultaneously high on all six components of this pattern; rather, the best examples of Involvement tend to be uniformly low on the Neutrality categories and high on four of the six Involvement categories. Denying Depression appears to be high most consistently.

The three major Neutrality categories have in common one important goal, to keep the relationship with the leader from becoming too intense. Withdrawing achieves this goal by its protestations of indifference and unconnectedness. Reparation achieves it by undoing and denying any hostility which might increase the intensity of the relationship. Denying Anxiety achieves it by its refusal to share in any perception of the leader as a threat, thus preserving a bland and unruffled orientation toward him. The minor loading of Level three on this factor suggests that the very fact of addressing oneself to case material and symbolic referents beyond the group can be part of a larger effort not to get involved with the leader.

Involvement. The performances high on Involvement display an eagerness to forge a unique and personal relationship with the leader. In each performance there are various indications of ambivalence, and the result is a highly complex message from member to leader. Harry's performance during a period of general revolt against the leader is a good example. In the span of two sessions he covered the entire range of the Involvement categories. He began with Denying Depression, mainly through avoidance of blame for disturbing people, then engaged in a slightly sadistic teasing of Frank who was complaining about being controlled by the leader (Harry to Frank: "There are five or six of us that were planted in here.") Next, he countered the exclusively hostile feelings of Frank and others toward the leader with the following remarks:

"We'll never be on our own, having been put in this situation . . . having been chosen by a father figure, and whether he's here . . . or should he not be here some day, his influence would be there, and I think it would probably be lots of fun if some day he got sick or something, or got run over by a car, I secretly would feel pretty happy about it . . . being able to be on our own, but his influence would still be felt strongly."

In the next session, he began with a hostile interpretation that the group saw itself as "a bunch of queers getting rolled," which provoked an immediate counterattack by Frank upon Harry's irritatingly noisy cigarette-rolling machine.

Frank: Oh. As long as we are on that topic, what are you doing in the classroom right now . . . rolling phallic symbols? (Laughter.)
Harry: It's really good. Take this 'shit' and play with it in your fingers and stuff it in this little machine . . . you roll it up and you've got it rolled, and not only are you getting burped but you got . . . you know, it's more complicated than that . . .
Frank: I think it's very amusing.

Janice: The mother and father all together.
Harry: Mother and father, masturbator, everything all at once. You can consume your own creation. . . . Very satisfying thing.
Janice: Does it make you feel more potent?
Harry: Very.

After more teasing of Frank about grades, Harry jabbed at the leader for using a "childish trick" in the opening session, and then announced that he and some others, at least, did not see the leader as "Great God Brown." Finally, as the leader leaned forward from his characteristic pose of chair tipped back, feet on the table, Harry told the leader to put his feet back. When asked why he wanted that, Harry replied, "It's a lot of anxiety, when you know he's going to take his feet down and say, 'All right, now, I'll be one of you guys,' with his smug little smirk."

The variety of Harry's responses to the leader in these two sessions have a common characteristic; they reveal an effort to stake out a distinctive mode of relating to the leader. Many Involvement performances contain precisely these elements of identification, trust and mistrust, heroic defiance, and high visibility. Frank, in shifting away from purely hostile feelings, puzzled over one reaction of the leader, uncertain if it had been said "on purpose," as the leader's way of "humanizing" himself, or if it was "spontaneous." He decided it was spontaneous, and this conclusion led directly to an increase in his involvement with the leader as a person. Several other members appear to "take on" the leader in only partially hostile ways, and one inference about what is going on in Involvement performances is that the members are flirting, in various ways, with the leader.

Harry's treatment of the Biblical story of Joseph is a good example of the complexity found in the Involvement performance. Joseph's fantasied dominance over the father and eventual mastery over him through control of the food supply were not cast in terms of defeating the father-rival, but in terms of reuniting on adult terms with the beloved father. In describing this pattern in terms of his own life, Harry anticipated with pleasure inviting his own father or father-in-law to visit, which would then give him the chance to say, "This is my house. You're my guest, and I'm feeding you martinis. We have made it. You can come here and we'll take care of you." In the light of his earlier performances, especially the manic fusion of "mother, father, masturbator," the pregenital quality of his image of the father-son relationship is evident.

Not all Involvement performances are as clearly ambivalent as th ones cited above. One of the rare Involvement performances by a fe male group member was clearly flirtatious, and it occurred in the fina session. The girl who three sessions earlier had reported the sexua dream discussed previously as an example of Loyalty resisted th group's ending by talking of after-life and by expressing the wish tha it were leap year and she could have the prerogative to make sexua advances. Her seating position, next to the leader, and her account o the seduction dream, combined to convince many group members tha at least some of her feelings were directed toward the leader. Som Involvement performances are primarily hostile but still express intens involvement with the leader. The aim of the hostile performances seem to be one of reducing the leader's strength and undermining his equa nimity by teasing or mocking him. Peter's taunting observation, "Loo at him. His hands are shaking, he's so anxious," is a good example o this aspect of this sort of Involvement performance. In each group th initial attempt to call the leader by his first name occurs within a Involvement performance, and these performances usually seem to b some sort of challenge to the leader, a challenge it is assumed he wi have a hard time managing calmly.

The best summary of these performances in member-leader term would be that the members are taking a large part of the initiative i building an intense or personal relationship with the leader. The may challenge him, announce their commitment to his point of view or behave seductively, but the initiative is meant to be seen as re siding in them. As such, the performances are clearly the opposite o the relationship-breaking and involvement-decreasing performance found in the Neutrality factor pattern.

In many ways, the Involvement performance seems like the mal counterpart of the Loyalty performance. Whereas females can mor easily move close to a male authority via dependency and indication of vulnerability, males tend more often to combine indications of affec tion with assertions of their equality with, or even superiority to, th male authority. The Involvement performance suggest very strongl the son's desire to pair off with the father, to the exclusion of all fe males. In nurturance terms, the son is more likely to try to replace th mother by providing for the father, than to admit his dependency upo the father, although interdependency would probably be preferabl to either of the other outcomes. The basis of the relationship tends t be built around the sexualized aggression that males use to move clos without appearing weak, feminine, or immature. Clearly the initiativ for the relationship is meant to reside mainly in the son's hands; w have seen how perturbed Harry became when the leader seemed to initiate the move toward equality by taking his feet off the table.

With so many competitors, the group member must find some way to be distinctive. For females, one path is to be the most loyal member; for males, the Involvement performance suggests another path: becoming the most vivid group member, the one most full of life. Before the males can pair with the leader on the basis of equality and friendship, the leader must see the member as someone to reckon with, someone with the vitality and uniqueness that would genuinely interest the leader. At the moment when the leader's interest seems merely to be some form of diffuse benevolence that fails to connect with the member as a special person, up come the hackles and the cycle of involvement begins again with hostility and counterdependency. Even among the relatively rare Involvement performances by females, there seems to be a similar wish, as seen in Lili's desire to have it be "Sadie Hawkins Day," a wish to be unique and to remain in control of the increasingly involving relationship with the leader.

Neutrality. The Neutrality pattern is found in performances from the first to the last session, but they tend to cluster in the first third of the sessions. Frank reacted to the first case discussion with a certain haughtiness, implying that the figures in the case were too immature and too alien to be bothered with. Part of Marie's reaction to the leader's first intervention, which suggested that she was identified with one of the case figures, was to search for a way to become less vulnerable. As she put it, "Yesterday we were all sort of put on the spot . . . we were honest, and now we want flexibility, objectivity . . . so that we won't be fooled, or appear to be. . . . What we're stressing is flexibility and always being able to extricate yourself." In the next session she was arguing the merits both of "parent-handling" and of avoiding potentially entrapping situations.

A clearer example of Neutrality comes from Anna, who discussed her feelings toward the group this way: "I don't know how to act because we have established no set relationships with any *one* person in here. . . . I don't think I feel any kindred bond between myself and the other 24 of you. (Looking at the leader) Twenty-five, excuse me." From this point on, for several sessions Anna alternated between a hopeless choice of the group's deviant hero (hopeless in that she knew he was going to be married in two months) and a self-absorbed discussion of how essential it was to be open and trusting in the group. The paradox of Anna's personal withdrawal and her insistence that others be open is common among those members who attempt to conceal their own feelings; perhaps they are waiting until others have become sufficiently vulnerable to afford general protection for all.

One rather dramatic example of Neutrality is found in the only case of explicit resignation from a group, after little over a week of the summer had gone by. The urge to withdraw, while at the same time denying the threat experienced in the group, is captured in this one quote from Naomi: "The group is too large. It's artificial and phony, petty and boring. I think I'd better just take something else."

The later examples of Neutrality deal with withdrawal from the hostile and threatening aspects of the group and finally from the group as a whole in the final session. In all these performances quite parallel measures are used to block personal involvement before it occurs or to drain out whatever involvement has been built up in the course of the group development.

In contrast to the Involvement performances, the member's efforts to keep his relationship with the leader distant and neutral seem not to have a clear developmental basis. The underlying, but unspoken assumption of these performances would seem to be that the relevant authority could be hurting or humiliating, if one were to be involved with him. The moments during a child's developing relationship with a parent when he might attempt to reduce the intensity of that rela tionship are hardly confined to any single stage.

What the Neutrality performances do indicate is the functional equivalence of withdrawing and the various attempts to deny hostility and anxiety. Not only can the child move away, but he can make it hard for the parent to pursue him, since his surface veneer is mani festly untroubled and unprovocative. The child who denies his fear blocks any remedial efforts; the child who denies his hostility not only blocks efforts to unravel the hostility but prevents such an unraveling process from leading him into a closer relationship than he desires or can manage. Beyond the overtones of these earlier techniques or avoiding the parent, the Neutrality performance suggests a scrupulous avoidance of all the personal aspects of the learning situation. The member who is thoroughly convinced that the classroom and the world of emotions should be kept separate must feel rather distant not only from the leader but also from his distressed and rebellious peers

❊   ❊   ❊   ❊   ❊

We are finished with the factor by factor review of the performances At this point, it might be helpful to recall the questions asked initially and to see what answers this analysis has provided. Our hope in study ing performances was that here we would find a manageable segment of the behavior initiated by one person which would take us beyond the descriptive level, even though the descriptive task was not thought to be easy or insignificant. By way of factor analysis, we arrived at six bipolar dimensions which combined the categories and levels into patterns of variables.

The task of interpreting the factors was transformed into a slightly different task, the interpretation of those performances that were particularly good examples of each factor pattern. The conceptual framework that developed out of this process, the thematic analysis of performances and the analysis of performances as strategies, is, in effect, what we have to offer as a partial answer to our second question: "What do the performances mean?" We suggest that any performance in these groups, and hopefully some performances in other settings, can be described in terms of six factors and interpreted in terms of the latent themes and observable strategies that emerge from this analysis.

Very few performances can be described by one factor alone; most require some assessment of how the various factors which are high and low combine to produce the overall picture. But this should not be surprising. The still active themes in an individual's life sometimes merge and sometimes collide, and the group member must be seen as employing a whole series of strategies as he attempts to pursue numerous goals and avoid numerous disasters.

The purpose of the present chapter has been twofold: to analyze the performance of an individual in terms of its underlying themes and strategies and to present the 12 factor patterns which will be employed in the increasingly complex analysis of the member, the leader, and the group. In terms of the first goal the chapter is self-contained, and we can rest our case on how adequate or useful a conceptual scheme this analysis has provided. We cannot hope to sustain the complexity of this chapter's view of the individual performance while adding new determinants such as the role of the leader, the nature of work, and the development of the group and its component subgroups. We must content ourselves with occasional references to the personal themes and the evidence of transference if we are to build a conceptual framework that will not collapse under its own weight. What we propose to extract from this analysis is mainly the set of 12 factor patterns, an appreciation of the four themes and their relevance to an individual's construction of reality, and the realization that each factor pattern can represent a strategy appropriate to each of the four themes.

Up to this point, we have concentrated upon the individual members.

But what about the leader? Certain qualities of the leader, his relative inactivity or his tendency to make interpretations, have emerged, but this is not enough. We have gone as far as we can without looking at the leader as something more than a blank screen in relation to which the members reenact various antecedent relationships. We can carry this analysis one step further and we shall discuss the following topics in Chapter 5: (1) how the leader reacts to these performances; and (2) how the leader's reactions might be seen as deriving from his own personal and professional goals.

Some Relevant Literature on Individual Performances

The search for basic dimensions which underlie an individual's performance in groups has proceeded along both statistical and conceptual lines. Thus Couch (1960), Mann (1961), and Borgatta et al. (1958) have all attempted to reduce the dimensionality of their observation categories to a few powerful and general factors, but the outcome of their work cannot help but reflect the particular observational systems which they employed and the different types of groups which they observed. The six factors extracted from the 20 variables employed in the present study do not greatly resemble the factors found in the previous studies, although one might wish, for example, to equate Loyalty with the positive-submissive and Rebellion with the negative-dominant fusion factors found by Couch (1960). However, since he was studying initially leaderless groups, he did not find, as we did, that submissiveness is associated with openness rather than concealment and denial.

It would be more useful to address this comparative review to the conceptual analyses of these and similar groups in order to place our analysis in its proper context. Our attempt to conceptualize individual development in relation to an individual's performance in the group has been much influenced by the work of Klein and Erikson. Melanie Klein's (1932, 1948, 1957) analysis of early mother-child interaction and her emphasis on the mechanisms of splitting, the relevance of ambivalence and depressive anxiety, and the tenuousness of the individual's emergent integration and defenses offer the student of group processes much that is relevant and thought provoking. An interesting application of these concepts is found in Bennis' (1961) study. We find parallels to her reconstructions of childhood in the group member's difficulty in tolerating the leader's ambiguous role without resorting to resentful jealousy, idealization, paranoid mistrust, fits of guilt and self-reproach, etc. Klein's notion is that development and maturity rest heavily on the individual's capacity to tolerate ambivalence and ambiguity, and when this capacity is limited, as Bion's (1961) analysis of group processes illustrates, there is great pressure toward regressive, partial, and covert gratifications. Bion's work bridges Klein's concern with the archaic impulse life of the member and Erikson's concern with psychosocial development, and we shall examine Bion's contributions in the next two chapters.

Erik Erikson's (1950, 1958, 1959) writings on the life cycle, although they certainly do not ignore the early stages of life, were useful to us primarily for their analysis of the dynamics of identity formation, fidelity, and productivity. His view of development as an epigenetic process in which each stage highlights certain distinctive dilemmas and stresses but also contains residues and forerunners of other stages seems particularly apt for the examination of young adults in action. The gradual crystallization of a self-concept, the uncertainty over where and to whom one should commit oneself, and the rising pressure to accomplish something—these factors in the life of a young adult must be understood no less than the triad of earlier themes which we have called nurturance, control, and sexuality. For a view of the value and limitations of a scheme that includes only the three early themes, the reader might examine Schutz's (1958) analysis of what he terms the need for inclusion, control, and affection. In contrast, White (1959, 1963) and Smith (1966) place heavy emphasis on the fourth theme, competence. In addition to the writings of Klein and Erikson to which we have already referred, the reader interested in the origins of the four themes might wish to examine the contributions of Freud (1953, 1955a, 1957), Murray et al. (1938), or the synthesizing efforts of Fenichel (1945) and Munroe (1955). The group therapy literature abounds with discussions of the notion that an individual's past will partially determine the gratifications and perceptions which will absorb him in a self-analytic group. The work of Frank et al. (1952), Beukenkamp (1958), and Durkin (1964) offer interesting examples of this effort to connect the member's behavior with his past history and current personality.

Chapter 5

The Leader

If Chapter 4 demonstrated nothing else, it certainly showed the considerable range in the content and intensity of the members' feelings toward the leader. This observation leads us to wonder about how the leader handles all this. How does he respond to the members' expressions of hostility or distress, or to their efforts to enact his role in the group? The response of the leader to the various feelings being expressed by members may be viewed as part of a larger strategy or style with which the leader entered the group.

We have named the three leaders of the four groups Drs. Allen (group one), Baker (group two), Charles (group three), and Dawes (group four), although Drs. Allen and Charles were the same person. In their roles as leaders, Dr. Allen (and Dr. Charles) tended more toward interpretation of group or at least dyadic phenomena, Dr. Baker toward a reflection and question-asking style at the group level, and Dr. Dawes toward the interpretation of both individual and group dynamics. Of the four leaders, Dr. Baker seemed the most remote and Dr. Dawes the most active and intrusive. Given his prior training in psychiatry, Dr. Dawes was more likely to focus upon the unconscious determinants of individual behavior, whereas the other two leaders, who had been trained in social psychology, were more oriented toward helping the group to understand its own processes and to move beyond impasses caused by more widely shared feelings of distress and resentment. Despite the many differences between the leaders, in goals, style, and personality, the question may still be raised whether their responses to the feelings expressed toward them reveal the existence of a common strategy and overlapping goals for the groups.

This may be an appropriate moment to recall that not all of the feelings scored are expressed directly toward the leader. We can assume that, like most people, the leader manages not to hear many of the feelings which are at least partially directed toward him. But we can also assume that the leader, like most other people, is often affected by communications whose import he had not fully grasped. He, too, may emerge from a group session with a headache or in a self-reproachful mood without knowing exactly why. However, whether or not he hears less than the scorer, he does hear something. Most of his responses reveal rather clearly his inferences about what the members are feeling toward him, as well as toward themselves and their fellow group members.

The member-leader scoring system records two aspects of the leader's response: (1) what feelings the leader seems to be ascribing to the member; and (2) the leader's evaluation of the member's feelings, ranging along the continuum from approval to no evaluation to disapproval.[1] From these data two answerable questions emerge. One inquires into what the leader is paying attention to and a second asks what feelings he tends to support. And there is a third question: how does the leader's attention to a given feeling relate to his evaluation of it.

The comparison of what the members express and what the leader reflects back to them can begin rather simply. We can correlate the two sets of percentages that describe the members' and the leader's distribution of acts into the 16 categories. The result, expressed in terms of the rank-order correlation between the members' and leader's percentage profiles, is not uniform across the groups. In group two, the leader's profile agrees very well with the all-member profile; the correlation is .91. For two other groups, the correlations (.58 and .72) are also statistically significant, but for group four the correlation (.46) fails to reach the .05 level of significance. It appears that there is a positive relationship between what feelings the members express and what feelings the leader ascribes to them, but there are some notable discrepancies. Sometimes the leader reflects back or interprets much more of a particular feeling than the members are expressing, sometimes much less, and this fact prompted us to devise an index of over- or under-attention.

---

[1] A further elaboration of the scoring system has been worked out by Mrs. Maxine Bernstein. In this scheme, the leader's feelings toward the members are scored using the same categories except for the exchange of Showing Dominance for Showing Dependency and Showing Counterdominance for Showing Counterdependency. This system is being used in our ongoing studies of Introductory Psychology classes.

The Leader's Attention

The attention index takes the percentage of all leader ascriptions falling in a given category and compares it with the percentage of all member-initiated acts falling in that category. If the leader's ascriptions are at double the rate of the member's acts, the index value would be 200%; if they were at only half the rate, the index would be 50%.

One question that arises is how much the leaders resemble one another in their inclination to overattend or underattend to the various categories. Table 5-1 shows the attention index by leader for each

Table 5-1
Leader Attention to the Member-to-Leader Categories

Categories	Group 1 Index	(Rank)	Group 2 Index	(Rank)	Group 3 Index	(Rank)	Group 4 Index	(Rank)	All Groups (Rank)
Moving Against	182	(1)	81	(9)	197	(3)	78	(7)	(3.5)
Resisting	106	(7)	174	(1)	82	(10)	56	(11)	(7.5)
Withdrawing	151	(4)	125	(3)	127	(6)	316	(1)	(2)
Guilt Inducing	155	(3)	122	(4)	83	(9)	29	(13)	(7.5)
Making Reparation	42	(13)	33	(16)	24	(13)	14	(15)	(15)
Identifying	24	(16)	49	(14)	6	(15)	17	(14)	(16)
Accepting	34	(15)	86	(7)	21	(14)	13	(16)	(13)
Moving Toward	68	(9)	70	(12)	173	(4)	186	(2)	(5)
Showing Dependency	171	(2)	173	(2)	214	(2)	144	(5)	(1)
Showing Independence	49	(12)	73	(11)	350	(1)	94	(6)	(9)
Showing Counterdependency	77	(8)	84	(8)	135	(5)	66	(10)	(10)
Expressing Anxiety	152	(5)	109	(5)	125	(7)	172	(3)	(3.5)
Denying Anxiety	56	(11)	87	(6)	56	(12)	71	(9)	(11)
Expressing Self-Esteem	35	(14)	57	(13)	0	(16)	50	(12)	(14)
Expressing Depression	145	(6)	74	(10)	96	(8)	148	(4)	(6)
Denying Depression	66	(10)	45	(15)	74	(11)	75	(8)	(12)

category and, in parentheses next to the index value, the rank of that category within the set of 16; a high rank signifies overattention, a low rank underattention. It is apparent that there are differences between the leaders, but the overall agreement among the four rankings, as measured by Kendall's index of concordance, W, is highly significant ($W = .64$, $p < .001$). Given the similarity among the leaders, the overall ranking of the attention indices across the four leaders, shown in the final column of the table, can be said to have some meaning. What this composite ranking reveals is that the leaders overattend to the feelings embedded in such categories as Showing Dependency, Withdrawing, Moving Against, and Expressing Anxiety, whereas they underattend to such categories as Identifying, Accepting, and Expressing Self-Esteem. Why should this be so, and what does it tell us about the leader's role in the group?

To the extent that the leader attends to any of the feelings expressed by the members, he is contributing to the construction of the group's agenda. At times, he may be saying that it is all right to talk about the feeling in question; at other times he may be saying that it is important to talk about it. To the extent that he overattends to various feelings, he is doing something more than legitimizing their expression. He is exerting pressure on the group to consider the existence, the relevance, or the consequences of the feelings to which he points. In most of the cases of overattention, our best guess would be that the leader feels that the group had better look at the underlying feelings of dependency, hostility, or distress in order to gain insight into the nature of these feelings and to move beyond the impasses caused by their disguised and unrecognized expression. The leader's interpretations often take the form of connecting one publicly accepted feeling with another that is less acceptable to the group at that moment. Where the members see boredom, the leader may see anxiety or avoidance of personal involvement; where the members see rational debate, the leader may see an undercurrent of resentment. Overattention to a given category may thus reflect the leader's effort to translate feelings expressed in other categories into what he hypothesizes to be the more fundamental feeling which must be examined.

There is another explanation of overattention that fits at least one of the cases. The leader in group three was particularly bothered by the dependent quality of the group. For him to overattend to Showing Dependency fits the explanation offered above, but for him to overattend to Showing Independence seemed to be a deliberate indication to the group of what he would prefer the members to feel. These efforts were neither numerous nor successful, but they do indicate that not all overattention is aimed at uncovering feelings; some overattention may involve efforts to encourage certain feelings.

Underattention may derive from a lack of urgency on the leader's part, a sense that it is not crucial that the group come to grips with the feelings involved. But it may also spring from quite a different source, which we might call the "kiss of death" phenomenon. The leaders uniformly look the other way when a member expresses affection by means of Identifying; they rarely imply that they are even aware of the message involved. The simplest explanation is that they seem to believe that for them to notice this would be tantamount to setting that member up as the teacher's pet.

By weighting and combining the categories in the appropriate ways, we can extend this analysis to the various factor patterns; we can ask not only which factor patterns are attended to but which pairs of factor patterns show the greatest discrepancies in leader attention. The results can be summarized briefly. The leaders tend, almost without exception, to pay least attention to the categories comprising the Enactment performance and the greatest attention to the opposite set, the categories that define Dependent Complaining. Of less magnitude, but still substantial, is the discrepancy between the leaders' overattention to Distress and underattention to the Colleague pattern. Thus the leaders focus on the feelings that tend to impede the member's independence and capacity to take over aspects of the leader's role, while at the same time ignoring the performances that achieve these two goals. The leaders pay more attention to both poles of factor two, which deals with the leader's authority, than to the two poles of any other factor. Evidently the leaders feel that both the Loyalty and Rebellion performances need to be examined, and the leaders' responses to these performances are designed to keep both sets of feelings clearly before the group.

The Leader's Support

The next issue is that of the leader's support for some feelings and lack of support for others. It may not be unfair to state that most leaders find it somewhat disagreeable to view themselves as rewarding or punishing the expression of any feelings. Interpretations of the effect of therapy upon patients or of training groups upon group members simply as evidence that people can learn to express the "correct" feelings and avoid the "wrong" ones are usually seen as betraying a hopelessly Philistine attitude toward the whole process. At least as the scorers view the leaders' interventions, the picture is a mixed one. Nearly two-thirds of all leader acts are scored as nonevaluative, which one might surmise is considerably higher than the corresponding figure for most teachers, bosses, or parents. But what about the other third of the acts? For each of the four leaders there is at least one category which is rewarded more often than it is received nonevaluatively and at least one other that is usually responded to in a negative or discouraging fashion. In order to summarize these responses the support index was constructed.

The support index is derived from the distribution of a leader's responses to a given category. A negative response is given the value of one, a nonevaluative response the value of two, and a positive response the value of three. The support index is the mean value of all the leader's responses to that category. Thus an index value of 3.00 would indicate that all of the leader's responses had been positive; an index value of 2.00 would result from having all nonevaluative responses or from a balance of positive and negative responses, and so on. Table 5-2 presents the support index values by leader for each category, and again the 16 categories were ranked from high to low support and the ranks shown in parentheses.

The amount of agreement between leaders regarding which categories are supported and which are not supported is very high. Kendall's W is .81, which is significant at beyond the .001 level. Thus the overall ranking, computed on the basis of the sum of ranks across the four groups, can be examined wih considerable assurance that it is meaningful to talk about leaders in general. It appears that Showing Independence, all forms of affection, and the expression of distress receive support from the leaders. The categories which are not supported are mainly the various expressions of hostility, especially Withdrawing, and the denials of anxiety and depression. There are a few exceptions; the leaders in groups two and four were more likely to support Identifying, and the leader in group three, whose interest in discouraging dependency has already been noted, was unusually supportive of Resisting and unsupportive of Accepting.

An even clearer picture emerges from the analysis of the 12 factor patterns. If one ranks these patterns from high to low support, the agreement between the four leaders is reflected in a W value of .86 ($p < .001$). Figure 5-1 displays these results factor by factor for each group. Of particular interest is the possibility that one pole of a factor

Table 5-2
Leader Support for the Member-to-Leader Categories

Categories	Group 1 Index (Rank)		Group 2 Index (Rank)		Group 3 Index (Rank)		Group 4 Index (Rank)		All Groups (Rank)
Moving Against	1.91	(8)	1.89	(9)	1.97	(7)	1.78	(9)	(9)
Resisting	1.56	(14)	1.64	(14)	1.93	(8)	1.25	(16)	(13)
Withdrawing	1.51	(15)	1.44	(15)	1.39	(16)	1.54	(14)	(16)
Guilt Inducing	1.73	(12)	1.75	(10)	1.56	(14)	1.50	(15)	(12)
Making Reparation	2.00	(5)	2.25	(3)	2.25	(2)	1.90	(8)	(3.5)
Identifying	1.85	(9.5)	2.50	(1)	2.00	(5.5)	2.21	(2)	(3.5)
Accepting	2.23	(1)	2.18	(4)	1.75	(12)	2.00	(4.5)	(6)
Moving Toward	2.05	(4)	2.00	(6.5)	2.04	(3)	2.09	(3)	(2)
Showing Dependency	1.73	(12)	1.74	(11)	1.76	(11)	1.56	(13)	(11)
Showing Independence	2.09	(3)	2.40	(2)	2.33	(1)	2.60	(1)	(1)
Showing Counterdependency	1.85	(9.5)	1.71	(12)	1.84	(10)	1.69	(10)	(10)
Expressing Anxiety	1.96	(6)	1.97	(8)	1.86	(9)	1.95	(6)	(8)
Denying Anxiety	1.40	(16)	1.65	(13)	1.62	(13)	1.60	(12)	(14.5)
Expressing Self-Esteem	2.20	(2)	2.00	(6.5)	2.00	(5.5)	2.00	(4.5)	(5)
Expressing Depression	1.95	(7)	2.17	(5)	2.02	(4)	1.93	(7)	(7)
Denying Depression	1.73	(12)	1.29	(16)	1.53	(15)	1.63	(11)	(14.5)

is supported more than the opposite pole. However, since the support indices for the two poles are computed separately, it may also happen that both poles would be supported or not supported. The figure shows the support for the positive and negative ends of each factor, and the longer the line connecting the two poles, the greater the discrepancy between the support which they receive.

We would interpret a high discrepancy between the support for

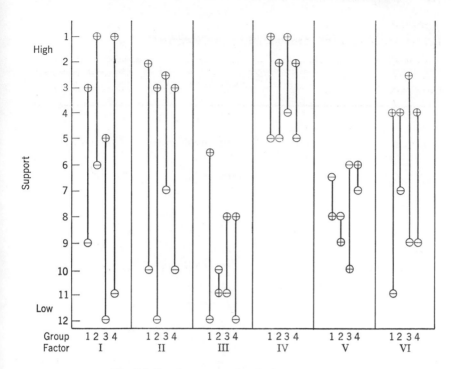

Fig. 5-1. Leader support for the factor patterns.

the two ends of a factor as evidence that the leader is exerting pressure upon the members to move from one end of the factor to the other. Thus there seems to be considerable pressure on the members to move on factor one from Dependent Complaining to Enactment, on factor two from Rebellion to Loyalty, and on factor six from Neutrality to Involvement. In contrast, both poles of factor four, Colleague and Distress, are supported, whereas there is little support for either pole of factor three, Counterdependent Flight and Resistant Complaining. The leaders are more balanced in their support of Anxiety versus Depression than for any other pair of factor patterns, although the support involved is relatively low in both cases. In an effort to summarize the findings thus far, we have prepared Table 5-3 to show the leader's attention and support for each of the factor patterns. The degrees of attention or support were simply divided into high, medium, and low thirds.

At this point, we can return to the richness of the transcripts and tape recordings in order to see more clearly what these results are

Table 5-3
Leader Attention and Support for the Factor Patterns

Leader Support	Leader Attention		
	High	Medium	Low
High	II+ Loyalty	VI+ Involvement	I+ Enactment IV+ Colleague
Medium	IV— Distress	III+ Counter- dependent Flight V+ Anxiety	V— Depression
Low	I— Dependent Complaining II— Rebellion	III— Resistant Complaining	VI— Neutrality

telling us. What do the leaders sound like when they support a factor pattern or when they put pressure on the members to move beyond certain feelings? We shall review how the leaders react not only to the various categories but to the particularly good examples of each factor pattern.

The pattern of attention and support for *factor one*, which deals with the issue of the leader as analyst, is more polarized than the pattern for any other factor. Enactment receives little attention but, when it is attended to, it receives high support; Dependent Complaining receives high attention and low support. The characteristic form of nonsupport for Dependent Complaining is noncompliance; the leader does not comply with the member's request that he give more structure to the group's proceedings and more protection to its members. The following interaction which occurred in the first minute of the first session of one group is as clear an example as any.

Jane: What is that you're supposed to do with the cases?
Leader: Well, we discuss them. (Pause.) There are many ways to discuss them.
Dave: With what reference, though? Are you looking for anything in particular? Personal opinions?
Leader: I guess this is something you'll need to work out. (Long pause.)

Dave: Should we attempt to coordinate the reading in this case? Will the reading follow the cases? Are the cases entirely separate?
Leader: I guess there will be reasons for making it one way or the other. Whichever way you do it, there—I think what you're asking for is a legitimate thing. You want some direction to know how to proceed—
Jay: Are you going to show us what to do, or are we going to show you?
Leader: That's the question, isn't it? Who's going to show who?

In this exchange the leader oscillates between rejecting and reflecting the dependency that the new situation has stirred up, but there is a teasing quality to this and the other introductory sessions, with the leader playing the role of the artful dodger. In throwing the responsibility for the group's fate back to the group, the leader may arouse a highly moralistic response from some members, a response that implies that the leader *must* perform his proper role. When Bion (1961) feigns innocence and amazement that the members could have expected him to lead the group, as if he of all people were especially qualified to do so, he is not only conveying his interpretation that the members are feeling dependent, he is telling them that such feelings are quite inappropriate to the situation in which they find themselves.

The leader's support for Enactment, however infrequently it comes, underscores the main alternative to Dependent Complaining. The interpretive style is sometimes cast as the antithesis of the judgmental style, with the implication that the group will make better progress if it tries to understand rather than judge what is going on.

When the leaders use words like impressive, productive, or beautiful to describe the empathic and interpretive approach of one member toward another, most members are unlikely to miss the positive evaluation of such activity. The message to the group, when the leader supports Enactment, goes beyond his support for the feelings involved. It is also a statement about the underlying themes, a hope that the members can move beyond the nurturance and control issues to the competence theme. Enactment, more than any other factor pattern, is supported because of its close relationship with one of the purposes of the group—to provide the members with an opportunity to learn by taking on the interpretive, analytic style of the leader in relation to the case material and the events of the group itself. The leader's support is indirect and attention to Enactment is low partly because the interpersonal nexus in which a person's own sense of competence will develop is necessarily one of distance and parallel effort.

The leaders pay attention to both poles of *factor two,* Loyalty and Rebellion, but the pressure they exert is toward the Loyalty end of the factor. The very thought that the leaders are punishing hostility and encouraging affection and dependency suggest several possibilities, one of which might be that the leader's own narcissism and counter-transference leads him to try to produce a group of loyal stooges. What *is* going on here? Only when the time dimension is added to these results does the picture become clearer. In the early sessions the leaders tend to pay attention to Rebellion, and the tone of their response is rather neutral. Consider the following early intervention by the leader:

"It seems to me that what we're really talking about is whether or not this group has got to suspend or somehow suppress the criticism it feels of what we're doing, or of me, or of the way the group is run, in order to survive as a happy, sensitive, joyous organization, or whether, as I think Harry is suggesting, you'd just better admit the fact that you don't like certain things that are going on. If you can only handle it by disassociating yourself from it, well, then, that's one way out, but at least the premise that you should know all the negative feelings that you have toward a situation is an important one. . . . We've talked about it in terms of society, but I think its more direct application to this group is: 'What are we going to do with the fact that we don't like each other, we don't like the way the course is going, and we don't like the way the reading tells us to feel, or one thing or another? Are we going to have a *Child's Garden of Verses* in here, or are we going to have something based on the honest feelings that are aroused by each other and by me?' "

In contrast to the intervention quoted above, which amounts to an open invitation to hostility, as the rebellion comes more and more into the open the leader's tone becomes noticeably more defensive and un-supportive. Even within the course of one interchange the shift is apparent.

Frank: My attitude was antagonistic because somebody tried to shut off the discussion that was going on in here, and I thought we were just going to talk about anything, you know?
Leader: You feel very badly that I interpreted, or tried to interpret the reasons why your discussions were taking place, tried to interpret

the things that you feel were interesting. You interpret it now as my intention to shut you off.

Frank: You weren't trying to shut me off. You were trying to shut the people off that were talking, and I thought this was wrong. I mean, unless you define what you're trying to do in a situation, you know.

Leader: You want to label what I was doing as shutting off as opposed to interpreting?

Although the major deviations from the nonevaluative response with respect to Rebellion come during the peak of the members' attack on the leader, the leader's support for Loyalty tends to come out only in the latter half of the group. In some instances, the leader supports those members who shift from a negative to a positive reaction to the leader. After days of seeing the leader as an "ice cube" or "smug," at the point when Frank decided that perhaps the leader was spontaneous, that he had "turned into a human being," the leader's response was to encourage Frank to say more. Beyond these instances, it is apparent that in later sessions the leader feels more at ease about rewarding the infrequent expressions of dependency, and his interpretations are designed to uncover the positive feelings that went out of style during the peak of the rebellion. Thus when the group is in its early "honeymoon" stage, the leader moves to uncover the hostility, and there is some evidence that he becomes increasingly threatened by and impatient with these negative feelings. Only later does he move to uncover and support the positive, dependent feelings, and this is particularly true when the prevailing group pressures make it as difficult to express positive feelings as it earlier was to express negative ones.

Factor three, which casts the leader as the manipulator, receives little support. The leader tends to react to both the Counterdependent Flight and the Resistant Complaining performances with acute discomfort. In effect, the leaders are being seen as devious, narcissistic, and usually maternal figures. Their response suggests that they want no part of this image. They are as likely to argue over its validity as they are to probe into the feelings that underlie the perceptions. Consider, for example, the following two exchanges during the eleventh session of one group:

Jacques: Every time we start to talk about cases and readings, you [the leader] seem to send us back to group introspection. Is this what you're trying to do?

Leader: What is the group trying to do?

Jacques: What side are you on now, group introspection or discussion of the readings and cases?

Leader: Does the group see me as intervening all the time?

Ed: Is it really fair for us to give away something of ourselves in a paper that's a requirement for this course?

Leader: Well, you're giving it to *me*.

Ed: I'm not sure it's fair to us, as a requirement of the course, to have to tell you something about ourselves. Does that strike you as legitimate?

Leader: How does the group feel about it? It is a requirement, so I'm not going to necessarily make it into a group issue. But I'm interested in any questions . . . *other questions?* (Cuts off Ed.)

In the first exchange, the leader attempted to dodge the issue of his manipulations by implying that the group is its own master. Later, when the privacy issue arose, the leader ignored the expressions of mistrust and the underlying moralism, and he attempted to redefine the issue in terms of his formal authority. No voyeur he; the paper is simply a requirement.

In another group, the leader was accused of identifying with and paying more attention to one of the members, thereby elevating that member above the others. The leader responded to this observation not by noting its high degree of accuracy, but by denial:

"I don't want to be put in the role of nominating people for the leadership positions in this group. My job is to try and interpret what I think are significant forces operating in the group at the moment."

Another member then pressed the point, and the leader's response, "Perhaps we can understand, as we go along, why it is important for you to see things that way," could be construed as an attack on the member's capacity to form veridical perceptions. These are the kinds of interventions that make members wonder if they might be slightly insane.

The leaders also resist the notion that the group is like an experiment. They pass the buck along to some higher authority ("I am a subject as well as you"), or they try to tease the members into seeing how foolish such a notion is. In general, it is fair to say that the leaders dislike being mistrusted. At one point, when the group became interested in why the leader put his feet up on the desk, the leader retorted:

"That's a very persistent theme in this group, that somehow I have more conscious control over my gestures and my behavior, etc. than anyone else in the room."

In one sense, the members turn the tables on the leader here: interpreting, digging, scrutinizing. And not unlike the members when they are on the receiving end, the leaders seem to feel constricted and irritated by the whole process. In short, the leader's annoyance and his tendency to deny his influence have some rather serious effects upon the group. The group learns that feelings in this area are not well received and might even be met with denials. By constantly redefining the issue and by minimizing his own influence, the leader may unwittingly postpone a synthesis of the two antithetical ideas that he influences nothing and that he influences everything. Not all the responses of any leader are of the negative form quoted here. The groups do make some headway on the issue of influence and manipulation, but the leader's role is not altogether a facilitating one.

The leader's response to the *factor four* performances, in which the members use him as audience for their expressions of value conflict or their distress is largely supportive, although his support for the Colleague pattern is infrequent. As might be expected, given the leader's aversion to being seen as manipulative, the leader rewards those definitions of the member-leader relationship that emphasize his own autonomy, his own lack of direct complicity in the turmoil and failures of the group situation. The Colleague pattern emphasizes the ego-integrative aspects of the member's task. One instance of the leader's support for this activity occurred late in one of the group's history:

Anna: It's either a matter of saying, 'How dare you be my authority, how dare you be my God,' or 'Please be my God,' and it seems like we're saying—we have said the one, we have said the other, and I think in a way we've said both, and now we're just in between.
Leader: I agree. There's a very fragile and tenuous middle ground between those two pleas. One, get down off the pedestal and become a member of the group, and the other, get way up there so we can really know what's right. Between those two, there is a middle ground being formed.

To be cast somewhere between an authority and a peer seems to satisfy the leader's definition of his role. His support for those who see him as different but similar, outside the group but inside the group, etc., also expresses his approval of the effort involved in sustaining these two views of him at one and the same time.

The leader's response to the Distress performances tends to be mainly neutral, but there is also much more positive support than explicit nonsupport. When one member said, "It's hard doing this all by ourselves," the leader agreed; when a whole series of members compared themselves with Joseph in the pit, the leader varied between reflecting the feelings involved and agreeing that they were valid and appropriate. To the extent, then, that the member gives the leader the impression that he is relevant, but not too relevant, the leader responds positively.

As the tables in this chapter suggest, the leaders' response to both the Anxiety and Depression performances of *factor five* are neither high nor particularly low on either attention or support. There are times when the leader rewards an expression of anxiety or depression, especially when it seems that to express the feeling took some personal courage or a willingness to run counter to the prevailing mood. There are other times when the leader becomes frustrated by the "unreachable" or self-isolating quality which the continuing expression of anxiety or depression conveys. In one such example, near the end of the group, Frank had been going on at some length about suicide, about how terrible it was for a psychiatrist to give Hemingway shock treatment, and about freedom. At this point, the leader began to express an unusual amount of hostility with unusual directness:

"It is just paralyzing to listen to what you are saying because any sort of rational opposition to what you are saying, I feel, walks right into the booby trap, as it were. I mean it walks right into the self-destructive, sort of bitter, resigned, self-defeating theme which in a way is an invitation to aggression and which, at the same time, is an invitation to tremendous guilt on the part of the attacker. What I hear you saying is: 'Here I am sitting way over here in the corner just killing myself, and nobody has a right to stop me, and I am going to say the most bitter, unhappy, nihilistic, lost, empty things, and no one has the right to touch me.'"

The leader's hostility at this point was probably derived from many sources. Perhaps he felt that Frank's performance was a discouraging note on which to end the group, or he may have been disappointed that Frank could so easily revert back to a mistrustful attitude that seemed to have lifted. Perhaps the theme had some personal relevance to the leader. In the light of Frank's subsequent behavior, it appears likely that there was a good deal of misperception involved. Suffice it to say that the leaders seem to have a limit beyond which the Anxiety or Depression performances produce a collapse of the usual neutrality and rather abrupt efforts to stem or deflect the flow of feelings.

The pattern of attention and support for *factor six* is somewhat unusual. Neutrality is the only factor pattern that is low on both attention and support. Involvement, on the other hand, is highly supported, but it is neither underattended to as in the case of Enactment or Colleague nor overattended to as in the case of Loyalty. The pressure from the leader is in the direction of Involvement, but the leaders tend to avoid the whole issue of the personal relationship between themselves and the members.

One early instance of the leader's pressure away from Neutrality occurred at a point when the question of revealing feelings was far from settled:

George: I don't think anyone should be afraid.
Leader: What are we talking about?
George: What's this?
Leader: What are we talking about now? What is going on? I understand these words you say; I'm wondering what they mean. What is the latent meaning of them?
George: The latent meaning is it's not to be revealed. This is just something to be thrown around.
Leader: Well, I really have the feeling that it's unproductive to operate on the level where everyone knows there is something else going on underneath, but we're performing this dance on a pane of glass above the real events which underlie it.

Another event which regularly raises the issue of withdrawal is an "outside meeting" or gathering of members who return to comment favorably upon how relaxed and yet meaningful are the exchanges that occur outside the group. One leader was particularly concerned to point out the negative consequences of such activity, as can be seen in the following summary of his interaction with the group:

The group began rearranging the tables and chairs so as to exclude the leader from the group. After a long discussion of an "informal" group which had been meeting for some time after the regular class hour, the leader commented: "Some people are deliberately excluded from these informal meetings. Perhaps those who are excluded raise issues that are too anxiety-arousing, and so we must run from them. I have the feeling that this informal group is a way to run from me and the kinds of insights that we have been trying to face here in the group." This interpretation was immediately rejected, and the session ended with further talk of the pleasant, convivial informal sessions. The leader abandoned his customary habit of titling the session and asked that the members title it themselves—a suggestion which they ignored.

Although the scoring system presents us with no record of how the leader responds to the use of various levels, it is apparent that the leader exerts pressure away from the "there and then" or Level three discussions to the "here and now" discussions on Levels one or two. The net effect of this pressure is toward Involvement and toward the expression of feelings that are currently being felt. Somewhat similar in its import is the following intervention which is aimed at the Neutrality implications of Making Reparation. The interpretation is directed toward the group's only ordained minister:

"I think that is very important. I think most times when you come in and talk, you come in and talk in the name of someone else. You really quite clearly were talking in the name of your neighbor just now, and on other days you've come in in the name of miscellaneous disturbed people who've come to you and said, 'I was upset by the discussion,' and you start off in a way to protect them. It's a very comfortable role for you. And really you are always able to dodge out from underneath some of the counterattacks by saying, 'It isn't really me who feels upset. I think sex is beautiful. I think our discussion was fine. It's just that two days is enough.' You're not attacking it, you're just saying, 'Well, let's call a halt to it in the name of someone else who is disturbed.' I think that one difficulty is that in addressing you the class has found that, in a sense, you are not there. Someone else is sitting there, perhaps the protected shadowy figures that stand behind you."

At the positive end of factor six is Involvement, and the leader's support for these performances takes various forms. The leader is confronted here with a member who initiates the move toward a close, but not exclusively positive, relationship. This scoring system does not record the greater alertness or interest that characterize the leader at these moments, but there is much evidence that these performances do intrigue and challenge the leader. The pressures on the leader to drop his role, or to stop being patronizing, put the leader on his mettle, lest he be rejected as nothing more than an empty, pompous person infatuated with his own status. One example of this issue arose when Harry shifted his behavior from the defiant, impulsive style he had adopted earlier to a style that was both more interpretive and more self-critical. The response of several group members to this shift was to urge Harry to return to the old ways, to become again the wild, irresponsible Harry. At this point the leader intervened, and on the surface his comments were an admonition to the group to tolerate the ambiguity of Harry's several styles. But at another level the message to Harry was that the leader, even if no one else could, was prepared to accept precisely the combination of heroic rebellion, ambivalence, and identification that had characterized Harry's performances thus far. When the leader was finished, the following exchange occurred:

Harry: Do you think it's a contradiction to interpret and to be an impulsive, libidinal self?
Leader: No, I don't.
Harry: Obviously not. But then where is the contradiction?
Leader: I think the contradictions scare each of us when we see them inside ourselves or when we see them in others, as much as they delight us and amuse us.

The leader's positive response to Involvement, far more than his support for any other factor pattern, brings up the issue of favoritism. The member whose Involvement is recognized and responded to is "in," but how much room is there inside the circle? When the leader pressures those whose performances are on the Neutrality side of the factor to become more involved, to what extent is he asking the members to abandon a strategy that is at least moderately safe for a strategy that has little chance of succeeding? How many members will the leader find especially interesting? To the extent that the leader is developing meaningful attachments, which can only partially be explained in countertransference terms, he may be raising the ante higher than some members can ever manage. To that extent, he is creating the conditions for the very Neutrality which he is simultaneously discouraging. The net result is a series of pressures of far greater complexity than the ones found for any other factor.

The Leader's Definition of Work

Now that we have reviewed the leader's attention to and support for the six factor patterns, it is appropriate to ask whether there is some overarching conception of the leader's role that would help make sense of the various pressures which the leader puts on the group. In our view, such a conception is provided by the notion of work. Many of the leader's reactions to the members' performances can be understood by considering the leader's definition of work and his role in the emerging work group. We propose to look at four aspects of work, each of which seems to be a necessary but not sufficient component of what the leader values and rewards in the name of work. These components are *enactment, independence, involvement,* and *expression.*

Enactment. From the evidence of the leader's support, it is clear that the leader wishes to have the members use his performance as a model for their activity. The members are encouraged to practice and take on, as one part of their total performance, the interpretive, intellectual style of the leader. Enactment involves seeing personal or interpersonal events as relevant; it involves an effort to make sense of these events by relating them to one another and to the slowly developing conceptual framework provided by the list of readings; and it involves testing the hypotheses that seem most fruitful by making one's inferences public, in the knowledge that most of the inferences will need to be modified or extended. The leader's support for those who enact his role and his nonsupport for those who are chronically disappointed or frustrated by it help to shape the group's definition of work. Not infrequently, the leader's pressure toward enactment takes the form of dogged perseverance in his interpretive style plus an inclination to point out and interpret the members' resistance. The leader seems to believe the members would more willingly take on his role if they were less inclined to cast the very act of interpretation in such a negative light. In the following interaction, we can see not only the leader's doggedness in the face of clearly expressed hostility but also a mixture of defensiveness and reparation. The defensiveness shows through most clearly in the teasing quality of the leader's responses and in his reluctance to have *his* actions interpreted; the reparation is most clearly seen in the leader's effort to differentiate between interpreting and not caring for someone.

Faith began the session by expressing her mistrust of the leader's "armchair psychoanalysis," complaining that she felt incapable of commenting on events in the group because she lacked the sophistication and experience of other members who were able to articulate their thoughts better than she. Doris attempted to avoid the issue, but the leader pursued it further:

Dr. Dawes: [To Faith] Perhaps you are frightened by some of the feelings that the group has aroused.

Faith: No, I think it's a question of not having the same psychological background and therefore not being able to speak in this kind of psychological language that you have, which is in any case quite arbitrary and usually irrelevant.

Dr. Dawes: Arbitrary?

Faith: Well that's just my opinion, I don't . . .

Carol: I think that Dr. Dawes has done a wonderful job of pointing out some of the feelings that we weren't ready to reveal, and I am finally able to see what he has been talking about since we began.

Ross: I want to agree with what Carol said. In the beginning, I was very resistant and so forth to this kind of analysis, but I now understand how it can help you to gain more awareness of what is happening in this kind of situation.

Dr. Dawes: What I would like to know is why Faith thinks that what I do is so arbitrary.

Faith: Well, like the time when Dolores didn't come and I was ten minutes late because my alarm clock didn't go off and you made a big deal out of it and kept saying that we unconsciously didn't want to come and that we unconsciously planned it that way. That just wasn't so, and you had no way of knowing anything about it, and so it's just an arbitrary assumption on your . . .

Dr. Dawes: Are there accidents in human behavior?

Mabel: Oh why don't you just shut up and leave her alone! That's mean and unfair. We've had this same discussion before, and most people decided that you were arbitrary and narrow-minded. And the other day you were late yourself—so what does that prove? (Charles enters.) Now don't you dare say anything to him about being late!

Dr. Dawes: The time I was late I couldn't find a parking place. It's hard to find . . .

Arnold: I guess you're in a special category of people who don't have to explain what they do because you don't make any unconscious mistakes.

Don: I think we are just attacking him because we know that he is omnipotent and above these things. I bet he spent years working on his personal flaws so he wouldn't have to watch himself all the time. He has such perfect control because he has perfected control to a fine degree.

Dr. Dawes: Are there fathers and mothers here with us today?

Pamela: We're finished with that. You had your moment of glory.

Dr. Dawes: Can we ever escape from transference?

Pamela: Someone said the other day that the concept of transference isn't very useful anymore. The focus now is on interaction.

Mabel: I wish he would just shut up.

Dr. Dawes: I wonder what is beneath all of this anger. Sometimes, when we don't trust people, we yell at them, or withdraw from them. I think that we have seen both reactions here. Some people have gotten angry, and others have withdrawn. Every day people come in a little later. Five minutes, ten minutes, fifteen minutes. Then we have parties and meet outside the group where we don't have to face up to what has been happening here. But you can't just run away from the unconscious, no matter how hard we try.

Audrey: I think if you wouldn't push at people all the time they might relax and reveal themselves in a more natural way.

Dr. Dawes: I think people are afraid that I don't like them or care about them when I try to point out some of the things that they are expressing through their actions, and that isn't the case.

Don: I think he's got us cornered and boxed up and we're just going to have to squirm around until he's finished with us.

Mabel: I hate his guts.

Bert: I have more respect for him now that I see how hard his job really is.

Mabel: He gets paid for it.

Faith: It's like being in the dentist's chair for an hour a day. It's not the course I thought it was going to be.

Ross: I think we're going to have to admit that what Dr. Dawes says is right, even though it hurts.

Don: Does a human guinea pig have any choice?

Dr. Dawes: Are parents too cruel and vengeful to be trusted?

Independence. The leader exerts pressure on the members to become independent and to relate to him not only as an authority but as a colleague. The conjunction of enactment and independence suggests the primacy of the competence theme in the leader's definition of work. The goal would seem to be to have the members achieve some form of individuated growth without undue preoccupation with the leader's expectations. The leader's concern over the development of competence is closely related to the central desire of nearly all socializing and educating agents, the wish to create life. The wish to be relevant to the development of autonomous, self-directed individuals may be contrasted with the fears that the learner will not survive being transplanted into another environment, that he will remain so parasitic or simply compliant that he will take nothing away with him. Enactment and independence, when combined, offer some reassurance to the leader that the member has taken charge of his own growth and that it will persist.

Involvement. When one considers the leader's pressure towards greater involvement, it is apparent that not all forms of independence are equally valued by the leader. Evidence of withdrawal and denials of hostility or anxiety seem to imply not autonomy but an unwillingness to engage oneself in the situation. The relevance of this reaction for our understanding of the leader's definition of work is that the leader evidently sees work as including some involvement and some tolerance of being exposed and vulnerable. As with most therapeutic and educational ventures, the group can be of benefit to the individual member only to the extent that he commits himself to it. Or so the leaders imply by their pressure on the group.

Expression. In turning to the fourth component of work, expression, we find a complex situation. On the one hand, the leader is encouraging the expression and opposing the denial of feelings. To the extent that the feelings come his way, the feelings are reflected back or accepted a great majority of the time. Closely related to this, the leader is often found attempting to remove the impediments that block the expression of feelings, especially the impediments raised by a moralistic or superficially judgmental atmosphere in the group. A good example of this is found in one leader's comments upon the climate of the group: "One thing that makes it hard to express feelings is that there is an air of judgment around. Some feelings are good and some bad, and, perhaps even more than that, feelings do not matter as much as the behavior they result in and the behavior is going to be judged good or bad."

On the other hand, there is a wide discrepancy between the amount of expressive behavior expected of members and the amount initiated by the leader. The pressure on the group to move toward enactment or independence asks little of the members that the leader does not ask of himself; in relation to expression, and to a lesser extent involvement, the leader urges, "Don't do as I do, do as I say." There are group leaders who emphasize leader expression as a form of modeling, but even in these cases it is not likely to reach the rate or intensity expected of members.

The picture is further complicated by the fact that some expressions are rewarded but some are not. The ones that do receive support from the leader seem to be the ones he might describe as set-breaking, honest, or courageous. When the feelings are seen as not helpful or "more of the same" or unproductive, the leader is less likely to support them. Whether the leaders recall or will admit the extent to which they discourage feelings that threaten or bother them personally we do not know. Implicit in the notion of work is the value on progress, on "getting somewhere." Disregarding for the moment the question of whether the leader's assessments of what will move the group along are correct, it is evident that the leader rewards those feelings which he thinks need to be expressed at that moment. In the early stages of the group he may reward or at least accept any feelings, even feelings of distance or dependency. As the group progresses, the leader's support for a given feeling parallels his interpretations; he tends to "go to the other side of the boat," to point to the less expressed as opposed to the commonly accepted feelings. This process of counterbalancing, of keeping the boat on a somewhat even keel, would make little sense if the leaders did not have a particular stake in helping the members to understand their own ambivalences. The support for expression is in part an effort to block premature closure, to prevent the group from settling on some partial awareness of its own feelings rather than a more inclusive and complicated picture.

The general rule that emerges from this analysis is that some expression is better than none, but the leader's support depends on when or in what phase of the group's development the member expresses a given feeling. And, as if this were not complicated enough, the leader's support for expression depends also upon the balance struck by the member between expression and enactment. When the member's performance entails expression at the expense of enactment, or enactment at the expense of expression, the leader's support, contingent as it is upon the multiple definition of work, begins to decline. There is a constant tension between the leader's value on generating data and his value on processing them. The leader's pressure on all aspects of work, and his decreasing support for partial solutions, places a heavy demand on the group. As we shall see, the leader is by no means alone in the construction of the work group, but we view his role as central to the normative developments that accompany its emergence. His attention to and support for the various individual performances help to define an exceedingly difficult and complex set of goals for the group and for its members.

Much of what we have said about the leader has been directed to the analysis of his role in the definition of work, but it would be needlessly narrow of us to close this section without recognizing the more personal aspects of the leader's style. These leaders differ among themselves with respect to the amount of distance they maintain, the kinds of interpersonal ties they feel are appropriate or desirable from both the professional and personal point of view. Nor are they entirely consistent over time. The leaders of the four groups seem to move closer to the members over time, making more and briefer comments and appearing more at ease and part of the flow of interaction, but on this score there was much variation. Although we are not in a position to gain much leverage from the difference between the leaders' personalities and interpersonal styles, we do not intend to exclude these factors from the range of attributes which can and should be studied in greater depth. The question to which we can address ourselves, on the basis of the data from this chapter, concerns the effect upon the group of the leader's conception of and pressure toward work.

Some Relevant Literature on the Leader

Before discussing in greater detail the numerous efforts to define the role of the leader in self-analytic groups, perhaps a few general observations might be in order. Much of the literature on the leader in self-analytic groups resembles the treatment given the psychoanalyst's role prior to the public discussion of countertransference and the analyst's actual behavior; the picture of the leader that emerges either tends toward the blank screen on whom the members project their early parental imagos or else toward an image of the diffusely benevolent, wise, and helpful professional. With a few notable exceptions most of the studies seem clearer about what leaders should do than what they actually do. The important issue of how differences between leaders affect the group seems somewhat neglected. Furthermore, unless one can assume, in contradiction to this study and the interesting case studies by Bradford (1946b) and Deutsch, Pepitone, and Zander (1948), that the leaders always do what they should, we are also lacking in information about the interventions that fail to help and the moments when the leader's feelings are other than benevolent.

There are numerous ways to conceive of the leader's role in facilitating individual growth and the productive functioning of the group. Most commonly emphasized is the leader's special insight into the crucial aspects of the group (Whitaker and Lieberman, 1964) and his special role as clarifier and persistent reminder of the realities which are affecting the group (Stock and Thelen, 1958; Coffey et al., 1950; and Benne, 1964). However, as Benne (1964) points out, the members' reality may not always coincide with the leader's view of their reality, and the leader should not block the group's capacity to arrive at veridical perceptions of its own proceedings. Beyond his interpretive function, it is often noted that the leader tends to frustrate the members' needs (M. Horwitz, 1964) and to increase their anxiety level (Whitman, 1964; Semrad and Arsenian, 1951) in order to foster growth and an understanding of their needs and feelings. Benne (1964) emphasizes, in addition, the leader's role in supporting the members in the face of the inevitable complexity and ambiguity of the group's situation. The leader's role as supporter and gratifier, as Semrad et al. (1963) point out, is part of his larger function in facilitating work in the group as a whole. Schutz (1958) examines the role of the leader in promoting work and, in the process, extends the range of appropriate behaviors by conceiving of him as providing the group whatever it is missing in order to remain an equilibrated, effective system. Finally, Coffey et al. (1950), among others, note that the leader's task includes that of helping the members to generalize their experience to the "outside world" within which the members must apply whatever they have gained.

Our discussion of the leader's role has emphasized his definition of work and his pressure in the group to move in the direction of work. The most eloquent descriptions of work are to be found in the writings of W. R. Bion (1961). He views work as a group process analogous to the ego mechanisms described by Freud. For the group to work it must integrate the disparate members into a cooperative, rational, and reality-oriented collectivity. In keeping with his emphasis on problem-solving and learning by experience rather than by magic, Bion views the leader as pressing for the maximizing of work functions and the minimizing of defensive, collusive arrangements among members that aim to block the group's awareness of its own processes. Throughout his discussion he implies that the group can overcome its need for illusions and thereby create the conditions for individual and group development.

The empirical study of the leader's behavior in this chapter led us to distinguish between four aspects of the leader's definition of work.

The first aspect of work, enactment of the leader's role, is clearly a pressure which Bion and most other leaders place upon the members. Kelman's (1963) discussion of internalization and identification seems particularly relevant for understanding how a leader attempts to influence the member, as do several other analyses of how the leader attempts to foster the member's self-awareness and accuracy in assessing others (Semrad and Arsenian, 1951; Schein and Bennis, 1965). The leader's pressure toward expression is widely recognized, but Semrad and Arsenian (1951) note that this pressure should not invite acting out but only the more constructive and manageable forms of self-expression. Gibb's (1954) discussion of the "participative" style reminds us that the leader may facilitate expression either through direct involvement and modeling or through sanctioning, unblocking, and uncovering the relevant feelings. By and large the leaders in the present study used the latter technique. The leader's pressure toward independence and his inclusion of this goal as one part of the definition of work seems to be a universal characteristic of leaders; at least, they tend to verbalize this goal. Semrad and Arsenian (1951) imply that the leader's interpretation of dependency needs aroused by the permissive leader is directed toward reducing this dependency, while Schein and Bennis (1965) note the implicit bias toward democratic forms found in the usual T-group setting. Benne (1964) adds quite another dimension to this process when he suggests that the leader must permit the group to succeed or fail on its own, thus indicating that the leader's pressure for independence is complicated by the familiar doubts and apprehensions of all socializing agents. One hears quite generally that the leader's position in the group does, or should, change from one of centrality and authority to one of resource person (Barron and Krulee, 1948) and member status (Frank, 1964). As leaders report this development one can almost sense the satisfaction and relief that is associated with a decline in dependency needs that block the group and burden the leader. We shall return to these matters in Chapter 6. No authors advocate withdrawal and denial on the part of the members, and involvement in the total situation seems to be widely regarded as necessary for individual growth. However, Bion (1961), Semrad and Arsenian (1951), and Semrad et al. (1963) go farther and suggest that the leader may usefully serve as catalyst and central focus for some of the member's efforts to feel, express, and understand how he is affected by at least one important person in the group, i.e., the leader.

Chapter 6

Group Development

Our purpose in this chapter is to determine whether there are uniformities in the development of the four groups under study. As we shall discuss at greater length in the concluding section of the chapter, many writers have noted that the members' feelings toward the leader become less intense and the authority issue less central as the group develops. In general, this observation seems correct. It follows, then, that we are studying not the most pressing concern of the members at every point in time but the continuous, changing relationship between the member and the leader. Within this narrowed but consistent focus we can set out to learn how the relationship starts off, what crises occur, and what transformations may result from various encounters with the leader.

The data for this chapter derive from the scoring of single sessions, pooling all members of the group (except the leader). The raw number of acts in each of the 16 member-to-leader categories was converted to percentage form, as was the raw number of acts at each of the four levels. In both cases the base number was the total number of acts scored for all members in that session. The resultant set of 20 percentages is the same set used to describe a single member's performance in a single session.

The next step in preparing the data was to convert the set of 20 variables into factor scores. One decision we made at this point was to eliminate differences in elevation between the groups which would result from variations in the average factor score across groups. We will present some of the group differences later; our present concern is the developmental trends within groups. Therefore it seemed sensible to set each group's average factor score, for each factor, at zero and then look for consistent variations around that zero-point over time. Since factor scores, by definition, have a mean of zero and standard deviation of one, this goal could be accomplished by computing factor scores separately for each group.

Each group met for 32 sessions, but in three of the groups the first session was not scored because it contained only brief, introductory remarks by the leader. Unfortunately, in two of the four groups the tapes for two sessions were inadvertently erased or else the tape recorder failed to operate properly. Thus the number of scored sessions per group is 29 in groups one and two, 31 in group three, and 32 in group four.

Using the six-factor matrix discussed in Chapter 4, a set of six factor scores was computed for each session within each group. Since the idealized factors were constructed to describe the performances of individual members, it is worth noting that when the whole group's scores for a single session are taken as the unit, the factors remain as nearly independent of one another as was the case for individuals. Only two of the 15 intercorrelations, using the group sessions as the data points, exceeded .15, and they were under .28.

In presenting the curves which describe how each group changes over time on a given factor, something had to be done to smooth out the wide swings from session to session. Otherwise, it must be admitted, the reader's first impression might be one of an erratic and meaningless jumble of data points. However, before we try to obscure these wide swings in the interest of discerning the underlying trends, we wish to emphasize the unevenness of the curve in its natural state.

It is certainly not surprising that the major group trends do not fully determine the events in a single session. For one thing, the first day of each week tended to be devoted to a case discussion, which permitted highly symbolic and sometimes quite novel themes to enter the group. In addition, certain events, such as a visitor's appearance in the group, the handing out of assignments, or even a particularly hot day, could deflect or reverse the evident momentum of the group to that point. Our hope is to muffle the unique, but transient, effects and to isolate the more important effects.

There are several ways to accomplish this, but our choice is three-session moving averages. This operation consists simply of averaging the factor scores on a given factor for sessions one, two, and three to form the first data point, then averaging sessions two, three, and four to form the second data point, then three, four, and five to form the third data point, and so on. The number of moving averages for any group would thus be two less than the number of sessions.

Figure 6-1 shows the four curves obtained by plotting the moving

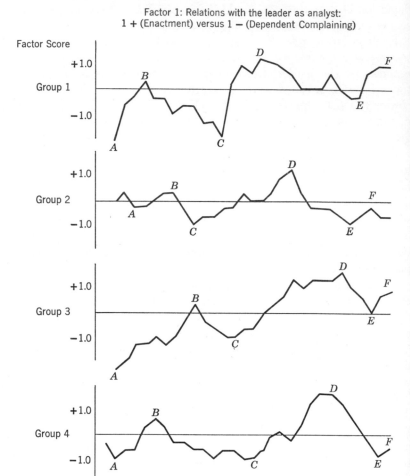

Factor 1: Relations with the leader as analyst:
1 + (Enactment) versus 1 − (Dependent Complaining)

Fig. 6-1. Three-session moving averages for factor scores over four groups.

averages on factor one over time. The correspondence between the curves is quite striking, and the graphs have been marked with points A through F, indicating that each group has three periods of Enactment (B, D, and F) and three periods of Dependent Complaining (A, C, and E). We shall have much more to say about each of these peaks and troughs, but a summary might be in order here.

Our interpretation of the three peaks of Enactment is that the first peak, B, represents an early, and to a large extent premature, attempt to take on the leader's role. The second peak, D, is the most important one and represents a sustained and concerted effort on the part of the members to perform the analytic tasks of the group. The final peak, F, reflects the group's tendency to end by reviewing and reinterpreting much of its prior history.

The three low points on the factor one curves represent rather different processes. The initial statements of Dependent Complaining, around point A, arise largely out of the shock of discovering how silent and passive the leader intends to be, but these feelings tend to be expressed mainly as complaints, on Level three, about case figures who are seen as weak and ineffectual. The group may recover and attempt to carry on, but the disappointment and resentment are left unresolved. The second wave of Dependent Complaining, around point C, seems to represent the unleashing of those feelings which could not be dissipated by displacing the feelings onto case figures or in some other way. The second surge of complaints is far more exasperated than the first, as if the members had run out of patience with their cold, retentive, and passive leader. The final complaints, at E, are interwoven with the issue of failure, as the group reviews its progress and begins to face its inability to accomplish all it set out to achieve. One recurrent theme at that point harks back to what seems, at that juncture, like an old issue for the group: the failure of the leader to provide direction and structure. Someone may have to take the blame for the group's failures, and the revival of Dependent Complaining is one attempt to place the blame on the leader.

Our summary of the major trends on factor one, across all four groups, suggests that while it is more or less true that Enactment increases over time, the increase is uneven, and we need to look at two important deviations from an upward, linear trend. One is the early Enactment, and another is the collapse of Enactment into a final wave of Dependent Complaining, from which no group rebounds back to the level of Enactment found in the middle or D phase. The emergence in each group, somewhere near or shortly after the midpoint, of a period of maximum Enactment is the finding we would like to emphasize. How can we account for its emergence? What do groups have to resolve, or experience, before Enactment can be solidly established? What accounts for the duration and eventual decline of this period? These are the questions which we will be trying to answer first in terms of the group as a whole and then in terms of the individual members.

At this point it would be possible to present factors two through six in the same manner as factor one, showing the curves for all four groups over time. However, this procedure would involve spreading out 20 more graphs. One economy might be effected by averaging the four groups to form one composite picture, and there appear to be two ways to accomplish this. One could simply average the four groups at each of the 29 data points to form a summary graph. But it is apparent from Figure 6-1 that this procedure would tend to obscure the uniformity across groups. Since the groups develop at different rates, such an averaging procedure would combine, for example, the major enactment period (D) of group three with the separation phase (E) for group two. The alternative procedure is to ask what is going on not during session number x, y, or z for all groups but during the comparable time periods defined by the six Enactment phases. We could then inquire about the amount of Rebellion or Loyalty during the major Enactment phase, or during the confrontation, etc. The major advantage of this procedure is that we can average groups across equivalent sets of sessions and produce a summary not only of a single factor but of that factor in relation to the six phases found for factor one.

The appropriateness of this mode of analysis derives in part from the fact that changes along the Enactment-Dependent Complaining dimension reflect changes in the members' willingness to perform an activity that is central to the work functions of the group: the taking over of the leader's interpretive, analytic role. Thus we may reduce the number of remaining graphs from 20 to five by pooling the analagous sessions across groups, asking how the other factors change in relation to the first and for our purposes most important factor.

Since we will be dealing with these enactment phases throughout the chapter, it would be well to give them some easily remembered labels.[1] We propose the following:

A—initial complaining
B—premature enactment
C—confrontation
D—internalization
E—separation
F—terminal review

Figure 6-2 presents the group development data for each factor, and these data were prepared in the following manner: first, the sessions of each group were divided into six phases, A through F; then the

---

[1] This list is a partial revision of an earlier attempt to describe group development (Mann, 1966).

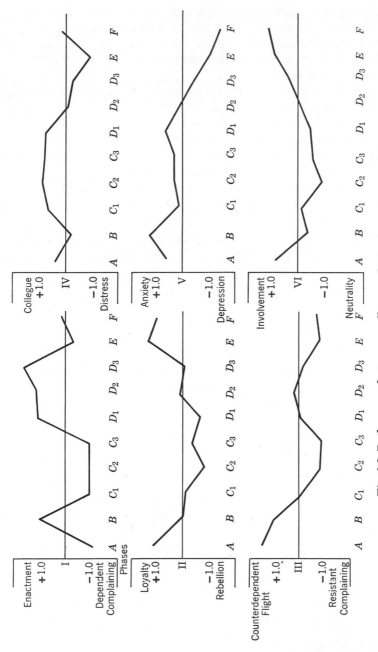

Fig. 6-2. Performance factors over all groups by enactment segments.

longest phases, confrontation (*C*) and internalization (*D*), were further subdivided into thirds; finally, for each of the ten points along the revised time dimension the values for the four groups were averaged. Each data point refers, on the average, to three sessions, but the range is from two to seven.

Figure 6-2 reveals much about the development of these groups. The picture for factor one is the clearest of all, which is not surprising since the sessions were divided with reference to that factor. One can see clearly in this graph the three phases of Dependent Complaining, each followed by a phase of Enactment. For factor two one finds a U-shaped curve. The groups start and end high on Loyalty, but in the middle, spanning the confrontation and the beginning of internalization, one finds Rebellion. The early sessions are the only ones high on Counterdependent Flight, whereas Resistant Complaining is characteristic of the confrontation phase and the final two phases. The Colleague factor pattern is particularly high in the first half of the group's development, especially during the confrontation phase, but this gives way to Distress, which is especially intense during the separation phase. Anxiety is high in the beginning, Depression in the end, but there is, in all four groups, a period of early Depression just before the confrontation and a second wave of Anxiety just as the confrontation shifts into internalization. Finally, after a brief, early period of Involvement, the groups reach their point of maximum Neutrality during the confrontation phase; during the remaining three phases there is a steady increase in Involvement.

Five one-way analyses of variance were carried out to test the significance of the differences between the means of the four groups' values on a given factor score across the ten points in time. For two factors, factors four and six, the differences were significant at the .05 level, and the remaining three differences over time were significant at beyond the .001 level. No test was carried out for factor one since the phases were defined by the rise and fall of values on this factor, but it is clear that the phases differ more on factor one than on any other.

Since the data for Figure 6-2 were prepared in terms of the six phases of factor one, the three Enactment phases and the three phases of Dependent Complaining, one way to review these findings might be to consider what the group as a whole is doing during each of these six phases. We might inquire what besides Dependent Complaining is going on during the initial complaining phase; Figure 6-2 reveals that this is a period which is quite high on Loyalty, extremely high on Counterdependent Flight, second only to the subsequent phase of

Anxiety, etc. But some changes are soon to take place, and in the premature enactment phase one finds not only an increase in Enactment but an increase in Anxiety and a shift from Involvement to Neutrality. In short, we have the beginnings of a description of group development, and it might suffice simply to elaborate upon the events which produce the group curves we have before us in Figure 6-2. All this could be done, and often is done in the analysis of group development, but such a procedure would seem to beg a central question in this field: Just what is meant by "the group?" For example, taking the group data just summarized, was there a meaningful entity, called "the group," which started off with Dependent Complaining, and was the entity also high on Anxiety and on Counterdependent Flight and Loyalty? Did that entity then change, becoming less involved, more anxious, and more able to enact the leader's role? One could assume an affirmative answer to these questions and proceed upon that assumption, but a closer look at the group interaction reveals that quite a different answer would be more appropriate.

The group curves presented in Figure 6-2 are in some sense like a tarpaulin thrown over the soon-to-be-revealed new model in the auto dealer's display window. The pedestrians stop and speculate about the shape and nature of the car under the wrapping, noting its bulges and overall dimensions. But what if there are two cars under the tarpaulin, or two cars and a motorcycle? It makes a difference. It also makes a difference whether one conceives of "the group" as one entity, or two, or more. Without sliding to the other extreme and declaring that "the group" is in fact nothing more than n individuals, it may be useful to view the group curves as revealing the simultaneous activities of distinctly different subgroups. To find that the group curves change from one phase to another need not lead us to wonder why everybody shifted gears and, for example, moved from Dependent Complaining to Enactment. A more appropriate explanation may be that one subgroup declined in its activity rate and its hold upon some of the other group members, while another subgroup gained in importance. We shall proceed to review the six developmental phases, and in the process we shall attend to the nature and composition of the major subgroupings. In particular, we shall note not only what they are doing but also what themes underlie their performances, what themes they tend to activate in others, and how the conflict between subgroups reflects the struggle over whose themes, strategies, and normative proscriptions shall dominate the group during a given phase. In discussing the various subgroups that are active during a particular phase, we will try to divide the members according to their actions during that phase without worrying about what they were doing or what they will be doing in the other phases. Only in Chapter 7 will we concern ourselves with the entire career of the individual; for now, it is enough to identify the primary subgroupings that give each phase its predominant tone.

Initial Complaining

As noted earlier, the group as a whole is high on Loyalty, Counterdependent Flight, Anxiety, and Involvement during the first or initial complaining phase. How shall we interpret these facts? As a start, it is helpful to know that this initial phase is usually devoted to case analysis; much of what we know about the members' feelings toward the leader is inferred from the way they discuss various case figures. More importantly, we should recall that the leader's behavior comes as a severe shock to some, but not all, of the group members. The nondirective, inactive style of the leader was rather unexpected, and we should be alert to the possibility that the members were trying, in various ways, to manage a new and somewhat unfamiliar situation.

In the process of describing the subgroups and splits among members which characterize each phase we shall ask two questions: (1) what themes are active during a given phase; and (2) what variations upon a single theme are present in the group? At any point in time subgroups can develop around shared concerns, and antipathies can develop to the extent that members fear that the group will be dominated by some issue that seems alien or uncomfortable to them. Thus during the initial complaining phase tension develops between those who are urging the group to see the new situation in terms of nurturance and control themes and those who are pressing for the centrality of the competence theme. Furthermore, subgroups and antipathies develop over the appropriate strategy to employ, even holding constant the thematic construction of the member-leader relationship.

A number of authors (Slater, 1966; Bennis, 1957; and Schutz, 1958) have noted the importance of nurturance issues in the early stages of group development, and these groups are no exception. In addition, the leader's unexpected passivity in the early sessions raises a number of control issues for the members. In the initial complaining phase we find four quite different modes of responding to the leader within the context of the nurturance and control themes. The high level of Dependent Complaining suggests that some members experience the leader's silence as abandonment and rejection. Case discussions tend to revolve around the unfeeling, weak, and unhelpful parents, and many of the overt communications to the leader amount to a plea for him to give the group more reassurance and structure. Meanwhile, a second subgroup adopts a different strategy, one involving more compliance and loyalty, perhaps in the hope that this behavior will pull from the leader what other members are pleading for. The third subgroup, which has minimal overlap with the previous two, is characterized by Counterdependent Flight. These individuals, to the extent that they view the new situation in nurturance and control terms, are bound and determined not to be trapped into a weak or easily manipulated position. In their heroic style, these members glorify the unencumbered, free spirit who has escaped from the devious, suffocating, and usually maternal figure. The implication is clear that the leader had better not try to approach them in that fashion, or else they will be out the door with lightning speed. Finally, there exists a subgroup whose solution to the nurturance and control issues is to adopt a stance of extreme self-sufficiency, a strategy that results in performances high on either the Colleague or the Involvement factor patterns and sometimes on both. This response to the leader amounts to an acceptance of two aspects of the leader's definition of his role: that he will resist dependency but encourage independence and that he will accept, but not necessarily reciprocate, involvement with him. Insofar as any members are urging that the group operate within the competence theme, they tend to be the members of the Counterdependent Flight subgroup, who are extremely touchy about being nurtured or controlled, or else members of the self-sufficient subgroup, who imply that they are far too mature to join with their dependent peers in asking for structure and leadership.

Several examples of these early interactions may convey the diversity of responses to the leader. In group four's discussion of the case material and some related issues that arose spontaneously we can see the conjunction of disappointment, distress, dependency, efforts to be independent of the leader, and the heroic or counterdependent style.

As the group became increasingly involved in a case discussion, the central figure in the case, a young woman, came to be seen as neglected and abused. A great deal of criticism was directed toward her "passive" father, who was accused of being "insincere" and "uncaring." Her mother, on the other hand, was condemned as "dominating" and "selfish." Psychiatry came under attack and was rejected as manipulative and exploitative. The group alternated, for the most part, between blaming the unresponsive or over-controlling parental figures for the young woman's difficulties and ridiculing her dependency and insecurity. Arnold attempted to establish a more aloof, expert role for himself by offering considered and dispassionate interpretations of the case and by describing his own loving and permissive attitude toward his own children. The group did not pursue his lead, however, and drifted into a depressed, inconclusive discussion of free will, fate, and predestination. Suddenly, Peter burst into the discussion with a heated defense of the street beggar as the only truly independent member of society. Since, he argued, a beggar has no possessions and lives from hand to mouth, he is free to live as he chooses, unencumbered by conventional restrictions. Several males joined the more dependent female members in rejecting his point of view. One member, while admiring the heroism of Peter's stance, felt that "you go crazy if you have complete independence." Another argued that "you can't just rebel like that." As the discussion continued, the group fell even further into depression, and the hour ended with widespread admission of and partial resignation to dependency and pleading for attention and sympathy.

One of the most disturbing aspects of the leader's role, especially as it becomes quite clear what he will and will not provide the group, is his failure to be the traditional and familiar leader who directs the group in its task activities. The control theme, as revealed in the variants of Anxiety and Dependent Complaining, is well illustrated in the following example.

In group three, which had the longest period of Initial Complaining of any group, the major complaint against the leader was that he was not providing information which made for what Alfred called "a smooth and satisfying relationship" in the group. In the first few sessions, the leader avoided giving in to the members' demands for structure, and by session five the complaints had grown more serious in their implications. The leader's lack of direction was seen as subjecting the group members to a highly dangerous situation from which they were doubtful that they could extricate themselves.

Pearl: You are aggravating the situation.
Dr. Charles: What is it you feel I'm not telling you?

Pearl: You are not giving us authoritarian guidelines that we need in order to function. We need an overall plan.

Dr. Charles: Well, there are several issues. First, is that request expressive of everyone's wishes?

Alfred: May we rely on you to tell us if we are diverting from the path we should be taking sufficiently to be dangerous either to the usefulness of the group or to our grades? I think it is useful for us to explore, but if someone has been over this ground before it would be very nice to know that someone was going to tell us if we were about to step over that cliff.

It would be inappropriate to attribute much cohesion or unity to these subgroups at this early stage in the group. They are composed of individuals who respond in a similar manner to the new situation, but this similarity does not go unnoticed by fellow "members" of the loosely defined subgroupings. We would also add that these groupings are not mutually exclusive; the fact that a member fits into more than one subgroup is simply an indication of his or her particular ambivalences and conflicting strategies.

In any phase there will be found not only the subgroups whose high activity and centrality are reflected in the overall group curves, but there will also be deviant members and deviant subgroups whose performances may be extremely important to the ultimate fate of the group. For each phase, we will attempt to locate the individuals whose performances, although deviant from the group at that moment, anticipate the next development of the group as a whole. The transition from initial complaining to premature enactment entails a shift on factor one and, in addition, a decrease in Loyalty and Involvement; Anxiety rises to its maximum, and there is a minor decline in the Counterdependent Flight and Colleague factor patterns. Whose performances during the first phase were exerting pressure on the group to move in these directions, and what do such performances tell us about the reason for the shift?

In group one, three members' performances were not only deviant during the initial complaining phase, but deviant in the direction taken by the group as a whole as it moved into the premature enactment phase. All three of these members were part of the Counterdependent Flight subgroup whose initial strategy regarding how to handle the nurturance and control issues was one of strident and heroic rejections of all affection and influence from above. Their performances suggest that they were disturbed about the alternative strategies being proposed, especially the ones which pleaded for or assumed the existence of a strong, protective leader. Their anticipation of the premature enactment phase suggests that this early enactment served two purposes: to block the efforts of other subgroups to obtain a nurturant and controlling leader and to direct the group toward the task of carrying on without the leader, thereby insuring themselves of an environment in which their autonomy would be unquestioned.

In addition to those deviants whose performances anticipate the next phase, there are, of course, other deviants. The early rumblings of rebellion can be heard. One finds individuals who are depressed while most of the group members are anxious. In addition, there are members whose performances seem to emphasize sexuality issues while most of the group is preoccupied with the issues of nurturance and control. But enough is enough. We must make do with the four subgroups whose divergent strategies do show through the overall group curves and one deviant subgroup that leads us into the next phase.

Premature Enactment

The premature enactment phase is characterized by a brief and usually minor surge of Enactment, by a continuing but lessened emphasis on Counterdependent Flight, by extremely high Anxiety values, and by values on factor six that fall between the Involvement of the first phase and the Neutrality soon to come. Several new elements enter the group in this phase. In contrast to the discussions during the first phase, which tended to revolve around case material and other Level three topics, the second phase contains the beginning of self-awareness as a group, the first sharing of what seem to be the dangers and the potentials of this new situation. A key word in these discussions is sensitivity: what is it, how necessary is it, and who is or is not sensitive? The second phase finds members beginning to verbalize how terrified and vulnerable they feel, how uneasy they are about revealing feelings or dropping previously acquired masks and roles. Thus one discernable subgroup focuses on the anxiety issue, and the message to the leader sounds like "Help!" Exactly how the leader could help varies. Certainly he could reassure the group members that their tension is usual, necessary, and transient. He might also dispel the anxiety by assuming stronger leadership or by distracting them with some assignment with which they could busy themselves. A second subgroup whose performances affect the overall group curves responds to the threatening aspects of the situation by remaining closed up. In member-leader terms, the Neutrality subgroup chooses to avoid the leader by withdrawing and by denying the distress and irritation which others are beginning to express.

One aspect of the premature enactment phase is, of course, the rise in Enactment, and we find not one but two important subgroups here. The first we might call the accepting enactors; these members, most of whom are females, give evidence of being satisfied with the leader's role. Their Enactment is usually set in a context of Loyalty, as if to demonstrate their confidence that nothing untoward will happen if members become more open and honest with each other. Many of the male members of this subgroup also tend to imply that they feel self-sufficient enough to get along without the leader and proceed to offer their services to any member in need of someone to run the show. The members are thus attempting to facilitate intimacy and sensitivity by expressing and accepting their own anxiety, by reassuring themselves and others that the leader is a benevolent figure who can safely be ignored, and by declaring themselves in opposition to the other enactors, the heroic enactors.

Only when we turn to this second subgroup of enactors do the events of this phase begin to make sense. Perhaps there is more than enough in the new situation to make most members anxious even without these heroic types, but these persons crystallize the entire issue of sensitivity and trust. In each group we find one or two males whose performances are high on Rebellion and Counterdependent Flight and whose Enactment takes the form of hostile interpretations of the sensitive, compliant, anxious, and complaining members of the group. The members of this heroic subgroup are given to such provocations as swearing, absenting themselves from the group "as a test," and outright scorn for those who express dependency upon the leader. Consider the following interaction between Harry, Frank, and Merv:

Merv: I find one of the greatest problems I've had, this is speaking of very intimate interpersonal relations, is that I tend to verbalize too much. I've always been afraid of really communicating in a very deep nature, and unfortunately it didn't really meet with very good results. . . . I mean, basically, I find that I'm really afraid, when it comes right down to it. It's a fear that I have of exposing myself too much to some other person; sort of, you might say, fear of rejection. If I were expressing my whole nature to some other person, and this person rejected me afterwards, I would feel that my whole personality had been rejected. . . . It's a very depressing feeling. . . . I just realized that maybe the reason I have this great motivation is because of the fact that I'm not intimate with my mother, or with my parents, so therefore I seek it outside the family.

Frank: I think I'd go by that, too. I feel everything you've said. I wouldn't even say a word differently.

Merv: That's good to know. It really is.

Harry (to Merv): Suppose someone offered you a breast.

Frank: What *is* this?

Merv: Now wait, I could be a little more specific.

Harry: Well, it goes back to what somebody said about looking outside your family for intimate interpersonal relationships. It seems to me that you're looking for a mother.

Merv: Oh, oh, I see.

Harry: And you wouldn't want it then. Being sensitive is kind of a way of avoiding biting or scratching the breast.

The heroic enactors, of whom Harry is a good example, quickly become central figures and a major source of intragroup contention. Interestingly enough, their special animosity toward the members of the deviant subgroup that is still expressing disappointment and frustration over the leader's passivity tends to drive that deviant subgroup and the accepting enactors together in the name of sensitivity. To the heroic subgroup's charge that some members are infantile in their search for protection and structure, the targets of these attacks and the accepting enactors retort that little can be accomplished when some members are so deliberately crude and insensitive.

Within the premature enactment phase some already established themes and strategies are maintained, and some new ones added. The tension between those who prefer a dependent solution to the nurturance and control issues and those who insist on absolute autonomy still remains. The latter group tends to demonstrate its autonomy by asserting its license to be insulting, crude, and honest without regard to the consequences, and thus the battle is joined with "the sensitive ones" who are counting on the leader to control these outbreaks of impulsivity. In addition to this split, a new issue arises around the sexuality theme. In one sense, the sensitives and the insensitives are displaying two familiar forms of seductive behavior: one gentle and considerate, the other assaultive and intimidating.

Without denying in the least the importance of these two seductive styles for the future course of member-member relations, we may examine their relevance for the member-leader relationship as well. Under the surface a serious battle is in the making, a battle over how to move close to the leader, with the heroic males on one side and the less heroic, more sensitive males together with many of the females on the other side. The females are more capable of moving in by way of loyalty and trust, more comfortable expressing their uneasiness, and more direct about their wishes for a sensitive, protective authority. The male heroes, on the other hand, need to feel that the initiative is theirs, that they are free agents. As a result, their performances are directed toward establishing their uniqueness and their superiority over those they deem to be the ineffectual males as well as toward fusion with the leader. It is at this point that the nurturance theme joins the sexuality theme. The male hero, despite the scorn he expresses toward his clinging, dependent peers, is likely to betray by his manic style a deep longing for unity with the leader. The heroic style, which alienates so many other group members, involves a denial of the member's separation from the leader. In that the hero offers the leader an alter-ego, or as one of the heroes termed himself, a "buddy," he is engaging in a struggle with the more compliant, loyal females for the leader's involvement.

In the following example of a group during its premature enactment phase we can see the diverse effect of the hero's early behavior. In struggling to handle the pressures he puts on them, the members make adjustments in their view of the leader: some find him untrustworthy and indifferent, others decide that he wishes them to take over the protective, directing role he seems to have vacated.

The sensitivity issue emerged toward the end of the initial complaining phase and continued throughout the phase of premature enactment. Peter precipitated the opening discussion when he first failed to attend a session, then returned to the group dressed in a suit and tie in place of his usual sandals and other casual garb. Doris was the first to confront him, taking him to task for his previously crude and provocative behavior. Carol tried to prevent the encounter by suggesting that the "misunderstanding" should be forgotten. But Peter insisted that he was inviting attack and suggested that the group's forthcoming attack on him would enable him to attack others more directly. Dolores raised the issue of "honesty" and expressed her feeling that apathy and depression were appropriate under the circumstances. Other members felt too anxious to participate in or even withstand such a hostile group atmosphere. Peter denounced all such expressions of "weakness" and urged others to be "tough" in facing the hostility and apprehension that the group would soon be forced to deal with. Although several of the female members grew uneasy over the leader's repeated failure to intervene, Paul assured them that the leader was concerned but was too "mature" to become concerned with Peter's "adolescent" displays and his attempts to "usurp" the leader's position in the group.

In the following session, Pamela and Carol began to explore the relationship between hostility and honesty. Peter and Ross emphatically denied any anxiety about "being hurt" in the group, but they were in the minority. The group puzzled over the problem posed by Carol—"how to be honest without offending people." Peter continued his scornful criticism of "tactful, dishonest people." Carol and Denise tried to maintain some distinction between a member's remarks ("a stupid thing to say") and the member's personal worth ("a worthless person"). Arnold and Paul sided with the frightened female members and assured the group that Peter was simply denying his own "sentimentality" and "sensitivity." Arnold in particular began to present himself as a warm, protective paternal figure, offering compassion and understanding to those in distress.

As the heroic enactors move to the center of the group, they raise for all members an urgent question: How will the leader respond to this hero? The transition from phase two to phase three is in large part a response to what some members consider to be the leader's unsatisfactory answer to this question. The leaders uniformly fail to control the hero and his crude, insensitive style. On the contrary, they often support some aspect of his performance in the name of expression, and they may also undercut the attack on the hero by inquiring whether some of that hostility might not be displaced from the leader onto the hero. Perhaps, the leaders wonder aloud, the heroic enactors, who are invariably counterdependent toward the leader, are expressing feelings that others feel but dare not express; perhaps the hero's pressure toward honesty at any cost increases some members' uneasiness about where the leader is taking the group, or letting it drift. The deviant subgroup during the premature enactment phase, the subgroup whose Dependent Complaining, Resistant Complaining, and Neutrality anticipate the group's next development, is particularly perturbed not only by the hero's insensitivity but by the leader's indifference toward or collusion with this menacing force in the group. In the absence of proper control by the leader, they assert, excesses of sexuality and aggression can be expected; a veritable state of anarchy will prevail.

Confrontation

Before turning to an analysis of the curves for the six factors and the subgroups that are active during the confrontation, we propose to describe in some detail the events in group four, which had the longest confrontation phase of any group.

In session ten, the group began by rearranging the tables and chairs in such a way as to exclude the leader from the group. There was a great deal of discussion of an "informal" group which had been meeting after the regular class hour, and several members felt forced to admit that their uncertainty about the leader's role had prompted their withdrawal from him. As several members began to offer apologies for their withdrawal, Peter initiated a relatively unbroken ten-minute period of whispering tête-à-têtes among the members, who sat with their backs to the leader. Pamela pointed out that the female members had "fallen in line" behind Peter and Ross, the heroic males. Paul, Don, and Roger joined forces to demand recognition of the fact that the leader was the sole legitimate authority in the group and should be respected as such. They blamed the leader's relative passivity on the more obstreperous males in the group and argued that if the group were able to sit patiently and obey quietly, then the leader would gladly take charge of the group. Audrey and Mabel were delighted with this prospect, but Carol joined with Peter in accusing Roger of "trying to take over the group."

A similar discussion ensued two days later. Louise opened the session with anxious questions about the grading of the papers, wondering whether the criteria would be "academic" or "personal." Some depressed thoughts on the recently announced departure of Naomi followed, and Bert charged that her decision to drop the course could be attributed to the leader's efforts to "drive her out of the group." Don expressed a great need for structure, support, and psychological counseling, but Carol reminded him that, after all, Freud had analyzed himself, and suggested that he do like-wise. Angus, Roger, Don, and Paul took advantage of Peter's absence to propose a series of rotating leaders. Then followed a long, fruitless discussion of the leader, which concluded with a request for firmer control of "irresponsible" members who threat-ened the stability of the group as a whole.

Session fourteen opened with Pamela's explicit attempt to "make friends" with the leader and learn more about his background and interests. She was joined by Mabel and Arnold, and Karen finally succeeded in persuading the group to discuss the problems raised by falling in love and enduring the rejection of love objects. As most of the members continued to court the leader, Peter attacked him viciously, describing him as overwhelmed with anxiety, in-sincere, and noncommital in his interpretations.

During the next three sessions, the group's discussion of its forth-coming party aroused a great deal of anxiety, and Bert pointed out the universality of the "incest problem." The possibility of the leader's attendance at the party was debated, and only Mabel felt certain that he would come. Peter suggested that the group organ-ize a militia to "tail" the leader and his wife (the leader was in fact unmarried) but then decided that such an effort would be pointless. Peter was criticized for "manipulating" the group, and Don was attacked for "acting bored." Arnold directed his anger at the leader, whom he described as "indifferent and uninvolved," then turned to Peter, whom he found to be equally "aloof" and "unhelpful."

When, in the next session, the leader announced that he would not attend the party, Ross asked Charles to take over the leader's role as chaperone. Peter attacked Don for not twisting and de-manded that there be dance music available at the party. Ross offered to bring the "Nutcracker Suite."

The day following the party, Paul and Lucy were the only members present for the first ten minutes of the session. The other members were hiding under the stairs nearby. They finally ap-peared, bearing refreshments. The leader received a beer, and Paul resented being served a Coke, arguing that priests are allowed to drink. The leader refused all offerings and later interpreted the beer as poison. Faith began to flirt with the leader, bringing him cookies and other snacks, and Bert attempted to involve him in a sociogram which he was developing. Carol, Mabel, and Don railed at the leader for "not letting your hair down." Carol then admitted that the group had acted childishly, but said that "the group and not the individual is at fault." Don described the leader as "an impenetrable fortress" and demanded increased "guidelines." A discussion of "spoon-feeding" followed, and Bert expressed a death wish against the leader. At the height of this anxious attack, Dolores described the leader as a wise, loving paternal figure whom she trusted and adored. This eulogy reactivated the group's earlier struggles over the dependency issue.

In session nineteen, after a long opening discussion of homosexuality, the incest taboo, and contraception, Pamela voiced her opinion that the group was behaving "preadolescently" and pointed out that "boys and girls are afraid to pair off." The group resented her disclosure and attempted to deny the validity of her observations. The leader commented that "there is celibacy at cocktail parties too," to which Carol responded by suggesting that Arnold and she were very involved with one another. The leader dismissed this argument and repeated his earlier appraisal of the party, and the session ended with a violent burst of angry denial.

The leader began session twenty-two by observing that Dolores had been afraid to attend the previous session. She refuted this interpretation, and argued that she had simply had another engagement. Mabel began with the first of many bitterly anti-introspective condemnations of the leader's style, accusing him of being "unfair" and "narrow-minded." Paul and Don contributed further sarcastic commentaries on the leader's style, and Bert suggested that he leave the group and sit in on the other group, which was meeting simultaneously. Don, Doris, and Denise accused the leader of taking absence and tardiness "personally" and of being uncertain of himself. Girls were criticized for being late for dates, and the leader was berated for coming late to several sessions. Arnold ridiculed the leader for having explained his lateness as a "reality issue."

The group curves shown in Figure 6-2 reveal that the confrontation phase is characterized by high levels on the Dependent Complaining, Rebellion, Resistant Complaining, Colleague, and Neutrality factor patterns. What these curves suggest, and what the tape recordings document, is that this phase involves a direct and hostile encounter between the group members and the leader. We have suggested that one issue that prompts this direct clash with the leader stems from the previous split over sensitivity and whether the leader should control the impulsive, heroic group members. One other facet of the confrontation should be noted. It is also a period during which the leader's pressure towards work is becoming both apparent and troublesome for some group members. We would therefore see the significance of this attack as: (1) a direct clash with the leader over the ambiguities of the control issue inherent in the task at hand; and (2) an attack upon the heroic members and upon the leader for not controlling such members. The group curves reflect the simultaneous operation of three dominant subgroups: one which accounts for the hostility of the phase, a second which is represented by the Colleague factor pattern, and a third which accounts for the Neutrality and much of the anxiety.

The hostile subgroup contains few individuals who can manage the full range of complaints and angers which emerge during this period. Many members enter the fray only when issues salient to them are predominant and then subside when the issues change. There are three aspects of the attack: disappointment expressed via Dependent Complaining, resentment and Rebellion, and mistrust which results in Resisting Complaining. If we look first at those members who can manage all three of these feelings, we find a broadside attack which, in distilled form, sounds something like this:

"You, the nominal leader, are supposed to be running this group and you are not. The result is chaos, unchecked impulsivity, and a strong possibility that, while you just sit there, someone will be upset and damaged by the group; also, you are constantly pushing us around, imposing your standards on us, ruling certain topics out of bounds, and generally exerting your power over the group in a dictatorial manner; and this raises another point, namely your inconsistency; either you should get out and leave us alone, or you should make your demands clearer; as it is, you are simply manipulating us, experimenting on us in the hope that we will follow some ill-defined path that 'all groups' are supposed to follow; we want an end to all these devious little efforts of yours to influence our group."

Before leaving the initiators of this exceedingly complex attack, it is worth noting that many of these individuals are male members who announce that they are acting as the spokesman for others, usually females, in the group. They are speaking for a band of individuals whom they represent to be lost, upset, or suspicious. While they are often expressing their own feelings more than they would care to admit, their effort to champion the subgroup we have labeled "the sensitives" has several implications. It is an attack upon the heroic members, an attempt to break their hold over many of the females and to disrupt or destroy the suspected coalition between the hero and the leader. In this context, it is worth noting that one spokesman who led the attack on the leader later referred to his activity during the confrontation as "romancing" the leader. It is not uncommon to find that the spokesman's hostility derives in part from his frustrated wish to feel closer rapport with the leader. The confrontation, to the extent that it involves an attack upon both the leader and the heroic enactors of the second phase, is thus a continuation of the earlier fight over sensitivity, with some insisting on control and delicacy and others insisting on the right to be insultingly honest. But there is more to the confrontation.

The attack upon the leader derives in part from the group's increasing awareness of the task pressures put on the group by the leader. We have tried to conceptualize this pressure in terms of the four aspects of work: enactment, independence, involvement, and expression. The negative response of the most active subgroup to these pressures is complex. They seem to be saying:

"In the first place, we cannot possibly enact your role because it is too dangerous, and in fact even you are not competent enough to interpret what we are doing without making us upset; in the second place, your pressure for independence is fraudulent since you are constantly undercutting what we are trying to do; we would, for example, like to talk about abstract topics or things outside the group without being pressured to express our feelings and without your absurd interpretations; finally, we find you so ineffectual, or else you arouse so much anxiety and mistrust in us, that we will not become involved."

It may seem paradoxical that so many individuals are capable, during the confrontation phase, of complaining that the leader is too passive and weak while at the same time complaining that the leader is manipulative and enervating. But we can find some of the reasons for this reaction in the nature of the group and in the leader's style. It is an extremely frustrating experience for some members. Their sense of autonomy, which they would gladly yield to the leader, seems to them in constant danger of being whisked away. Any pressure from the leader, especially if it is not announced by blaring trumpets, may turn out to be the solvent in which their sense of independence will dissolve. Their paranoid-like concerns about being controlled fit poorly with a situation which, for all its lack of structure, is definitely not without its pressures and rewards. Given the complicated nature of the leader's pressure toward work, it is not surprising that some people become increasingly uneasy. They are unable either to please the leader or to feel free of his disapproval and influence. The confrontation phase gives these members a chance to unload the accumulated feelings of disappointment, resentment, and mistrust.

Meanwhile, another development takes place; another subgroup which is not feeling particularly hostile begins to move toward center stage. The members of this subgroup are high on the Colleague factor pattern, and their contribution resembles that of "the independents" described by Bennis and Shepard (1956). They verbalize their own personal goals for the course and clarify the overarching values from which they derive these goals. Characteristically, they tend to support the goals of sensitivity without joining the attack upon the crude, heroic enactors. They assert the importance of being self-reliant without needing to test their autonomy by attacking the authority structure. They seem more interested in coexisting with the leader than in replacing him. These individuals anticipate the group's next development and provide both a normative and behavioral alternative to the confrontation phase.

Beyond those who contribute directly to the confrontation and those who offer an alternative path, one can detect a subgroup that is primarily interested in pulling out altogether. These individuals are usually high not only on Neutrality but on Anxiety, from which we may infer that they also find the main issue to be the threatening leader and the ambiguous situation. Where they diverge is in their unwillingness to get involved in confronting these perils; they construct a facade of indifference and denial which effectively removes them from the storms that are raging around them.

Finally we must turn to the deviants, the members who are not entirely caught up in the many aspects of the confrontation. The most important deviants at this point are "the heroes." Not only are they being attacked for being crude and insensitive, but they are also under attack for their interpretations, especially the scornful interpretations with which they dominated the second phase. How do these heroes perform during the confrontation? They continue their interpretive, enacting style, taking particular aim upon the Resistant Complaining aspect of the attack. It is quite common to find the now deviant heroes mocking the implied impotence and paranoid quality of the attack on the leader. Some members' assumption of weakness and defeat at the hands of the devious leader is too much for them, and they answer all this by reasserting their potency and freedom. But the heroes are very much part of one aspect of the confrontation, the rebellion. If anything, their urge to move against the leader is stronger and more directly expressed in this phase, and two explanations can be offered. In part the attack on the heroes involves the charge that they are in collusion with the leader, that they are being protected by the leader. The heroes are in danger of being dubbed "teacher's pets," and they respond to this by disassociating themselves from the leader by means of direct attack.

The second explanation of the hero's rebellion at this point takes us in the direction of Slater's (1966) thesis that the revolt is a totemic process by which the males attempt to replace the leader and gain access to the females. We have some evidence to support this contention. The confrontation phase, whatever the curves for the group as a whole may show, includes some of the most blatantly dependent and sexualized approaches to the leader on the part of some of the females. The issue of thralldom is raised by declarations such as the following:

Jane: He [the leader] is sitting there for a long time and really thinking about it, you know? It's very upsetting.
Marie: I think he thinks about it. It doesn't really upset me. It's kind of comforting because when you go to your little therapist, I'm not trying to be scornful—but when I say sage, I'm not trying to be scornful either because sage is a term of great praise with me, sort of tongue-in-cheek praise, I guess. But, you know, he thinks about it, and I get very disturbed, say, and we talk on and on and on. And you sit there glued to the chair, and you're really tense, and you never can gain weight because you're always tense, and things like this, and then he interjects these little sage words, and then you realize things, and then you're calmed after a while.

The strident, abusive hero finds common cause with those members who attempt to speak for the sensitive females even though they violently disagree over *why* the leader should be less powerful. The hero finds no reason to oppose thralldom in general, but the spokesman is pressing for a less magical, less charismatic mode of attracting others. The hero wishes to break the leader's magic spell, but he would substitute one of his own; the spokesman would break all such spells. The common cause in which they unite, however briefly, is the destruction of the leader's charisma. The hero is more likely to attempt to accomplish this by belittling the leader. The spokesmen, who are not only involved in Rebellion but in Dependent and Resistant Complaining as well, are trying to desexualize the entire situation, and their opposition takes all possible forms. What they offer as an alternative to the leader's magical power and to the hero's potency is tenderness and consideration for those in distress.

By way of summarizing the exceedingly complex events in this phase, we may turn to the various themes and their variants. We are struck by the virtual disappearance of the nurturance theme. Control and sexuality issues are much in evidence and, in addition, some members for whom the question of competence is important are becoming increasingly central to the group. The confrontation per se, the attack upon the leader and/or upon the heroic enactors, is an attempt to reduce the ambiguity of the leader's control, to remove charisma as an issue from the group, and to provide the less flamboyant but more sensitive members with an environment in which they can achieve power and interpersonal success. To the extent that the majority of the group decides it has been manipulated and trapped by the leader, the hero tends to move against the group, affirming his potency to be still very much intact. To the extent that the issue is not enervation but domination by the leader's magic and the leader's standards, the hero joins in the attack and attempts to destroy the leader's charisma.

At this point it is difficult to distinguish between the control and the sexual implications of the hero's behavior. He wishes to replace the leader, take over his mana, and gain access to the females. But for the rest of the group, there is a strong indication that were they to gain control they would outlaw mana as a means of gaining centrality. We found ourselves wondering whether Freud's description of the period after the overthrow of the father, as elaborated by Mills (1959) and Slater (1966), is not in need of some revision. Is the banding together of the brothers and the failure of the victorious sons to capitalize upon their newly won license evidence of guilt? On the basis of these groups we would expect more guilt from the victorious rebel-hero than from the victorious spokesman and his followers. The purpose of the revolt for the latter group is to remove the leader (and his potent cohorts) in order to change the ground rules. The failure of this subgroup, upon overthrowing the leader, to advocate increased sexuality could have been anticipated since their initial purpose in attacking both the leader and the hero was to drain the aggression and sexuality out of the situation, or at least to redefine sexuality in less assaultive and more delicate terms. Those individuals who felt that only under different conditions could they succeed, or even survive, acted to change the leadership structure, and from them one hears not a reaction of guilt but of relief upon altering the interpersonal environment to their liking.

If we could use these data to amend the theory of totemic processes, we would expand the *dramatis personae* to include the nonheroic males. To cast it all in mythic terms, their existence under the oppressive father seems to have convinced them of the need not only to overthrow the primal father but to overthrow the charismatic principle which he embodies. Their affect upon joining together in a successful revolt is less one of guilt than of pleasure mixed with anxiety: perhaps the father is not dead; perhaps his ghost will return. Paranoia, not melancholia, seems to be the fate of the less ambivalent, more inhibited males upon defeating the father. Guilt and reparation might be expected from the more heroic sons; their identification or magical fusion with the father antedated and continues beyond the revolt. In this view, it would be important to know the role, during and after the revolt, of the more and the less heroic sons. Revolts could have quite different outcomes. The heroic sons would have an interest in sharing their guilt with the others, and, given the power to do so, they would attempt to make reparation by deifying the dead father. For the less heroic sons, the major task is to complete the revolt by insuring that none of the sons attempts to carry on the charismatic tradition; beyond their pleasure in being rid of the father, it would only remain to manage their fear of revenge, and some efforts at appeasing the father's ghost might be instituted. To the extent that they dominate the post-revolt phase, the new controls on sexuality and aggression would express not their guilt but their original purpose in joining the revolt.

The behavior of the females during this phase serves to trigger the whole sexuality and thralldom controversy and to sustain the latent split between the heroes and the spokesman. Some females steadfastly resist being rescued from their distress and from their fascination with the hero and/or the leader. Others, especially those explicitly rejected by the heroes, tend to band together with the spokesman, allowing him to use their discomfort as evidence that everything must be altered if "some people" are not to have a nervous breakdown, or worse. A third group of females becomes directly involved in the confrontation, and these performances deserve further attention.

Female rebellion serves two functions, or at least two that we can observe with some regularity. For some females it is an effort to transcend their initial inclination to succumb to the leader, an attempt to move beyond the role of "Daddy's little angel" which they often perform with painful awareness of both their success and their anger in such relationships. There is anger at "Daddy" for enticing them into this cul de sac, mixed with shame and anger at themselves over their complicity in recreating this dyadic relationship yet another time. For other females, and even for some of those just described, rebellion is a delicate mixture of efforts to save their male peers and to shame them by initiating hostility which the males had not managed, but should have. In a peculiarly modern inversion of the Grimm fairy tale, the "sister" saves her "brothers" not by abandoning her claims to masculinity but by demonstrating to them how one might go about challenging and defeating the oppressive father.

Finally, we must underscore the development which assumes great importance during the confrontation phase and beyond, the ascendance of the competence theme. The attacks upon the leader's competence are more manifest, especially in the Dependent Complaining performances that view the leader's interpretations not as positive contributions but as pathogenic bumblings. For the loyal members, the leader becomes the intellectual hero; for the resisters, the leader and his pressure toward work must be blocked at every opportunity. But it is those whose performances tend toward the Colleague pattern who anticipate the group's next development. It is they who press upon the group the crucial, competence-related questions: What would we be doing if we were only serving our own ends? And what would our proper ends be if we could escape, even for the moment, our endless absorption with the leader?

Internalization

What distinguishes the fourth phase is both the duration and the high level of Enactment. It is also a period during which Anxiety gives way to Depression, Colleague to Distress, and Neutrality to Involvement. In terms of member-leader relations, the most prominent feature of this phase is the dramatic increase in Identifying, and we are led by this and other evidence to call this the internalization phase. In no other phase is the leader's definition of work so clearly shared by the members, and indeed a fuller sense of the events during this period would be captured by calling it the work phase. But we had earlier decided to label the phases by their level on factor one, and there is more to work than Enactment. Not only do the members' capacity and willingness to interpret the events of the group increase markedly, but the group has moved into a period of considerable independence and involvement. The earlier voices of dependency and withdrawal either were transformed or are now edged to the periphery of the group. In addition, the leader's pressure for expression, which never had been an injunction to dwell only upon the member-leader relationship, is reflected now in the attention paid to issues of sexuality and intimacy.

Looking back to the issues of the earlier phases, it appears that neither the heroes nor the spokesmen for "the sensitive ones" are completely victorious. The groups are never as uninhibited and orgiastic as the heroes seem to imply is their goal, but neither are they as desexualized and delicate as some of the sensitive ones would have preferred. It is now more acceptable to talk about sexual feelings. Some pairing occurs in each group, but we are equally impressed by how diffuse the sexuality remains, how tentative and easily side-tracked it is. We must focus upon three obstacles, real or apparent, to sexuality in these groups: (1) the differential readiness of members to operate in the sexual domain; (2) the issue of morality as it emerges under the pressure of increased sexuality; and (3) the now salient issue of how the leader shall be integrated into the group.

In group two the sexuality theme remained dormant following a premature and thereafter unmentionable eruption of sexuality, an evening party which the leader opposed and from which many unresolved guilts remained. With the exception of this group, we find that the sexuality theme rises to the fore and generates two new forms of deviance. One deviant we might identify as "the sexual scapegoat" and the other as "the moralist." These deviants are the cause of, or at least the occasion for, much of the Enactment which occurs in this phase. The dominant subgroup is characterized by Enactment which is designed to provide these deviants with insight, however welcome or unwelcome it might be, into the apparent nature and causes of their behavior. There is a fine line between interpretations that seem like impatient efforts to "cure" the deviant with one rapier-like thrust and those which convey some genuine compassion and understanding. It would be stretching a point to say the latter type was exclusively in evidence, but there is at least more gentleness and tact in many of these later interactions than we heard from the heroic enactors during the second phase.

Returning to the interchange between the enactors and the deviants, we may start with the most commonly observed phenomenon, the isolation of the sexual scapegoat. In the earlier phases the deviant or discordant member tended to be the highly sexualized and aggressive hero. In this phase one deviant who receives a considerable amount of attention is the member who seems particularly immature or inhibited in some aspect of the sexual domain.

In group one, Lloyd, during a lull in the discussion of the group moralist, stated his opposition to a previous reference to Anna as castrating. As the ensuing discussion developed, the level of excitement, laughter, and mockery rose to an extraordinary pitch.

Lloyd: I'm not fully ready to accept the interpretation given to Anna's behavior either. I can't recognize her system of emasculation. I can't see that this is a natural thing. I don't see women going around performing this operation. I would inquire as to their attempted method and I think that reading this into Freud's discussion is more or less having been propagandized by his having repeated this often, but he has yet to give a specific example where any one woman has performed this operation on any one man. (Mounting background noise of objections and laughter.) I think that the reason for the operation being performed is rather as a punishment and generally imposed by a father figure or other men as a punishment for improper behavior or for preventing furtherance of behavior which the father figure had considered improper and giving Anna this right is something which women just don't do as a natural thing.
Marie: Oh yes they *do*! (Laughter.) I think what Anna did was not uncommon.
Lloyd: What *tools* do they use?
Dr. Allen: Are you looking to be spared?
Janice: It's interesting. There is a child guidance clinic in Boston, the Judge Baker Guidance Clinic, which is for boys, and one of the things that they are most cautious about in hiring women on the staff, and they make no bones about it, is that they don't want castrating women around. And they are extremely careful—
Lili: Well, how do they find out?
Janice: I don't know.
Lili: That must be quite a task. (Laughter.)
Lloyd: What I'm saying is that Freud has given us this interpretation. Therefore we believe it. But give us a specific example where the actual operation has been performed. Used as a figure of speech to imply a feeling for a person it is fine, but to assume that therefore they want to do it is another thing.
Harry: Did you read *Lady Chatterley's Lover?* In there, Mellors,

the gardener, is describing to Lady Chatterley some of the women that he has slept with, and there is one who he said was like a coffee grinder inside. She wanted to grind up his genitals. Ah . . . that's a well done example.

Lloyd: But did she *do* it?

Frank: Yeah, but wait a minute.

Harry: He got out in time. (Laughter.)

Lloyd: This is what I am trying to say. Who has succeeded in accomplishing something?

Joanne: Delilah accomplished it.

Frank: That is a fiction.

Joanne: Other people have, too.

Marie: What about the eunuchs? Bettelheim by no means agrees with everything Freud says, and he says that the reason they have eunuchs in the harems is the desire of the women in the harem to have men servants over whom they have this sort of power. Otherwise, why wouldn't they have women servants?

Lloyd: I'm not willing to accept that.

Marie: Well, *I've* wanted to do it sometime. I don't want to do it right now, but I might pretty soon. (Laughter.)

Dave: I can't see the emphasis on: 'You don't know, you haven't seen anybody do it, you haven't heard anybody do it.' Certainly, you have *felt* the difference if you compared two women that you know very well. This doesn't mean that you have slept with them. But in my case, yes. There are some women that really make you feel like a man, other women feel very uncomfortable after a while, they are trying to get the reins all the time. They really threaten you and you know what they are after—your masculinity. This doesn't require a knife or anything. It's what you *feel* which is much more important than—

Lloyd: What I'm trying to say is that this more or less figure of speech is giving us the feeling that someone is actually attempting—

Jane: It is giving *you* the feeling—

Anna: I think you are diverting the discussion. Frankly, I kind of got lost when you started all this.

Frank: He has his legs crossed. (Laughter.)

Anna: I think you must be diverting the discussion from what it would *mean* to be castrated.

Lloyd: Well, I'm saying that your idea was that you wanted to temporarily prevent his sexual attainment, but not *finally* as implied by emasculation.

Anna: I think that now what you want to talk about is *actual, literal, physical, concrete* objects.
Lloyd: Yes.
Harry: How about what this threat that is felt *means*?
Marie: I think you are so terrified by the threat that you cannot *admit* what it means.
Frank: The power of suggestion might be making this poor guy feel this way. Let's look at it this way: You might ruin his whole life by telling him . . . (Laughter.) No, wait a minute. Maybe he does have a certain amount of this feeling, but you're going to magnify it.
Marie: Well, no. But he's obstructing the discussion.
Lloyd: I think that perhaps my dwelling on this comes from having performed the operation on numerous animals. You do this for the purpose of preventing their engaging in sexual behavior at any time in the future. And what Anna is attempting to do is prevent it at this immediate time, not for the indefinite future, and I think there's a very great difference there.

What is the cause of this polarity? At one level it would seem that some members feel constricted in the presence of these deviant members. All members, the enactors seem to say, must enter into the general spirit of flirtation and adventure or else the group cannot progress. Or is this an attempt to bolster their unsteady self-esteem in this area? These interactions do occasionally seem like hazing, the process of distancing oneself from the weak and the insecure in order to appear mature to oneself and others. These deviants are not unlike the scapegoats who are nudged off the wagon, amidst much hilarity, just as the hayride is about to begin. Beyond these observations, we might note that there are member-leader implications in these events. For some members the leader is also a deviant in that he seems unwilling to join the mood of increased intimacy. Other members seem to fear that the leader views their first attempts at pairing as immature, just as they find certain members to be less mature than themselves. We are suggesting that two factors are operating: the attack upon the scapegoat may be a displacement by some members of their feelings toward the leader, while other members are pointing an accusing finger at the member who most properly deserves what they fear is the leader's condescension and ridicule.

While we are on the subject of sexuality, we will point out that the place of the leader in a group undergoes some important changes during this phase. To the extent that some members continue to see him as above the group, his role drifts toward that of chaperone. And as with any chaperone, the limits must be tested. For many of the same reasons, the most moralistic group member becomes an important deviant for the group. As with the sexual scapegoat, the group becomes absorbed with the inhibiting effects of what they consider to be outmoded and psychologically naive standards of behavior.

An example from group four might illustrate this process.

At the start of session twenty-five several members still had not arrived. Carol was concerned about the possibility that they were losing interest in the group. Peter asserted that "all of this is just a rationalization for not talking about sex" and demanded that each member reveal the sexual attractions and fears which the group had aroused. Paul, the moralist, took offense and suggested that each member describe his hobbies and other interests, such as religion, music, and politics. Carol disagreed and seconded Peter's proposal, provided that some distinction between sexual and affectionate interest could be maintained. Two sessions later, Paul argued that, "All of this psychological probing may hurt someone very deeply. In fact, I have talked with several people, outside of class, who feel that they are on the brink of a serious personal disaster." He quoted a statement of the leader's to the effect that repeated interpretation was not always appropriate, but the leader quickly intervened, implying that the precedent was not applicable.

In the following session, Peter and Carol suggested that Paul relinquish his role as defender of the anonymous sufferers and allow them to "vote their own stock." Bert later pointed out that Paul had identified with the protective aspects of the leader's role without making a serious effort to enact his interpretive role. Several other members continued the analysis of Paul's behavior and his function in the group, while Paul suggested that the group was avoiding the problems raised by the impending termination.

To the extent that the leader is seen as a peer, and his own behavior often contributes to this shift in the members' perceptions, the leader's role includes the potential of becoming a sexual object for some and a sexual rival for others. It is not uncommon for those members who had previously defined themselves as the sensitive ones to decide that the leader is less threatening, insensitive, and aloof than they had previously thought. In the next phase this transformation is carried even further. The single most important antecedent of this transformation occurred, we suspect, during the confrontation. We would point to the discrepancy between the expected consequences of the members' attacks and the leader's actual response. Not that the leader absorbs all the hostility; there are signs of impatience and irritation. But the leaders do manage to absorb most of the angers and complaints, emerging less as ogres than as fairly patient and accepting human beings, and this has two consequences of great importance to the group. The members become more willing to trust the leader and even to be attracted to him under conditions other than thralldom. In addition, this increase in trust and affection contributes directly to the members' willingness to internalize the leader's style and to begin enacting his role. In contrast to earlier identifications through which the members, and especially the heroes, took on the most threatening aspects of the leader's role, here we find what Slater (1961b) would call personal identification, the willingness to identify on the basis of affection and esteem. With one exception, the split between the enactors and the resisters during this phase is compounded by the tendency for the enactors to be high on the Colleague and Involvement factor patterns, whereas the resisters, particularly the moralists and the sexual scapegoats, are high on Distress and Neutrality.

We have dwelt at length upon the increased relevance of sexuality in the internalization phase. Of equal or perhaps greater importance is the rise of the competence theme. This is the period in which many of the members try out the interpretive style of the leader. It is the period during which norms that legitimize and regulate the work functions of the group are being developed at a rapid rate. Those members who are in the enacting subgroup are becoming clearer and clearer about the nature of the task, its dimensions, its challenges, and its built-in frustrations. The competence theme is relevant not only to the enactment that occurs but to the increasingly noticeable signs of discouragement and depression. The intractability of some of the deviants, the rapidly mounting fear that more harm than good will result from interpretations, the fact that it is not easy to make sense out of group events in which one is embroiled, all these factors combine to raise the specter of failure. The possibility of failing, which becomes an issue only when one feels autonomous and responsible, and of discovering one's incompetence constitutes the major source of depression during this period. Out of these tensions, and from the increasingly salient issue of separation, derive the forces that transform this internalization phase into the next phase, separation.

Separation and Terminal Review

The two final phases are similar, and thus it makes sense to discuss them together. In contrast to the internalization phase, the separation phase is notable for the abrupt drop in Enactment, for the increase in Loyalty and Involvement, for the switch into Resistant Complaining and Distress, and, above all, for the Depression. In the final review phase, Depression and Involvement become even more extreme, but there are minor shifts back to Enactment and away from Loyalty and Distress. The major event of these phases is, of course, the end of the group, but even at the finale we are not spared the task of locating and analyzing quite divergent reactions to this common stimulus.

Since the most notable process during this separation phase is the mounting depression, it would be well to turn first to the subgroup that accounts for this development. The final sessions are alternately wild and heavy, euphoric and sad. If these groups can ever be said to achieve unanimity in the feelings held and expressed by the members, it would be during some of the depressed and manic segments of these sessions. Both the expressions and the denials of depression seem to be affected by all the themes. There are numerous references to food and hunger, and there are intimations that the group now expects the leader to provide "the word" which he had retentively withheld all these weeks. To some extent the final separation reactivates the feelings of loss and abandonment aroused in the earlier sessions, and just as those early discomforts were attributed to the leader, so too it is the leader who now must prevent the end of the group. Some of the depression harks back to the early discussions of impulsivity, as the group reviews the wounds inflicted during the course of its history. For some members, the power of the group norms and the leader's sanctions fails now to prevent an eruption of guilt, and many instances of scapegoating or scorn are reviewed with shame. Not all members join in these self-accusatory ruminations, but much of the terminal depression results from the sudden awareness of those standards of behavior and etiquette which had been temporarily suspended in the name of honesty and "work." The issue of termination seems also to stir up feelings of failure in the competence area, and members may berate themselves for working and learning less than they should have. The final collapse upon the all-knowing leader is acompanied by a decrease in self-esteem that contrasts markedly with the pride developed during the internalization phase. Finally, the depressive and euphoric bursts represent divergent responses to the termination of member-member and member-leader intimacy. Of greatest relevance to the member-leader relationship is the fantasy, expressed in various forms, that between them the members and the leader have created a progeny that is immortal and uniquely valuable to the world beyond. Fantasies of rebirth, reunion, and proselytizing arise, and there is much concern over what people will take away inside them. All told, the members and the leader seem to share equally in the role of procreator and carrier of the group's future value.

Beyond the depressive trend that is quite general there are several other developments that can be traced to dominant subgroups. For one subgroup the separation phase is a time for direct approaches to the leader. Some females, especially those who have been high on Loyalty throughout the group, become even more explicit about their affection for the leader. These females seem to be staking out a special role as carriers of the group's progeny and the fruits of its labor. Another subgroup emerges at the end to challenge the general agreement over the group's fertility and value. For them the experience has been draining or painful. These performances convey more hostility than depression; through a combination of Resistant Complaining and Distress they convey both a sense of emptiness and resentment over efforts to change them. To the extent that changes have occurred, they imply, the changes have been a subtraction from rather than an addition to whatever they value in themselves. In the final phases these individuals attempt to recapture the *status quo ante* and to expel the worthless thoughts and judgments which they have internalized. All the experiences are cast in control and nurturance terms and are seen as one long process of brainwashing and poisoning. Finally, there are indications, particularly in the Dependent Complaining performances, that some members are in a mood to hand the group back to the leader, often blaming him in the process for the failures of the group. In a variety of ways, the group is trying to pinch off and cauterize their connection with the group and the leader.

Some members regress to much earlier concerns, as if to find security in the outworn complaints and reasons for rejecting the entire situation. Others focus narrowly upon the competence issues that can be discussed with less intensity and greater distance: What did we learn from it all? Or how useful will this course be to us in the future? It is this latter surge of reviewing and draining the intensity out of the experience that accounts for the final upward turn of factor one toward the Enactment pole. Three of the groups ended with a form of round-robin confession and testimonial which provided a number of members an opportunity to share with the group either how much they had observed and understood all along or how much they had left unsaid.

One example of the unexpected reversals of form which sometimes occur during the end of the group is found in group three.

Ida was the member who had been most consistently against "soul-baring" and had resisted all efforts of the group to enlist her aid in the mutual enterprise of sharing feelings. Yet on the last day of the group, she was able to express some of her feelings.

Ida: I'm a speaker but the silent members are too, now. But I don't want to commit myself. I'm sad I left this impression. But I'm involved and emotional, but not *here*—not in this group. And you don't care about Georgia because she doesn't bug you!
Alfred: You're involved, but you don't want to rock the boat. I don't mind rocking the boat, I just want to have a life jacket on first.
Molly: She's involved.
Hank: I think she is, too.
Malcolm: I feel satisfied with Ida. I know you now.
Ida: That's so *simple*. All these perceptive people think they know me. It shakes me.
Pearl: You are comfortable enough to talk about it . . .
Ida: I'm foolish! (Cries.) I wish I could delete this.
Hank: It doesn't need explanation.
Ida: When people attacked Judith, I saw me in her place.
Judith: (Cries.) I'm crying now.
Pearl: The crying is insignificant. It's the emotion that we all feel.

Whether they end with a heavy and muffled session or with a giddy rush, the members do manage to arrive at the final gong of the bell in a position to leave as they came, individually. One unique feature of these groups, as opposed to most training and therapy groups, is the final exam. Undoubtedly this affects the final phases. But what is impressive is that, unlike most ordinary classes, these groups do not end with a burst of pre-exam dependency and anxiety. There is some of this, but despite the impending exam it has still been their group to an extent that is both reflected and accentuated by the final depression. To a large extent it was their group to make and theirs to mourn.

It is fitting to end our account of group development with an abridged version of group one's last session. One can see that many of the themes and feelings which have occupied the group for 30 sessions come tumbling out in the final moments of the group's history.

Marie: It seems that all the acting out we've been doing isn't efficient, but I don't see why we should bother to be efficient now.

Frank: I just had a funny experience. I was thinking about the group, and all of a sudden this tune started running through my head: 'I'll be seeing you in all my dreams, dear.'

Lili: You too?

Frank: It's funny, I can't remember what I've been dreaming. (Long silence.)

Gino: I had a dream last night. It didn't seem to be about this group at all. Some friends of mine passed, and I would see each one of them; each one I'd see I'd like for a few seconds, then I'd say, 'Well, there's the same thing wrong with this person that was wrong with this person before,' on and on and on, people were coming into my dream, . . . you probably don't know who they are. There were scenes of some of my friends' faces, and so forth, my mother looking confused, and portions of one face attached—one portion of one woman would be attached to another woman. And I tried to remember—the phone rang many, many times this morning, and I got up and I was just about to remember the purpose of the dream, the importance of this dream to my mind, and the phone rang and it was time to get up. My feeling was one of being dissatisfied with a group of people, not necessarily in this course. (Long silence.)

Janice: One of the first things you said to the group, Dr. Allen, was 'It's hard to begin, isn't it?' I have the feeling now that it's even harder to end.

Ellie: Nothing seems significant enough to say at this group.

Jane: It seems so sad to waste the last hour of the class.

Janice (to Dr. Allen): I was thinking that, I guess it was the day before yesterday, I felt a tremendous amount of anger toward you 'OK, the game has gone far enough. When is he going to take off the mask and tell us what the hell has been going on?'

Dr. Allen: I was wondering when *you* all were going to do that (Laughter.)

Frank: We're the 'Hallelujah Chorus,' and we're just sitting here saying, 'And he shall reign for ever and ever,' even though he won't

Alvin: You mean Dr. Allen?

Frank: Yes.

Gino: Who knows? (Laughter.) Maybe Dr. Allen—

Frank: Long hair and a forked beard.

Gino: A friend of mine had sort of Christ fantasies. He had a beard. He was on the West Coast. He has sort of very curly hair, a big mop of it, a tall thin guy, you know. He would put a sheet on himself and walked up and down the beach at night. He would do this for hours, and then he would get tired.

Janice: Did he walk on the water?

Gino: No, he could never seem to get into the water. . . . I think there's a reason why I started talking about somebody out of the class, sort of a bridge to the outside world.

Frank: I had a funny impression. I heard Lili singing in the Summer School Chorus. It was very good. There was this line about the dead leaves, the autumn leaves are falling, and we are sad. What—what—what is this?

Lili: I don't know where it's from.

Frank: It's very beautiful, and I had a strange connection with this group—autumn leaves—light too, and everything. . . . What I think is that I draw an analogy between this group as a small life and the world as another small life, somehow I draw an analogy between this and that. But the endings are different.

Merv: How is the ending going to be different?

Frank: We won't all walk through the door.

Merv: This is our own wake—when the bell strikes, that's it.

Frank: When we walk out that door we'll still be able to remember and to think and do other things.

Lili: Maybe there is an after-life after all.

Frank: I don't know. I couldn't say, myself.

Alvin: Are we saying, dead is a kind of being, and perhaps the best kind?

Harry: Perhaps.

Gino: You felt as if you were dying. When the time comes to die, you die, and it's real.

Alvin: You just die?

Merv: You haven't been judged yet. We don't know whether we're going to heaven or hell. . . .

Lili: Is there a leap year coming up?

Frank: Why do you say that?

Bob: Do you want the prerogative?

Lili: Either that or to have had the prerogative and not used it. Look at it both ways.

Jane: Maybe we could sort of evaluate ourselves.

Harry: You read that somewhere. You really don't want to, do you?
Jane: No, what I really wanted is—I feel sort of incapable. Somebody else might be able to say something.
Merv: About you?
Jane: No, just about the group.
Frank: How do you mean?
Jane: Well, I don't always feel—I feel that it's been a very good experience. I recommend it to practically anybody, but (laughter) when I try to describe the group to somebody else, I can't. I can't find anything to say, and I have to say, 'Well, you just wouldn't believe it.' And they say, 'Well, try me.' And I can't say a thing.
Merv: I found the same thing. Someone says, what is it like, and I find it almost impossible to describe.
Lili: Are you asking Dr. Allen to describe it?
Jane: Yes.
Harry: Life is a well. It's a well.
(Several mumble "Huh?")
Gino: Sort of a nice existential joke.
Merv: I just had a song run through my mind too, 'The Party's Over.'
Jane: It must be fate. How about, 'It Was Just One of Those Things.' (Laughter.) (Long silence.)
Merv: Did anyone ever notice, the further you sink into a silence, the harder it is to get out of it?
Jane: Thank you very much.
Merv: Dr. Allen always has those tapes. There's the group on those tapes.
Kamala: I think there should be a television, to get gestures.
Janice: You are really asking for a last minute salvation, an immortality.
Kamala: Yes, but the immortality of the group; you will not perceive it in concrete terms, but it will still be there, in everyone's mind. It will probably sink deep down to the subconscious or the unconscious.
Frank: Deep down inside.
Alvin: I have the feeling that the group or the influence of the group will be spread further, because for instance, I feel my own experience that I have grown in knowing everybody in the group and have taken something of the group while we were here. I think that's true of most of us here. We will take this growth out into our lives and really to my way of thinking, this will be an extension of the group and the influence of it—what we have felt.
Merv: It seems as if time is going much slower to me.
Gino: I was going to suggest we leave a few minutes ago.

Jane: Sort of, 'Let's get this over with.'

Frank: Yeah.

Jane: No need to starve to death. (Laughter.)

Gino: Dr. Allen, can I ask you a question? This is, I hope it doesn't embarrass you too much. When I'm at work, I go from smoking cigarettes to drinking bottles of pop, eating. All night long, I'm putting something in my mouth. I think I'm consumed by endless orality. (Laughter.)

Dr. Allen: What's the question?

Frank: All of a sudden I started thinking about this thing down in the subway, you know, that big sign on the wall that says: 'Stop a moment and pray to Jesus through Mary.'

Gino: The point actually was, I think it's a bad thing; I think it is regressive. This isn't how a twenty-year-old man should act. But I don't think that enough to stop.

Harry: Well, sort of coming right back to the beginning of the problems with orality.

Ellie: I'd like to note that there's one last resistance to this class, at least, and I guess there's probably more to it than I noticed just before. Somebody had said something, I don't remember what it was, and I had sort of an interpretation to offer, but I figured, by God, I'm not going to give in to the group standard now, and I didn't say it, and I thought this was rather funny.

Hanna: What are the group standards? (Laughter.)

Joanne: Isn't it interesting that we are not really offering interpretations, but we're just laughing.

Bob: Maybe they are supporting.

Harry: *You* are not interpreting. Other people do seem to be interpreting.

Kamala: What Ellie said about the group standards, I think we never came to discuss the group standards that all of us took or implied, in the course of our discussion.

Marie: I think we feel like damn fools for not doing it.

Kamala: Isn't that conforming to group standards?

Marie: No, not at all. We didn't know what the group standards were.

Kamala: I think there was at least one assumption that we must not discuss values and everytime we came to discuss values we got away from there because it irritated us. We must not really discuss values. It seems as if it was an implied group norm that we developed in the class.

Marie: That's true, but the way we dealt with the task, we didn't decide exactly; we never actually did decide what was constructive. We decided what was not constructive. It was all this saying, 'This isn't constructive, but what was it? We have to do what we're supposed to do, well what is it?'

Harry: The biggest group standard seems to me being nice to everybody, that over the last week we've found some sort of jovial if fragile acceptance of each other, kind of laughing around and staying away from the id.

Bob: I'm not sure I would agree that's such a fragile acceptance.

Harry: Well, we laugh an awful lot.

Bob: I know—I feel uncertainty in the laughing, but I don't know if there isn't a much deeper acceptance.

Harry: So we've made an agreement not to threaten each other.

Marie: I think the id—the id is all very fine, maybe we could show it, but I think there would have been less exhausting ways, for instance, we could have, if we were a little bit more sophisticated when we started, we could have talked about it a little bit better.

Jane: But if we didn't act out, there wouldn't be anything to analyze.

Bob: Do you feel strange for having acted out?

Marie: No, well I just say, well, it's good old Marie again. She always acts out.

Alvin: I think there has been more of an understanding, if not an acceptance of each other. I don't think you always accept when you understand. I feel that I have a deeper understanding of people, but I don't know that I completely accept what I understand.

Marie: Narcissism is the defense against all kinds of things, including very sad separations like—(the bell drowns out her words).

Frank: It's not the end of the world.

Summary

We have now completed our narrative of the groups' development, and it is time to consider how best to summarize these results. As a start, we have prepared Table 6-1 in which are arrayed the various dominant and deviant subgroups which emerge in the development of the groups. The dominant subgroups account for the major characteristics of each phase, and their diversity reminds us that "the group" is in fact a collection of diverse forces and cliques of at least this complexity. Some of the subgroups can be labelled with a phrase suggesting an ideal type, "the heroes" for example, but for the most part the

Table 6-1

Subgroup Characteristics by Phase

		Phase		
Initial Complaining	Premature Enactment	Confrontation	Internalization	Separation and Terminal Review
Dominant subgroups:	Dominant subgroups:	Dominant subgroups:	Dominant subgroup:	Dominant subgroups:
Dependent complaining	"The sensitive ones" Withdrawal and denial	Rebellion and complaining (including "the spokesmen")	Enactment and work	Depression and manic denial
Loyal compliance	"The accepting enactors"	Independence		Personal involvement
Counterdependent heroics	"The heroic enactors"	Anxiety and withdrawal		Complaining and abdication of responsibility
Self-sufficiency				
Deviant subgroup:	Deviant subgroup:	Deviant subgroup:	Deviant subgroup:	
Enactment in the service of autonomy	Disappointment and resentment	"The heroes"	"The scapegoats"	

table contains a brief description of the feelings and actions that characterize the members of the particular subgroup.

We would propose to extend our major effort at summarizing this group development chapter by considering the emergence of the work subgroup, to adjust Bion's phrase slightly to fit our data. This task leads us to inquire how the members define work and how the members' definition differs from the leader's definition outlined in Chapter 5. In addition, we are led to wonder whether some of the subgroups are not pressing the group in the direction of work and others dragging it away.

If we consider only the leader's pressure toward work, then clearly it would make sense to look first at the internalization phase. All four aspects of the leader's definition of work are in operation: enactment, independence, involvement, and expression. That is, the dominant subgroup has put them into operation. Despite the work subgroup's dominance of this phase, there is still a subgroup that might be called the antiwork subgroup. Just as the work subgroup fits all four aspects of the leader's notion of work, the antiwork subgroup deviates on all four aspects of work. Was this split always present? How did it come about?

Our conclusion from these data is that much of the early history of the groups finds a split not solely between work and antiwork subgroups but between subgroups each of which champions one or more but not all four aspects of work, as defined by the leader. In the first phase, the Dependent Complaining and Loyalty subgroups are quite expressive, but they reject the notions of independence and/or enactment and reject, as well, many expressions of hostility. The Counterdependent Flight subgroup also starts off in an expressive mood, but the goals of independence and involvement are particularly alien to their frame of mind, as are others' expressions of dependency. The subgroup that starts off high on the Colleague and/or Involvement factor patterns may understand and implement all the other work goals, but they are usually quite low on expression, preferring to assist others in their distress rather than expressing their own. The major antiwork subgroups, in their dismay over the leader's passivity and distance, seem to resist particularly the goal of independence. If there were, in fact, the kind of unanimous sharing of feelings that Bion alleges, we would look here for the dependency group, but we find no such unity and it seems best simply to note the existence of a subgroup that is disappointed, usually anxious, and still quite dependent. In the premature enactment phase, the antiwork subgroup seems most alarmed by the notion of expression. The heroic enactors, it may be remembered, stir up this alarm, but even they seem to resist expressing some of their feelings. Mixed with their hostile interpretations of others' dependency and weakness are high levels of denial, particularly denials of depression and dependency. Although they may be high on enactment, their strident assertions of independence and their frequent denials define for them a rather invulnerable position, and for quite a while the attacks on them by other members fail to penetrate the wall they build around themselves. In contrast, the other early enactors, those that we call the accepting enactors, are often not fully prepared to accept the independence aspect of work. Their enactment is part of a larger and fundamentally dependent strategy.

By the confrontation phase the four aspects of work are becoming clearer to the group. The work implications of the hostile subgroup, the one that leads the attack upon the leader and the heroes, are most interesting. Every aspect of work but expression is explicitly rejected, yet the very fact that the attack is launched represents an important reversal of one common feeling during the previous phases, that the expression of hostility is to be avoided at all costs. The leader of the revolt propels the group into its most heated expressive phase, and the members are able to test their predictions about what disasters will befall the group if they do express some real feelings. Two other subgroups are active during this confrontation period. The heroes, who persist in their enactment and involvement, now increase their expression by joining the rebellion aspect of the confrontation. What they, in their counterdependent mood, fail to espouse about work is precisely what another subgroup develops at some length, i.e., the goal of genuine autonomy and independence. The independents' subgroup may still be somewhat short on expression, but it does help to define one part of the path that leads toward the period of work. What we are suggesting is that it takes the entire development of the group up to the internalization or work phase for the four aspects of work to be advocated and carried out simultaneously by any dominant or deviant subgroup of the whole. We are suggesting, in addition, that the antiwork subgroups may object to one or another aspect of work without opposing all four aspects of the leader's pressure on the group. The major cleavage during the internalization phase, on the other hand, reveals the extent to which the separate aspects of work have become integrated into one coherent whole, and members tend to line up on one side or the other of the pro- versus anti-work schism.

Thus far our analysis has assumed that the members' definition of work is the same as the leader's definition. To a large extent this is true, or becomes true over time. Those who imply, during the early phases, that to work is to enact but not to express, or to express but not to be independent, etc. are arguing for a definition of work. In their eyes it is not a partial definition. It is their idea of work. Why do these early definitions of work, which are partial only with reference to the leader's definition, give way to a more inclusive definition? The first explanation might be that the leader's support for all four aspects of work and his occasional nonsupport for partial definitions exerts the crucial pressure, but a second explanation should be added. The final definition of work that emerges from the work subgroup is a compromise, a synthesis developed by the newly formed coalition among previously distinct subgroups. Each of the contesting subgroups seems to give ground. Those who enact but do so as a means of denying their own feelings become more willing to live with the expressions of others and even to begin to echo them; in turn, the expressive members become willing to let the enactors carry on in their preferred style and begin to share the analytic task with them. The members of each subgroup discover, as it were, the appeal, the legitimacy, and the merits of several other subgroups, each with its own particular notion of work.

The final definition of work, as developed by the members, is not a perfect replica of the leader's four-part definition. Even the subgroups most favorably disposed toward work in this setting have a hard time incorporating and then making public their understanding of the assigned readings. The intellectual material of the course is mentioned off and on, but extensive use of it seems to the members perilously close to becoming the dependent teacher's pet or the cold, distant observer whose lack of involvement and expression disqualify him from membership in the emergent work subgroup.

The members' definition of work, as it emerges from the grand coalition developed during the major work period, puts sensitivity high on the list of criteria. In contrast, the leaders, although not opposed to sensitivity per se, have spent too much of their time supporting expression, even abusive expression, to make any substantial contribution to this part of the definition of work. In the early phases the leaders seemed to respond primarily to the possibility that if sensitivity were made the cardinal virtue, progressively more and more expression might be ruled out-of-bounds. It is the members who are the victims of insensitivity, and the final work subgroup either includes many of "the sensitive ones" and their spokesmen or else is much influenced by their concern for the consequences of honesty.

One crucial development in the work period is the formulation of norms that crystallize the members' sense of what does and what does not constitute work. That is, the members do more than perform in ways that seem like work; they become increasingly self-conscious about what they are doing. By codifying and thereby making public their changing attitudes toward work, they create a source of standards that seems to reside not in society, not in the leader, but in "the group," although there are always deviants who frustrate the desired show of consensus. It is when the group has developed to this point that the moralist, with his explicit connections to society's standards, becomes a relevant and a vulnerable deviant for the great bulk of the members and not simply the butt of the hero's attacks.

What we have tried to show in this chapter is the regularity found across groups with respect to each of the six factors and the four themes underlying them, and we have suggested that the major cause of the changes that are found, as captured here in terms of six phases, lies in the shifting nature, power, and composition of various competing subgroups. Although the developments can be interpreted from many angles, we chose to look at the emergence of a work subgroup and a set of work norms that coincide in large part with the leader's definition of work, insofar as we could infer his definition from his pattern of attention to and support for the members' performances. The major addition by the members to the leader's definition of work was the inclusion of sensitivity, and this expansion of the definition permitted many of those who were previously outraged and alienated by the hero's assaultive style to join with the hero in the major work subgroup. The work period breaks up under the pressure of the impending separation; the drop in Enactment and the increase in dependency testify to the members' fatigue, to their uncertainty over re-entering the world beyond, and to their uneasiness over what effect the group has had upon them. At this point, the main effect of the antiwork subgroup, the members high on Resistant Complaining and Distress, is to puncture the groups' belief that the experience has been beneficial to all. In their effort to erase the effects of the group, the antiwork subgroup is merely responding to termination in a different way than those who are absorbed with the expression and denial of sadness, guilt, and helplessness. Even if the latter group is still attempting to pursue the members' own goals of work, their efforts are usually in vain.

This chapter has examined the group as a whole and the various subgroups that emerged within each phase and has ignored, for the most part, the question of who belonged to this or that subgroup across phases. This permitted us to observe the shifting alliances as the group split over the issues of dependency, sensitivity, work, etc. What was necessarily unclear in all this was why a particular individual starts off as he does, who alters his performances and who does not, and how the entire career of an individual can be seen as a coherent and meaningful entity. This will be discussed in Chapter 7.

Some Relevant Literature on Group Development

In comparing our analysis of group development with other contributions in the field we may distinguish among the various conceptions of the developmental process per se and the specific phases that are demarcated and described. As Chin (1961) and Dunphy (1964) have noted, some authors portray group development as a gradual succession of stages from early disorganization and frustration to eventual harmony and productivity. Tuckman's (1965) synthesis of numerous studies of group development is a clear example of this model; his summary specifies four stages: forming, storming, norming, and performing. In contrast to the successive stage model emphasized by Tuckman and many of the researchers whose work he summarized, the recurrent cycle model suggested by Bion (1961) and Schutz (1958) emphasizes the enduring absorption of groups with the same issues, and these authors imply that the resolution of certain issues can never be more than partial and temporary. We suspect that a fusion of the two models, as found in Bradford (1964a), would be acceptable to those employing either the successive stage or recurrent cycle model; the difference is primarily one of emphasis. For example, although Bennis and Shepard's (1956) description of group development is in terms of the progression of six stages, they are not unaware that regression and recycling occurs; on the other hand, Bion (1961), whose analysis of group process Tuckman rather inappropriately forces into his successive stages of approach, is not above concluding that the work group is likely to prevail over earlier, less mature forms of group organization.

The next property of developmental models worth noting is whether they leave the group at its apex or, alternatively, provide a sense of the group's decline and death. The latter approach, which we might term the life cycle model, is found in the work of Mills (1964), Slater (1966), Dunphy (1964), and Mann (1966). An interesting mixture of the recurrent cycle and the life cycle models is suggested by Schutz (1958), who notes that the members' earliest and final concern is with inclusion and the location of the group's boundaries. Again, we find it hard to believe that any observer of group development would boggle at distinguishing between the group's most productive period and the group's final sessions; certainly all the empirical studies of group development have indicated that members behave and feel differently near the end of the group's history.

Finally, we would note that, except for such studies as Stock and Thelen (1958) and Bennis and Shepard (1956), few analyses of group development depart from the notion that either "the group" develops or the individual members change, or both. What is missing, in our view, is any sense of the issues that create the conditions for subgroups to emerge, compete, and combine, thereby altering the direction of the group's development. This empirical study suggests that only rarely is a shift in the predominant tone of the group shared by all members equally. On the contrary, our results lead us to construct a life cycle model that allows for clearly specifying which subgroups are primarily responsible for the various alterations in the group's center of gravity.

Without listing all the studies that portray the first and subsequent stages in a fashion similar to our analysis, it may be useful to indicate how at least some of the other authors have described the various phases they have found. As Tuckman's (1965) review reveals, most observers agree that the early sessions are characterized by heightened anxiety (Bion, 1961; Stock and Thelen, 1958; Whitman, 1964), by a sense of loss and depression (Slater, 1966) which arouses dependency needs that cannot or will not be satisfied (Bach, 1954; Bion, 1961; Bennis and Shepard, 1956; M. Horwitz, 1964), and by a desire to test the limits and reality of the new situation (Mills, 1964; Semrad and Arsenian, 1951). No previous study has noted the development found for all four groups wherein enactment rises immediately prior to the confrontation but then collapses because it is premature and provacative in ways which contribute to the rush of hostility toward the leader and his role in the group.

Slater's analysis of "the revolt" is by far the most extensive and complex discussion of the development we have described as the confrontation phase. In his view, the attack on the leader occurs when the group members are sufficiently aware of their ambivalence toward this depriving, frustrating figure, and the revolt signifies both an effort to destroy the leader and to create the conditions for his incorporation and deification. The members' efforts to gain autonomy from their irritating but overly valued leader, if successful, enable them to deal with the intermember issues of sexual attraction and the revised hierarchical structure of the group. Other authors, notably Bion (1961), Bennis and Shepard (1956), Miles (1964), and Semrad and Arsenian (1951), have discussed the hostility that arises toward the leader and among members in self-analytic groups. Whitman's (1964) discussion is particularly relevant in that he notes sex differences that accompany the rise in hostility generally, with the males fighting the leader and each other and the females tending less to initiate such activities than to attach themselves to the aggressors or the victims at any given moment. Up to and including the confrontation phase, this study agrees with most previous accounts of group development. Where it differs, at least in emphasis, is in its view of what happens next.

Except for those employing a recurrent cycle model, there is a strong tendency, most clearly seen in the work of Bennis and Shepard (1956), to conceive of the confrontation as resolving "the authority issue." Some see intimacy issues as coming to the fore (Bennis and Shepard, 1956); others see a period of increased openness (Bradford, 1964a), collaboration (Semrad and Arsenian, 1951), and normative integration (Mills, 1964; Tuckman, 1965). We would certainly not disagree with these descriptions of changes in member-member relations. Our analysis is focused on the continuity of the member-leader relationship, and our only quarrel with the previous studies is over their treatment of this aspect of group development. The problems raised within the member-leader relationship by dependency, mistrust, resentment, etc. are treated within the present study in the manner suggested by the recurrent cycle of approach, i.e., as issues that are never fully resolvable. The internalization phase is only relatively free of these early feelings, and it is against the background of such feelings that any evidence of identification must be viewed.

Many of the phenomena to which we point during the period of maximum work have been noted by others (Stock and Thelen, 1958; Herbert and Trist, 1953; Slater, 1966; and Mills, 1964). It is a time for expression and experimentation (Semrad and Arsenian, 1951) but also for the sharing of insights and the analysis of what has gone on in the group thus far. We find that our discussion not only emphasizes the persistence of early feelings more than most, but we are also more inclined than most to make explicit the continuing relevance of the leader. We have tried not to overemphasize in our minds the relevance of the leader to the group's decision to work; it is, of course, a time when the member's own desire to achieve a sense of competence is liberated, and the members do make the work goals their own to a large extent. Without denying these observations, we may wonder if some contributions to the field do not reflect the leader's own ambivalence about how much he should control or has controlled the development of the group. In Chapter 5 we saw how touchy and defensive the leaders in this study became when they were perceived as having a covert influence on the groups. Might it be possible that somewhat the same reluctance to perceive one's own influence affects leaders when they write that at a certain point the group moves beyond the authority issue? After the confrontation phase is over, it is easy to be distracted by the highly relevant and often dramatic alterations in member-member interaction, which again we emphasize we are not discounting, but we feel that the continuous if changing relevance of the leader deserves a different treatment than that afforded by the authority-then-intimacy model suggested by Bennis and Shepard (1956).

Finally, we note the relatively rare accounts of the group's terminal phase. Mills (1964) sees the members as striving to establish the fact that they have produced something of enduring value, and this attempt is viewed by Dunphy (1964) as contributing to the rise of the messiah-hero myth. Mills (1964), Coffey et al. (1950), and Schutz (1958) all emphasize the difficult task of dissolving the group boundaries and preparing for re-entry into "the outside world." A number of authors, e.g., Slater (1966), note the regressive quality of many of the final discussions which signals the rearousal of earlier wishes for gratification in the nurturance and control areas.

Chapter 7

The Study of Individual Careers

Chapter 6 traced the gradual emergence of the major subgroups and pointed out the shifting coalitions and the various recombinations of those subgroups which culminate in the formation of work and resistance factions during the phase of internalization. The primary purpose of this chapter is to describe more completely some of the key members in these subgroups. We intend to discuss in some detail the characteristic interpersonal styles of these individuals: how they perceive the group and the leader; what they hope, fear, and expect from the group; their conscious and unconscious goals and strategies; and their relationships with other members. This suggests a typology of interpersonal styles or roles, but the typology offered is neither exhaustive nor even very systematic. Instead, the focus of this chapter falls on the most salient group members, around whom most of the principal events in the group revolve.

Individuals become central figures for many different reasons. Some are consistently and often dramatically equated, whether explicitly or implicitly, with one or more aspects of the leader. Others are quickly recognized as the most articulate or persistent proponents of a particular view of the group and the leader. Alternatively, they may offer a viable synthesis of the opposing ideologies and strategies of warring subgroups. Some are highly visible deviants at one or more points in the group's history. These several routes to centrality do not, of course, preclude one another. It is not at all unusual, to cite but a single possibility, for an individual to exert significant influence for a variety of reasons in different phases of the group's development. In short, it is impossible to state any general rule which could improve upon the simple observation that a central figure is always seen as a representative of at least one dimension of a current, group-wide concern.

The dual process of selecting regularities to focus upon and then assigning individuals to what we have called member-types was accomplished with reference to the statistical summaries of each member's total career and our assessment of what kinds of active participation catalyze, crystallize, and resolve important issues in the group. We do not mean to suggest, however, that these are in any sense universal member types. Other groups, developing in different settings with different goals or different leader styles, may well be characterized by quite different arrays of member-roles than we encountered in these groups. What we do hope is that this general approach to the individual's thematic concerns and interpersonal strategies will be found helpful regardless of the context in which it is employed.

It is helpful to begin by recalling the earlier discussion of the work and resistance subgroups and their antecedents. In the three phases prior to that of internalization, different factions within the group endorse somewhat conflicting definitions of work. These conceptions of work are brought together and partly fused relatively late in the group's history. It is important to note that one reason why it is so difficult for the member to integrate the several aspects of work is that the leader himself provides a model for some of them, but not for others. He asks, in effect, that they identify with his independent, interpretive approach to group life; yet he also encourages them to express feelings and provide evidence of their involvement, even though he maintains a calmer, cooler, and more detached stance. One principal source of conflict in the member-leader relationship is the member's frequent refusal to identify with the model presented by the leader or to accept his demands for expression and involvement.

Another, and often more tenacious, form of resistance arises when the member redefines work by distorting the leader's injunctions, or when he identifies with aspects of the leader's role which the leader implicitly reserves for himself. The sensitive subgroup, for example, may pay lip service to the goals of enactment, but it usually condemns the interpretations of others as "too deep," "too personal," "too hostile," or "irrelevant." The sensitive ones justify their opposition to interpretation by appealing to moral principles which they assume the leader shares and which they insist are applicable to the conduct of a self-analytic group. They may, at other moments, agree that the leader does not or would not support them, but only because he is cold, insensitive, and undeserving of emulation. Some members identify only with the leader's aloofness, his mysticism, his relatively inactive style, or his personal mannerisms. Whether they argue that such resistance is their only available defense against omniscience or malevolence or take the position that the leader too is defensive, they often remain firmly entrenched and inaccessible to further influence. A closer analysis of these individual deviations from the norms of the work group, only a few of which have been touched upon here, will help to illuminate the developmental processes and interpersonal compromises which produce and sustain or oppose and restrict those norms.

In addition, a simultaneous developmental pattern must be considered. As the group passes through the phase of confrontation and into that of internalization, many members become less preoccupied with nurturance and control issues and more capable of maintaining an atmosphere in which sexuality and competence are given priority. A study of individual development will serve to explain this transition and will provide a wide range of examples of the ways in which competence issues are interwoven with other themes, sometimes facilitating but often impeding work.

This chapter, then, is an attempt to explore the interrelationships among the individual's thematic concerns, his ability to work, and his role in the group. Such a case study approach entails an evaluation of: (1) initial perceptions of the group situation; (2) individual needs, fears, goals, and strategies; (3) the individual's position vis-à-vis other members and his commitment to subgroups; and (4) the intrapsychic and interpersonal forces which encourage or block positive adaptation to the situation. Again, our aim here is not to formulate an all-inclusive theoretical framework, but to bring together in a more speculative, open-ended fashion our thoughts about interpersonal styles and group development. This analysis will fall somewhere between a typology of individual members and a case study of group development and will necessitate somewhat different emphases for different individuals.

Our point of departure is the subgroup split which characterizes the internalization period. In general, those members who come to participate in the work group are those who begin by endorsing some aspects of work, then expand their repertoires to include others. One of these is the *hero*, whose role in the early phases has already been noted and whose career will be discussed in more detail a little later. Toward the middle of the group, the hero is joined by and to some extent subordinated to the *independent enactors*. Whereas in the initial phases the independent enactors may have been somewhat too loyal and accepting, too distant and unexpressive, too concerned with consideration and sensitivity, or too much preoccupied with sharing in the hero's glory, they tend to emerge from the confrontation with a clearer notion of what constitutes work and a greater willingness to undertake it. They are able to synthesize enactment and sensitivity as neither the hero nor the sensitive ones can. They establish an atmosphere in which an optimal degree of expression and involvement can be preserved. There are some important similarities and differences between male and female enactors, and these will also be examined.

Those members who eventually become the most active members of the resistance subgroup cling to incomplete definitions of work and maintain a rigid, unwavering, and extremely defensive position which is incompatible with the goals of the work group. Although there is an infinite number of alternatives to work, we shall direct our attention to two relatively stable behavior patterns around which most of the resistance is centered. The *moralistic resister,* who often leads the Dependent Complaining of the initial phase, is invariably an important contributor to the resistant and sensitive factions during the perod of premature enactment. He is often the leading candidate for the role of spokesman during the confrontation, and he continues his defense of the weak and the distressed throughout the internalization phase. The *paranoid resister* may follow a similar career, though his initial assumptions are rather different from those of the moralist. He expresses concern not over the abstract principles which the moralist invokes but over the malevolent and insidious influence which he attributes to insight and interpretation. While some paranoid resisters speak out in behalf of those in danger, others retreat and utter dire predictions which serve to evoke the anxious questioning of other members. In adopting the term "paranoid" to describe one of the principal resisters, we do not mean to imply that members who tend to adopt this role are necessarily on the verge of psychosis or even troubled by a neurotic, paranoid character disorder. On the contrary, we feel that it is entirely possible for a member with relatively few paranoid preoccupations to assume this role under the appropriate circumstances.

Finally, there are members who are neither active workers nor major resisters. Some are involved but distressed, others remain silent and plead total neutrality and disinterest. Although they are often quite expressive, they seldom become central figures for more than a session or two. We will comment briefly on a few such minor types— the *sexual scapegoat,* the *anxious female,* the *depressed female,* and the *collapsing colleague*—since they are of primary significance as members of an amorphous and unstable subgroup which becomes the prize for which the enactors and resisters battle. Are they to be protected, or is their distress open to further interpretation?

These, then, are the individuals with whom this chapter is concerned, and before proceeding further, we shall indicate the kinds of data, empirical and observational, which enabled us to study their roles in the group.

The basic data are the tape recordings and the observers' notes and summaries of each session. In addition, we studied each individual's category scores, both for single sessions and for longer time periods, sometimes consulting the act-by-act scoring sheets in order to understand a particular sequence of acts. As the factors were extracted, factor scores for performances were obtained. Somewhat later, it was possible to look at an individual's factor scores for a given enactment phase. Finally, the group factor scores for a given phase were taken as a baseline against which the individual factor scores could be compared. Each group was analyzed separately and each individual and all-member profile in the first five phases of group development was given a factor score on each of the six factors. The data for the brief terminal review phase were omitted from this analysis. The mean of all the factor scores for each factor was zero and the standard deviation was one, but the all-member factor scores varied from phase to phase, in accordance with the findings presented in Chapter 6. Each member's factor score was thus compared with the all-member factor score for that phase to determine if, regardless of how high or low the group as a whole might be during that phase, the member was above or below his fellow group members on that factor. The deviation scores produced in this fashion were only approximate, since the group means were based on the individual's own acts as well as on the acts of the other members. Even so, the deviation scores made it possible to estimate the individual's position relative to the group as a whole on all six factors. A careful study of these data took us a long way toward clarifying the relationship of a given individual to the various subgroups and to the group as a whole.

It seems unnecessary, however, to present all of these data or to dwell at great length on all of their subtle ramifications. Instead, we have simply prepared tables of phase-by-phase deviation scores for the heroes, the major resisters and enactors, and the sexual scapegoats. We shall attempt to explain the most significant developmental patterns suggested by the deviation scores in terms of the role relationships operating within the group. Of the major types, we found that the heroes, the resisters, and the male enactors could be identified with little difficulty. The selection of the female enactors presented more problems, though we shall postpone for a while our discussion of those problems. Of the minor types, only the sexual scapegoats seemed to emerge with any degree of regularity. The short descriptions of the anxious and depressed females and the collapsing colleague are best viewed as convenient illustrations of distress which could have been replaced by a number of equally representative case studies. We did stipulate that any member whom we were considering as a possible example of a member type have enough acts to be factor scored in at least four of the five phases. Although we were forced to exclude a few important individuals for whom we had insufficient data, we were satisfied that the careers of all the major types and the sexual scapegoat were adequately represented by the individuals chosen.

It will soon become obvious that whereas this typology of members is based on an analysis of all the groups, the vignettes in this chapter are taken from a single group, group four. This procedure is not without its disadvantages, but we felt that its use was justified and even demanded by the task at hand. We plan not only to illustrate a typology of group members but to demonstrate how interrelated individual careers really are and to reflect upon the ways in which individuals come together to form a particular group. Toward the end of the chapter, we shall return to a wider focus in order to consider the most crucial changes in the relative positions of the various member types over time.

The Hero

In at least three of the groups there was one highly conspicuous male member who very early captured the attention of the group, as well as the leader, and who remained a central figure throughout the summer. Harry in group one, Kurt in group two, and Peter in group four maintained undisputed possession of the hero role. In group three both William and Malcolm were seen as heroes, though neither exhibited the full range of heroic attitudes and behavior characteristic of the others. Because of this complex splitting of the hero position in group three, these generalizations are somewhat less applicable here than to the other groups. We shall delay our consideration of this important group difference until Chapter 8 and concentrate instead on the most salient similarities among the five heroes.

The deviation scores for the heroes (as can be seen in Table 7-1) point to some impressive correspondences. In fact, the heroes appear to be more alike, in terms of both factor profiles and observational comparisons, than any of the other types, a finding well worth keeping in mind. The hero is consistently higher than the group as a whole on the Enactment, Rebellion, Counterdependent Flight, and Involvement factor patterns. This is the case, with few exceptions, for all five individuals over all phases; and the majority of these exceptions are attributable to the dual heroes of group three, who are less rebellious and less involved than are the other three individuals. The heroes are

Table 7-1

The Hero

Phase	Member	Group	I	II	III	IV	V	VI
Initial	Harry	1	+++	---	+++	+	+	+++
Complaining	Kurt	2	+++	--	---	0	--	++
	Malcolm	3	+	---	++	++	+	0
	William	3	+++	+	+++	++	-	++
	Peter	4	++	---	++	++	0	-
Premature	Harry	1	++	---	+++	-	--	-
Enactment	Kurt	2	+	--	+++	--	-	+
	Malcolm	3	++	---	+++	+	+	--
	William	3	+	+	+++	--	--	++
	Peter	4	+	---	++	+	+	+++
Confrontation	Harry	1	++	-	++	+	---	+++
	Kurt	2	+++	--	+++	-	--	++
	Malcolm	3	+++	-	+++	---	--	---
	William	3	+++	-	+++	-	0	+
	Peter	4	+	---	++	-	+	++
Internal-	Harry	1	++	-	++	--	+	+++
ization	Kurt	2	+++	--	+	+	---	++
	Malcolm	3	++	0	+	++	+	-
	William	3	++	-	+++	0	-	+
	Peter	4	++	---	++	---	+	-
Separation	Harry	1	++	-	++	+++	---	++
	Kurt	2	+++	-	+	-	+	++
	Malcolm	3	+	++	++	-	--	++
	William	3	++	--	+++	-	--	+++
	Peter	4	+	0	-	+	+	-
All	Harry	1	++	--	+++	-	--	+++
	Kurt	2	+++	--	+	0	-	++
	Malcolm	3	++	--	++	0	-	-
	William	3	+++	-	+++	-	-	++
	Peter	4	+	---	++	-	+	+

Factor Titles

I+:	Enactment
I−:	Dependent Complaining
II+:	Loyalty
II−:	Rebellion
III+:	Counterdependent Flight
III−:	Resistant Complaining
IV+:	Colleague
IV−:	Distress
V+:	Anxiety
V−:	Depression
VI+:	Involvement
VI−:	Neutrality

Symbol Key

0:	Member's factor score = group mean.
+ or −:	Member's factor score less than .5 standard deviations from group mean.
+ + or − −:	Member's factor score less than 1 standard deviation from group mean.
+ + + or − − −:	Member's factor score more than 1 standard deviation from group mean.

somewhat higher on Depression than is the group as a whole, though they occasionally pull the group toward Anxiety. The factor four deviations are less consistent but equally revealing. There is a significant incidence of Distress, particularly after the first phase. This alerts us to the possibility of a serious threat to the hero's initially invulnerable position somewhere around the confrontation, internalization, and separation phases, and this hunch is substantiated by our observations.

For the most part, the hero stands alone. Although he is supported and echoed by a small contingent of male followers and lesser heroes, he is emphatic in his initial presentation of himself as unique, superior to and free from all restrictions and cumbersome commitments, and capable of defending himself from any attack on his position. He welcomes supporters, but at first refuses to compromise to insure their continued respect and allegiance. As a result, the hero becomes the first major deviant in the group. His initial centrality and deviance, which last until and sometimes even beyond the phase of internalization, precipitate a widespread attack on the hero and alienate him from the rest of the group.

It is this alienation which is reflected in the burst of distress toward the end of the group, and the alienation passes only when the hero is partly integrated into the work group. This resolution is to some extent accomplished through an intensification of the attack on the hero by the independent enactors. He must ask forgiveness for his "domination" and "manipulation" of the group, he must confess that he too is capable of feeling anxious or depressed. At the same time, however, other members are able to accept some responsibility for the hero phenomenon. They have "used" him, "put him up to it," or "let him get away with it." It is the more or less successful resolution of the conflict between the hero and the emerging enactors, who, more than any other subgroup, anticipate and express the dominant mood of the internalization phase, which consolidates the work group and signals the downfall of the resistance subgroup. The resisters, unable to accept any part of the hero's program, fade rapidly from prominence and come more and more to resemble a bitter, indecisive, and fractionated opposition party. We will illustrate this developmental sequence, admittedly somewhat idealized, through a study of the career of Peter, the hero in group four.

Peter quickly rejected the dependent, distressed climate which prevailed during the first two phases of the group. In the first three meetings he was witty, sarcastic, and patronizing. He immediately assumed responsibility for some minor administrative decisions with which the group was grappling, a move which was followed by Charles' anxious warning that "this man should be noted." Peter contradicted any suggestion that the group experience might prove frustrating and unrewarding. He identified himself with Jack, the aggressive leader of the band of hunters in Golding's *Lord of the Flies,* and he was consistently hostile toward any member who attempted to lead the discussion. At one point, he interrupted an intense outburst of dependent complaining with the assertion that:

"The truly independent person is the beggar. He never works, doesn't eat too much, and never has to pay for anything. He is free from all social constraints and so is superior to all of those rich fat slobs who have to earn their living."

This classically counterdependent statement touched off a wave of angry rebuttals from Dolores, Faith, and Ross, who argued that dependency feelings could not be dismissed so flippantly. Peter ignored their protests and continued with other, equally provocative remarks, ridiculing the dependent, loyal, pleading stance which many members had assumed. He dressed in the "beat" fashion currently popular— sandals, dungarees, and long, unkempt hair. In session four, he was inexplicably absent and was discussed for several minutes. He had clearly won the attention, and the fearful respect, of his peers, but a full-scale attack on him was postponed until his return to the group.

Peter returned in session five dressed in a suit and tie. He sat quietly as the group questioned him about his absence, then revealed in a calm tone of voice that he had intentionally stayed away from the group "to see what would happen." He went on to explain that he was attempting to demonstrate the "constructive" uses of hostility and suggested that the group should be considered an unstructured experiment in which everyone could act as he chose in order to satisfy whatever emotional needs and intellectual curiosities he desired—"let's just use each other." Paul, the moralistic spokesman, pointed out the group's fear that Peter was becoming a "usurper." This led to a group-wide concern with exploitation, manipulation, and integrity. Cynthia and several other females wondered why the leader remained silent in the face of this "crude, calculating, callous" person, but Peter observed that their trust had been misplaced and that the leader would not intervene to assuage their fears.

In the next several sessions Peter presented himself as a fearless, insistent questioner of whatever caught his attention. He was scornful of any "filtering of anger through tact and politeness." He accused Carol, who had cried after being criticized by Don, of "phony dramatics." He diagnosed Don's preference for detachment as "a massive defense." He then invited the group to "attack me if you like, then I'll be able to bear down on you even harder." When Naomi announced her decision to leave the group, many members turned to the leader and requested that he take a more active role in the discussions and thus help to "hold the group together." Peter hastily rejected this motion, scoffed at Naomi's "fear of getting close to people," and argued that "the privilege of being the scapegoat should be distributed more evenly." Peter admitted that he enjoyed a free and unrestricted environment in which he could operate as he chose, and he praised the "informal" group which had begun to meet after the official class hour. He continually reminded other members of the hostility which he had aroused and urged them to rail against him at every opportunity. He assured the group that "the potential for pain isn't really too great here." Paul and Arnold, both older members, began to express a tolerant, understanding view of Peter. While stressing their own maturity, self-confidence, and stability, they contended that Peter's "adolescent antics" would soon pass and urged other members to wait patiently for the storm to abate. Peter in turn accused the older males of stifling the expression of feelings which he was trying to encourage. Several female members, led by Mabel, repeatedly asked that Peter explain himself. Finally, he consented to present the rationale for his "plan for the group."

"Hostility is a basic need in each of us, but we hide it under our masks. I'm playing the Devil's Advocate here because we have to break up this damn tact and gentility. . . . We have too much respect for feelings. Hostility is enjoyable; we all enjoy hurting people who irritate us. And maybe after we've beaten away at others we can get to work on ourselves. . . . Besides, if one feels the urge, one should just let it out. Self-control is unnecessary if you are mature."

It was through proposals such as this that Peter continued to frighten other members, particularly the more distressed females. Despite Paul and Arnold's effort to force Peter to admit that he was simply hiding his own "sensitivity" and "sentimentality," he continued to support the counterphobic notion that anything, no matter how anxiety-arousing, can be faced and endured, if one is sufficiently bold and courageous. At one point, however, he seemed depressed and said that he was "seeking pity." This surprising revelation was not pursued by the group.

This, then, conveys some of the flavor of the hero's initial presentation of himself and points to some of the reactions on the part of other members in the phases of initial complaining and premature enactment. Let us consider briefly the several facets of the heroic style which are so threatening and which provoke so much resentment on the part of other members.

First of all, the hero endorses impulse expression as the primary goal of the group. He will not accept "tact," "gentility," "apathy," or "consideration" as valuable contributions. He is blunt, forceful, and direct and will tolerate no restraints on his own verbal expression. At the same time, however, he will not permit the expression of dependency, anxiety, or depression. He does not deny the existence of these feelings but simply asserts that they must be overcome through heroic countermeasures. He provides a model of counterdependency by refusing to consider himself "just another member." He maintains an aloof, critical, scornful position and may profess a distaste for group membership and a disbelief in the desirability of cooperation and compromise, at least for himself.

He presents himself as a probing, intrusive, and somewhat sadistic interpreter of the myriad "defenses" which he finds arrayed against him. He sets himself the task of powering through them, opening the way to the buried impulses which others cannot or will not see. The phallic symbolism implicit in this kind of interpretation elicits an intensely ambivalent reaction on the part of many female members.

On the one hand, they find the hero's interpretive thrusts quite exciting, but they fear that in the end they will be "exposed," "ripped apart," or similarly ravaged, destroyed, and then cast aside. They do not know where to turn. Can they continue to trust the leader, or must they rely on one of the older, more sensitive and gentle males? Is the hero really a callous, insensitive monster, or might he one day prove to be a trustworthy, if somewhat uncontrollable and erratic partner? The hero's behavior, however, is anything but reassuring. He creates an impression of sexual competence and interpersonal "toughness" and refuses to alter his style to accommodate those who cannot match his aggressive, sexualized search for "what is really going on here."

The hero is often equated, consciously or unconsciously, with the leader. Once the first attempts to persuade the leader to silence the hero have met with undeniable failure, most members begin to sense that the leader is not totally opposed to the hero's activity. There are, indeed, many real or apparent similarities between the leader and the hero, and they are ferreted out and introduced as further proof of their underlying identity. Both occupy a somewhat special role—seemingly untroubled, unconcerned with what others think of them, interpretive, and "above the group." The hero's quest for uniqueness is, for many members, completely unacceptable. Others are more disturbed by the fact that his interpretations are not only caustic and amusing, but frequently correct. The hero seems to be controlled, though relatively uninhibited. He says what he pleases. The leader, though much less active, also feels free to change the subject at will, to talk about taboo topics, to enter and withdraw from the discussion without notice. The paranoid spokesman may announce that the hero is, in fact, a "plant" and thus represents those aspects of the leader's personality which the constraints of his formal role prevent him from displaying. Characteristically enough, the hero does not deny this report but confirms it and adds that the group is thoroughly infiltrated by other bogus members and agents of the leader. These fairly well systematized apprehensions reinforce the hero's fantasy of fusion with the leader and intensify the more diffuse anxiety of the other members. The group cannot escape the conclusion that the worst has actually come true. If there is order or purpose to the group, then it is malevolent. If there is no controlling influence, then the weaker, more sensitive members will surely be overwhelmed by the destructive impulses soon to be unleashed.

Even a counterattack against the hero holds little promise, for he presents himself as a deliberate provoker of anger. Angry attack, however often it occurs, is never fully satisfying, for the hero simply accepts it as a further indication that his plan is working. Complaints that the hero is "toying with the group" are paralleled by similar complaints against the leader, that "he is just trying to get us mad at him."

One more effective solution might be to ignore the hero entirely, but such a strategy is obviously impossible. First of all, the hero simply cannot be ignored. When he is not talking, he is involved in some equally distracting and irritating activity. He may absent himself for a session, or sit in a corner of the room, or roll his own cigarettes on a primitive, noisy machine. More important, the members cannot stop thinking about the hero any more than they can deny the leader's presence and their ceaseless concern with what he is thinking and feeling. The hero, like the leader, is soon experienced as something of an addiction. The group cannot endure with him or without him. He becomes the focus for a great deal of discussion and provides the group with many of its most discomforting preoccupations.

In summary, then, the hero's principal strategy during the first two phases centers on his efforts to establish for himself a permanent position of centrality in the group. He is at first more concerned with gaining the constant attention, rather than the affection and support, of his peers. He presents himself as the primary representative of the leader's goals, though he avoids appearing dependent and often scoffs at the leader's passivity or "defensive" retreat into silence. He often acts as if the leader were unnecessary and alternates between asserting his identification with him and seeking to replace him as the principal focus of group discussion. He is most tolerant of those who join in his attacks on the leader and the dependent and loyal subgroups and most critical of those who plead helplessness or uncertainty in the face of the relatively unstructured group situation.

It is not difficult to see how deviant the hero actually is with respect to the group's attempted solutions to the major issues of the first two phases. First of all, the hero steadfastly refuses to accept any definition of the situation which entails a recognition of many members' dependency feelings, though his manic excesses point to a less obvious need to fuse with the leader. In addition, the hero strives to overthrow early agreements, explicit and implicit, to keep firm control over impulses, and he even begins to introduce sexual topics, a step for which most members are not at all prepared. Finally, he introduces a further source of concern by equating competence in this classroom situation with the uncovering and open expression of sexual and aggressive feelings, a definition of work which clashes directly with the gentler, more repressive views of the loyal, dependent, and sensitive members, who are largely concerned with the nurturance issues so crucial in the early sessions.

The reader may feel that our reporting of these events is overly dramatic, just as we have often felt that the group's response to the hero is not entirely genuine. Why should one rather uncouth member, a stranger to most of the others in the group, have such a devastating effect on the group? It is difficult to understand the hero phenomenon unless one is acquainted with the intense anxiety which many members experience in the initial phases of the group. Fears of losing one's identity, of being swallowed up, of being overwhelmed by impulses from within and without, are commonplace. The hero, like the leader, often seems content to stand by while other, less self-reliant members are destroyed by the chaos which he has helped to create. Yet it is also true that the group ignores the hero's occasional expressions of distress and will not acknowledge the possibility that the hero might be more troubled, and the distressed members more in control of their reactions, than they appear. The polarization of the group and the deviance of the hero serve to justify the group's continued refusal to interpret group events and thus are not entirely unwelcome.

The hero's performance during the confrontation is in many respects a continuation and elaboration of his previous role in the group. He remains aloof from and critical of his peers and is persistent in his assault on the loyal, the distressed, and the sensitive. He is particularly critical of the spokesmen, whose Resistant Complaining contrasts so dramatically with his own Counterdependent Flight. The confrontation does, however, reveal more clearly two aspects of the hero which were less evident in earlier phases. As the hostile subgroup steadily mounts a barrage of Dependent and Resistant Complaining, the hero becomes more and more rebellious. This rebellion casts in doubt the assumption that the leader and the hero are in essence two sides of the same coin. Equally important is the hero's increased expression of passive yearnings and of distress, feelings which he had previously succeeded, for the most part, in denying. Since this increased expressiveness is often tentative and symbolic, it may be ignored or misconstrued by the other members, who are as yet unwilling to listen. The hero's distress becomes a major issue only during the internalization phase, but it is anticipated, to varying degrees in different groups, throughout the period of confrontation.

The departure of Naomi and the group's depressed reaction to the loss of a member touched off a wave of dependency, led by Audrey and Denise. Many of the females were beginning to flirt, as subtly and inconspicuously as possible, with the leader. There were many coy pleas for his assistance and advice. Peter, who was sitting directly opposite the leader in session nine, joined with Ross to organize a group cocktail party, to which the leader would not be invited. Peter and Ross were at first forced to battle against several female members, who wanted the leader to attend, and then against the leader's efforts to undermine the party plans with interpretation. Then, apropos of nothing in particular, Peter offered the following story:

"I read about a guy who had all sorts of things wrong with him. His mother slept with him when he was 13 or 14, and he had taken eight courses at a time, getting A's in all of them. He would go on binges when he would eat garbage. He was pretty sick. Every time he tried to have intercourse with a girl, it turned out that he was impotent, and they traced it to an experience he had had as a kid. He had been playing in his parents' bedroom, and his parents came in and went to it. Somehow his father caught him and beat him . . ."

After relating this story, Peter began to ridicule the leader's passivity and his efforts to "con" the group. He continued this attack for several sessions. He first urged the group to ignore the leader altogether, pointing out that "he leaves the room right after the bell rings, avoids us in the hall, keeps no office hours—let's just forget him." He continually reminded the group that it was being observed and tried to show that the leader was unworthy of respect: "See how nervous he is; look how his hands are shaking!" He assured the group that the leader was married (he was in fact single) and thus could not possibly have any sexual interest in a group member. On one occasion, he rearranged the tables and chairs in the meeting room to exclude the leader from the group. He initiated long periods of whispering withdrawal and reasserted his authority over the informal group, which was now meeting daily after class. He continued to probe into the personal lives of other members, but he often pointed out that the leader's nondirective style was equally "manipulative." In one session he became exasperated with the high level of thralldom expressed by the females and said to Pamela, "Don't you see he won't really talk to you? He's just tricking you into revealing more of yourself than you think you are." He threatened to form a group "militia" to "tail" the leader around town, then concluded that "his personal life doesn't mean a damn thing to any of us. Let's just let him be."

All of these tactics, which occupied the greater part of Peter's energy during the confrontation, seemed to be directed toward the destruction of the females' preconscious fantasies of intimacy with the leader. He constantly denied that the leader was the actual authority in the group. He demanded that all displays of dependency and depression be ruled off limits and labeled such expressiveness "regressive" and "unconstructive." While many members were begining to discuss affectionate feelings toward parents and parental figures, Peter continued to dwell on hostile feelings and argued that outright rebellion was the only effective way of dealing with authority. He stated, over the objections of some, that there would be dancing at the party and suggested that no one who refused to twist be allowed to attend. He specifically excluded Don, who said that he would not be forced to twist and who professed boredom with Peter's discussion of orgies, incest, and intermarriage.

Peter's efforts to replace the leader as the major focus of concern were not entirely futile. He did win some displays of allegiance, particularly from Carol and Pamela, who offered sporadic support for his rebellion. Pamela was certain that most of the females had "fallen in line behind Peter," but her estimate of his support was contradicted by some.

Peter was, on the other hand, frequently accused of being "cold" and "manipulative," complaints which echoed his own assessment of the leader. After one especially bitter attack on Don's "aloofness" and "failure to participate," Peter became depressed and admitted that his own attempt to manipulate the group was "a defense against loneliness and detachment." Cynthia, Karen, and Ross received this admission quite warmly, but most members failed to respond. Peter again turned to Don and chided him for his lack of involvement. Two sessions later, he criticized Arnold for failing to offer his therapeutic services to the group. Peter then apologized for his rising hostility and offered to leave the group if asked. The group again failed to respond, but Peter did miss a meeting two days later.

Peter's attention turned to the group's increasing concern with sexuality toward the end of the confrontation. The day after the party, he expressed relief that the leader had not attended and stated that he had enjoyed the "freedom" of the party. Other members were less defiant and seemed depressed. Many felt guilty for having come to class 20 minutes late that day. The next day, Peter suggested "group free association" as a means of overcoming embarrassment about sexual matters and began his associations with some references to the incest taboo. He was joined by Cora and Dolores, but most members chose not to become involved in the free association. At the following meeting Peter asserted, over the protests of most of the other males, that "love between homosexuals is much more passionate than heterosexual love" and defended homosexuality as a way of life. On the final day of the confrontation phase, Peter was again absent. The group devoted several minutes to an angry denunciation of him, finding no justification for his behavior in the group or for his occasional absences.

As we have seen, the hero continues, throughout the confrontation, to demand greater impulse expression from the group. More specifically, he hopes now to replace the leader as the focus of sexual as well as of aggressive feelings. He is handicapped by the fervent loyalty of many female members and takes advantage of every opportunity to point out to them the leader's inaccessibility, indifference, and impotence. He thus supports, to some extent, the hostile females who are responsible for much of the Dependent and Resistant Complaining of this phase. But he also ridicules the weaker, more apprehensive males who refuse to join in his more open and defiant rebellion and who feel sexually inhibited in the presence of the leader. The hero strives to bring together a cohesive band of brothers, with himself as the unquestioned leader, to overthrow the father. The resisters are opposed to all such heroics, and they are torn between attacking a passive, unhelpful authority and continuing to support him as the only possible alternative to the hero's domination of the group.

At the same time, the hero presents himself as somewhat more sensitive and vulnerable than he has previously appeared. It is striking that in all four groups the first person to refer to homosexuality was a hero, and the introduction of this topic seems to serve more than one purpose. It is in part simply a further elaboration of his characteristic crudeness and his gift for shocking and frightening other members. Yet the hero is admired for raising the issue. The other members, especially the males, clearly see the hero's expression of homosexual feelings as courageous, as something of which they are incapable. The hero, whose masculinity has been demonstrated to most people's satisfaction, is free to discuss homosexual attraction, while the other males are still struggling to assert their masculinity and independence or else are avoiding the issue entirely.

On the other hand, however, the hero's homosexual preoccupations are but another indication of his growing sense of inadequacy. He senses that his rebellion, with all its oedipal overtones, will inevitably end in defeat, or at least in an unsatisfactory compromise solution. He feels guilty for his domination of his peers and angry at himself because his attempt to lead the group has not been more successful. Finally, the hero's rebellion necessitates some recognition on his part of his increasing separation from the leader. While his more obvious strategies are predicated on the assumption that the leader must be overthrown and replaced, at some level the hero wishes to remain fused with the leader. He thus views the loyal, enthralled females not only as potential sexual objects who must be won over but also as sexual rivals. The hero is uncertain whether to attempt to maintain the earlier appearance of fusion with the leader to the exclusion of his peers or to organize and dominate his peers in order to carry out the oedipal rebellion. In either case, the persistence of the females' thralldom is unwelcome. It presents a challenge to his fantasy of an exclusive relationship with the leader, and threatens to obstruct the rebellion. The hero may well entertain the hope that he can, by rebelling against the leader and winning over the females, preserve his fantasied relationship with the leader, since the rebellion will at least have diverted the females' interest from the leader to himself. In fact, however, the oedipal guilt and the sense of alienation from both leader and peers is too great to be endured.

Nevertheless, the hero does not surrender his facade of invulnerability during the confrontation. Instead he alternates between further "manipulation" of the group and expressing guilt for such manipulation. Perhaps more important, the group is not yet prepared for the collapse of the hero. Other members sometimes overlook his protestations of distress and continue to view his confessions as both heroic and crude. Many have a vested interest in preserving this image of the hero as insensitive, callous, and assaultive. He continues to represent the evils of interpretation and of "going too deep," and by pointing out his excesses they justify their own refusal to work. The one subgroup which deviates from this view is the independents. To some extent, they are able to listen to the hero without becoming judgmental. They demonstrate some support and sympathy for him despite their impatience with him, and they prepare the way for his integration into the work group during the internalization phase.

Following his failure to attend the previous session, Peter apologized for his absence, which he described as "impulsive and juvenile." The group was, however, more interested in condemning psychoanalytic theory than in dealing with Peter's guilt, and he was again ignored.

Peter repeated his apology, but Pamela insisted that he was simply searching for additional ways to "run the show." Peter was supported by the leader, who felt that his intentions were honorable and that he was speaking sincerely. After this intervention, Arnold and Ross praised Peter for his many worthwhile contributions to the group. Charles, who was soon to become the sexual scapegoat, became anxious, said that Peter was not to be trusted, and moved his chair to a corner of the room. Since his chair rested on a raised portion of the floor normally reserved for the instructor's desk and chair, he ended the session by sitting above the rest of the group.

The next day, Peter argued that the group was continuing to avoid sexual issues and became angry when Carol and Paul countered that sexual feelings were "irrelevant" and "too personal." Peter attacked Charles and Cynthia for sitting outside of the group circle and refused to allow the group to proceed until they moved closer to the rest of the members. Charles refused to move his chair, though he had not chosen to sit above the other members. Carol then began to defend Peter, who admitted that he felt that he had incurred the leader's displeasure. Pamela praised Peter for organizing and leading the informal group, and Peter urged the group to "forget about" the "insoluble problem" of authority relations and to concentrate instead on sexual feelings between group members. He then demanded that each member state his own sexual feelings about the group and name those members "that you would like to sleep with." Carol agreed that this kind of revelation might someday be possible for the group but added the thought that for the present it might be helpful to distinguish between sex and affection. Peter rejected this distinction, which he considered "phony and evasive." Charles entered the discussion with a long expression of his admiration and envy of Peter's "intellectuality." Ross admitted that he had originally resented Peter, but had come to respect him for his insights into the events of the group. He concluded by stating that he "worshipped" Peter. Carol ended the session by commenting that many people felt this way about Peter but few were brave enough to admit it.

When, in the next session, Faith questioned the appropriateness of psychoanalysis, Ross, Carol, Pamela, and others defended the leader's interpretive style and said that Peter had done much to make the leader's interpretations seem more relevant and meaningful. At this point Ross noticed that Peter had not said a word, and this stirred Peter to initiate a critical appraisal of Arnold and Paul, whom he again charged with stifling the expression of feelings in the group.

When the leader pointed out the transference implications of Peter's attack on these two older members, Pamela and Audrey argued that the group had moved beyond transference and asked that the leader refrain from making further transference interpretations. Faith wondered aloud whether Peter was "lonely" or "tough" and asked if he had "the guts to stand naked before the group." Pamela returned to her criticism of Peter and asked him whether he had been "hurt by our failure to carry out your program." Peter replied that the group was, in fact, continuing to carry out his program. This rejoinder was greeted with silence, and the remainder of the session was devoted to a review of the theory of the female oedipal complex, with much questioning of its validity.

In session twenty-five, Peter joined with Carol, Pamela, and Ross to lead a lengthy discussion of Charles' relationship with his mother and his feelings about Lucy. In the following meeting, the same foursome, which was coming to constitute the nucleus of the work group, turned against Paul, the spokesman, and demanded that he allow his followers to "vote their own stock." Paul objected to their demands and argued that his campaign for sensitivity and compassion had been sanctioned and even encouraged by the leader. A timely intervention by the leader squashed his objection, and the ensuing discussion reflected the work group's attempt to rescue the group from Paul's moralism. Throughout the next sessions, the group assessed the relative strength of the forces of inhibition and suppression, represented by Paul and Don, and announced that the "era of interpretation" had arrived. Ross and Carol continued to praise Peter's initial interpretations of events in the group, which they felt had encouraged them to become more open in expressing their own feelings about the group.

In session twenty-seven, however, Peter sat quietly, seemed depressed, and wrote constantly for the entire hour, recording almost every word that was spoken. Although several members were immensely critical of this performance, for the most part Peter was praised for his leadership. When Peter was again silent in the next session, the group argued whether this silence should be interpreted as encouraging independence—"We should be able to work without him"—or as manipulation and abandonment—"He really doesn't care; he's just toying with the group again." Several members sensed that Peter was depressed and wondered what could have "offended" him so deeply. Pamela was alternately angry and supportive, and Carol felt that, "We all owe Peter a great deal. This has all been very difficult for him."

Late in the group, Peter emerged from his silence with an angry denunciation of the group, which he described as "totally unproductive." He talked of his own need to maintain an "illusion of control through detachment and manipulation . . . a combination of power and virtue that helps you keep people on strings." He longed for what he termed "a passive peace," which he felt could be found only through drugs—"only then can you cut through layers of phoniness and get down to the mystical oneness—immortal, nonaggressive, loving." He spoke, on the other hand, of the group's unwillingness to allow him to change, to assume any role other than that of the provocative, deviant hero. This touched off a long burst of depression, during which several members bemoaned the difficulty of self-change and their defensive need to prevent others from changing.

These session summaries illustrate three interrelated aspects of the hero's role during the period of internalization: his partial integration into the work group; his increasing distress and withdrawal into an angry, self-absorbed depression; and his ability to elicit not simply accusations that he has "toyed with" the group but also cries that he does not love the group, that he has abandoned it at its moment of greatest peril.

The hero's distress is partly attributable to his feeling that he has failed to achieve the goals which he had set for himself and for the group. The resistance subgroup has not been annihilated, and many topics are still considered unmentionable. He comes to the realization that the group has let him down or that he has not been strong enough to dominate it. Perhaps equally important is his growing realization that the group has, in fact, moved toward enactment, but in so doing has deprived him of his uniqueness. He is no longer the deviant, isolated enactor struggling against overwhelming resistance. Quite to the contrary, he is now a principal subject of concerned inquiry. His distress has been opened up to interpretation by the independent enactors. He has lost his centrality and his exclusive relationship to the leader; he must now endure the somewhat patronizing attention of the independent enactors, who at once sympathize with him, carry on his work, and chide him for being too militant, too doctrinaire, and too exhibitionistic.

The hero's withdrawal from the group reflects both his collapse into depression and a last desperate attempt to regain his centrality. To some extent he succeeds, for he comes to represent not only the probing intrusive image of the active leader but the cold, rejecting image of the passive leader. Whereas many members are equated with one or another aspect of the leader, only the hero seems capable of eliciting both responses. This later centrality is not, however, as striking or as satisfying as the original position of deviance, and it disappears after one or two sessions.

The hero's integration into the work group is only partial and is dependent both on the willingness of the independent enactors to accept the validity of many of his contributions and on his ability to accept the loss of centrality which they demand. In group one, Harry was less insistent on occupying a highly deviant role position than was Peter, and the independent subgroup was less opposed to his interpretations than were their counterparts in group four. Consequently, Harry was integrated into the work group with much less effort than was Peter, and the cooperation between Harry and the independent enactors was much more lasting. In group two, on the other hand, the hero continued to raise "controversial" issues well into the internalization phase, and the group's apprehension and anger subsided only during the period of separation.

Throughout the confrontation in group two, Kurt was accused of frightening the female members with his "sexiness." A massive attack on Kurt ensued, and he was again labeled "crude," "arbitrary," "aggressive," and "authoritarian." He was judged "morally depraved" and found guilty of "destroying any possibility for a worthwhile discussion."

The separation phase, which was quite protracted in this group, began with a further review of the "damage" which Kurt had "inflicted" upon the group. He responded by withdrawing for a session but returned the following day and continued to assault the sensitive ones with highly charged interpretations. He was equated with Hitler and was described as "a great charismatic leader" and "a personification of evil." At the same time, however, he began to lead the discussions and was finally goaded into delivering a lecture, throughout which he was jeered.

The summer ended with a relatively objective appraisal of Kurt's role in the group, marked by widespread guilt for having "given in" to his charisma and for having helped to perpetuate his deviance.

This study of the career of the hero provides us with one measure—though there are many others—of the group's ability to move toward work. Perhaps the single most important index of the level of work attained is the range of issues which are finally considered appropriate for discussion. A closely related question involves the degree to which the members are able to reveal and discuss previously unacceptable aspects of themselves without projecting them onto others. In no group was this move toward greater honesty and self-understanding completely successful. It is important to note that in some groups the internalization phase is characterized as much by an attempt on the part of the independent enactors to disassociate themselves from the defensive resisters and the inadequate scapegoat as by an attempt to understand what is going on in the group. A parallel consideration is the extent to which the polarization of interpretation and sensitivity can be attenuated, and the success or failure of this resolution is reflected in the hero's position vis-à-vis the group after the confrontation has been accomplished.

The Resisters: Moralistic and Paranoid Spokesmen

We turn now to the two resisters who together constitute the hard core of the resistance faction in the group. Their initial presentation of themselves suggests that they do not consider the group an appropriate setting in which to undertake or reveal personal change, and so it is not surprising that their thematic preoccupations and interpersonal strategies are relatively stable. They remain actively resistant throughout the entire development of the group, though their influence wanes after the group has passed beyond the confrontation.

As Tables 7-2 and 7-3 indicate, the factor profiles of the moralistic and paranoid resisters are quite similar in most respects. Both member types pull the group toward Dependent Complaining, Rebellion, Resistant Complaining, Anxiety, and Neutrality. However, there are several interesting differences between the two groups as well as some variability within each group.

Whereas the resisters fall below the group mean on the Enactment factor pattern, there is some tendency, particularly among the moralistic resisters, to rise above the group as a whole during the early and late phases. Our two case studies from group four, Paul and Don, are somewhat atypical in that they were both high on Enactment in one or more phases. Still, no resister was above the group mean during the most intense work period, the phase of internalization; only Alvin, a moralist, is high on Enactment during the confrontation.

The moralistic resisters are less rebellious than the paranoid resisters, though this difference is due in large part to the more loyal performances of Alvin and Paul, the two priests in the study. All of the resisters

Table 7-2
The Moralistic Resister

Phase	Member	Group	I	II	III	IV	V	VI
Initial	Alvin	1	0	++	−	+	−−−	−
Complaining	Alfred	3	−−	++	−−−	0	++	−−−
	Paul	4	++	−	−−−	−−	−	0
Premature	Alvin	1	−−−	0	−−	++	−−	++
Enactment	Ed	2	0	+	−−−	+	−−−	0
	Alfred	3	−−	−	−−	+	+	−
	Paul	4	+	−	−	0	+	−
Confrontation	Alvin	1	++	+	0	−−	++	−−−
	Ed	2	−	−−−	−−−	+	+++	−
	Alfred	3	−−	−	−−	+	0	−−
	Paul	4	−−	+	−−	−	−−	−
Internal-	Alvin	1	−−−	+	−−−	+	−	−−−
ization	Ed	2	−−	+	++	−−	+++	−−−
	Alfred	3	−−	−−	−−	+	++	−−−
	Paul	4	−−−	++	−−−	−−−	−	−−
Separation	Ed	2	+	−	−−	−−−	+++	−−
	Alfred	3	−−	−	−−	++	++	−−
	Paul	4	++	−−−	−−	−	−	−−−
All	Alvin	1	−−	+	−	0	−	−−
	Ed	2	0	−−	−−−	−	+++	−−
	Alfred	3	−−	−	−−	+	+	−−
	Paul	4	−−	+	−−	−−	−−	−−

Note: Individual factor scores for a phase are not computed unless the individual has twenty or more acts in that phase. Ed in the first and Alvin in the last phase failed to meet this criterion.

Factor Titles

I+:	Enactment
I−:	Dependent Complaining
II+:	Loyalty
II−:	Rebellion
III+:	Counterdependent Flight
III−:	Resistant Complaining
IV+:	Colleague
IV−:	Distress
V+:	Anxiety
V−:	Depression
VI+:	Involvement
VI−:	Neutrality

Symbol Key

0:	Member's factor score = group mean.
+ or −:	Member's factor score less than .5 standard deviations from group mean.
++ or −−:	Member's factor score less than 1 standard deviation from group mean.
+++ or −−−:	Member's factor score more than 1 standard deviation from group mean.

Table 7-3
The Paranoid Resister

Phase	Member	Group	I	II	III	IV	V	VI
Initial Complaining	Frank	1	−	− −	− −	+ +	+	− −
	Angie	2	− −	0	− −	+ + +	0	+ +
	Ida	3	+	− −	− −	+	− −	+ +
	Don	4	+ +	−	− − −	+ +	− −	0
Premature Enactment	Frank	1	−	− −	+ +	− −	− −	−
	Angie	2	0	− −	+ +	− − −	+ + +	− − −
	Ida	3	+	− −	−	+	+ +	− −
	Don	4	−	+	− −	−	+	− −
Confrontation	Frank	1	− −	− − −	− − −	+	+	+
	Angie	2	− −	+ +	− − −	+	+ + +	− − −
	Ida	3	−	− − −	− −	+	+	−
	Don	4	− − −	+ +	− −	−	+	+
Internalization	Frank	1	−	− −	− −	+	+	−
	Angie	2	−	− −	+ +	+	+ + +	0
	Ida	3	− −	− −	− − −	−	+ + +	− − −
	Don	4	0	− −	0	− −	+	− −
Separation	Frank	1	0	−	−	− −	− −	−
	Angie	2	−	− − −	−	+	− − −	+ + +
	Ida	3	− −	− −	− − −	+ + +	−	+
	Don	4	− − −	0	−	+	+ +	− −
All	Frank	1	− −	− −	− −	+	+	0
	Angie	2	− −	− −	−	0	+ +	−
	Ida	3	−	− −	− −	+	+	−
	Don	4	− −	+	− −	−	+	−

Factor Titles

I+:   Enactment
I−:   Dependent Complaining
II+: Loyalty
II−: Rebellion
III+: Counterdependent Flight
III−: Resistant Complaining
IV+: Colleague
IV−: Distress
V+:   Anxiety
V−:   Depression
VI+: Involvement
VI−: Neutrality

Symbol Key

0:   Member's factor score = group mean.

+ or −:   Member's factor score less than .5 standard deviations from group mean.

+ + or − −:   Member's factor score less than 1 standard deviation from group mean.

+ + + or − − −:   Member's factor score more than 1 standard deviation from group mean.

are strongly committed to Resistant Complaining, their common specialty. Two of the moralistic resisters are more anxious than the group, as are the paranoid resisters, but Alvin and Paul are above the group mean on Depression, a reflection of the guilt which the experience precipitated and which they attempted to induce in others. The resistance subgroup is clearly on the side of Neutrality, with the moralists providing the most forceful opposition to involvement with the leader. All in all, these two sets of factor profiles suggest that the moralistic and paranoid resisters are in agreement on the central issues of the group and are capable of working together to obstruct the activities of the enactment subgroup and to resist the pressures which the leader places on the group.

Although moralistic and paranoid resistance are certainly not mutually exclusive styles, we found an obvious example of each type in all four groups, and in none of the groups did a single person assume both roles for any length of time. It is not unusual, however, for one or another to monopolize the spokesman function. In group four, for example, Paul was intent upon being recognized as the major protective power in the group, whereas Don tended to abdicate and retreat to a withdrawn, distressed, and premonitory position.

It seems clear that both are capable of serving as spokesmen when the total group situation permits. Their subgroup allegiances as well as their performances over time are very similar, and they tend to support the same partial definition of work. The spokesmen are often among the most vocal members of the loyal or the complaining subgroups in the initial complaining phase. They usually dominate the resisters and the sensitive ones who emerge during the period of premature enactment. They are prominent in the hostile subgroup during the confrontation phase and can always be located among the bitter, dissatisfied subgroup in the separation period. The resisters endorse only two of the five aspects of work, sensitivity and expression. Even their support for expression is limited mainly to their encouragement of various dependent and resistant complaints against those who urge the group toward greater enactment, independence, and involvement. The career of the moralistic spokesman is best exemplified by Paul, and that of the paranoid spokesman by Don.

Paul, a Roman Catholic priest, began by spending the first few sessions seated in a raised section of the classroom, occupying the position normally reserved for the instructor's chair and desk. He offered occasional comments on the inadequacy of the leader's opening remarks and found his explanation of the formal and informal requirements of the course utterly mystifying. When the leader made it quite clear that he would not respond to Paul's indignant requests for direction, he lapsed into dreary commentaries on "the impossibility of really getting anything done here." At one point he stated that he was "going on faith" and went on to ask, "Aren't we important here? Doesn't anyone care that we may fail miserably?" Throughout the summer he bemoaned the "purposelessness and pointlessness" of the course and argued that without strong leadership the group would never get off the ground.

Paul's most effective weapon was his highly moralistic guilt inducing. He presented himself as the defender of "balanced, sane discussion," "moderation and compromise," and "respect for the rights of the individual." He was particularly troubled by the group's potential for changing people, and he demanded that all attempts at influence be forbidden. Early in the group, he expressed the fear that unjustified pressure was being put upon him to cast aside his priestly identity and enter into "petty self-revelations" and "collective examinations of conscience." He proposed an alternative program, a sharing of past and present experiences "in the real world outside of this room."

Paul's reaction to Peter's heroics was one of unequivocal dismay, and much of his guilt inducing was directed against Peter's crass disregard for the feelings of the sensitive ones. In session twelve Paul summarized his position:

"I think that some of the things that have happened here are really unfortunate. I myself have done and said things of which I was later ashamed. Authority actually makes people more responsible, because it prevents their acting foolishly. Haven't we been going too much on the assumption that we are searching only for the truth? Knowledge is not virtue."

Paul was acutely disturbed by the absence of an authoritarian leader who could insure the maintenance of a safe, repressive group climate. He felt unable to participate fully and constructively without compromising his perception of himself as a proper, if progressive priest, and the prevailing sentiment did not permit his style of polite, ordered examination of intellectual and philosophical issues. He felt that the only way for him to avoid behavior which he would later regret was to relegate himself to the somewhat unappealing role of "old preacher." He began, though not without some reluctance, to accuse the "majority" of punishing the "minority" which he represented. He complained that the helpless minority was being swamped by the "coalition" which had started to form under the leadership of Peter and pointed out that his constituency could not be expected to match the coalition's "hostility and intimidation." Finally, he turned to the leader with the charge that "the price of admission has gone up in this group. We are given only two minutes apiece every day, if we can be heard at all. I question the value of total anarchy."

During the internalization phase, the group's forays into the domain of sexual feelings only intensified Paul's sense of exploitation and abandonment. Several members' questions and criticisms made him painfully aware of what one member termed his "marginal identity as a sexual being." Faith concluded that, being celibate, he was "unsexual." He retaliated with more vehement criticism of Peter and the emerging enactors. "All of this free association is going too far. It's like showing yourself to the whole mob. This kind of verbal promiscuity must stop." He opposed interpretation as a dangerous endeavor to "expose weakness and guilt" and proposed that the group's attention should be focused on the "positive" attributes of members rather than on their shortcomings and neurotic problems. At the height of the internalization phase, he suggested that the group discuss hobbies and other personal interests and accomplishments, but most of the other members considered his proposals "boring."

Paul introduced many of his moralistic assessments of the group's development by quoting a remark of the leader's to the effect that the interpretive work of the group must never be allowed to serve as a front for malicious personal attacks on another member. He insisted that the group's increasing reliance on "wife-beating questions" had brought several members to the brink of "deep personal pain" and argued that the leader should intervene in behalf of "four unhappy youngsters" who were swiftly approaching a "crackup." He blamed the impending catastrophe on the leader, on Peter, and on the enactors, but he refused to identify the distressed individuals whom he had offered to defend. Paul's attempt to initiate a discussion of "non-genital sexuality" met with little success, the leader quietly dissociated himself from Paul's moralism, and Peter and Carol ridiculed him for not allowing his charges to speak for themselves and "vote their own stock."

Paul and Roger were the first to raise the issue of termination, and they would not allow others to escape from the growing depression which ultimately replaced the enactment of the internalization phase. For Paul, the group's entry into the period of separation marked the end of a phase of distress, and he felt more at ease in the lugubrious climate of the closing sessions. In the last session, he admitted that he had experienced an inner battle with his own "rigidities" and made reparation for his failure to come to terms with those who had espoused the leader's style of psychological inquiry. Still he defended his resistance as unavoidable: "I'm sorry I've kept so many of my original defenses, but I'm not sure that's a bad thing. After all, we must all return to the old roles and superficial relationships that our professions demand."

One might have anticipated that Paul, one of the oldest members of the group, and a priest at that, would have had more difficulty than most in adapting to a classroom situation which was radically different from any that he had ever known. It is worth noting that three of the four moralistic spokesmen whom we studied in some detail were significantly older than the majority of the group and that two of them were priests. The role of a repressive but benevolent spokesman is a familiar one for them, and the temptation to present themselves as judicious protectors is almost irresistible, despite whatever ambivalences and partial openness to new experiences brought them to the group.

As we have seen, the moralistic spokesman is primarily concerned with nurturance and control, both of which he finds are in extremely short supply. He cannot acept the leader's relative passivity or the unstructured nature of group discussions. He is particularly incensed at the hero, in whom he sees all of the destructive and chaotic forces which he opposes. For the moralist, the group offers little opporunity to pursue the kinds of interests which he values and which are most closely related to his sense of competence. As time passes it becomes increasingly difficult to comment on issues which are not directly tied to group events; the calm, intellectual discussion of the external world is deemed "evasive" or "defensive." He feels that only by sheltering and speaking for others can he demonstrate his competence in this unfamiliar and uncomfortable situation. The moralistic spokesman comes to feel that he is operating in a constant state of emergency, and he tends to argue that although nothing can be learned under such circumstances it is at least possible to salvage some self-respect and restore a semblance of dignity and order to the proceedings. He presents himself as a necessary antidote to the leader's aloofness and the hero's insensitivity. He attempts to provide the compassion and discipline which they withhold. At times he condemns both leader and hero, but he often takes the position that were it not for the hero's ruthless domination of the group, the leader would be able to lead. In the early sessions he is likely to argue that the leader is making an effort to direct the discussion. Later he joins the paranoid spokesman in making explicit the latent equation of hero and leader, thus virtually abandoning his hope that the established authority will ultimately provide solutions to the group's problems.

The moralistic spokesman is often the champion of the antiheroic functions of the premature enactment phase. He continues to exert a great deal of influence throughout the confrontation, but the advent of the internalization phase is accompanied by a marked loss of support for his style of resistance. The independent enactors' ongoing integration of enactment and sensitivity undercuts both the hero and the spokesman. The spokesman often becomes a prime candidate for the role of sexual scapegoat, and he discovers that the enactors, many of whom had previously shared his apprehension about the dangers of interpretation, now wish to have nothing to do with him. It is not uncommon for the enactment subgroup to contribute more time and energy to a repudiation of the moralist than to an attempt to understand the events which preceded and necessitated such a total rejection. Under more favorable conditions, however, the enactors are able either to move beyond their denunciation of the moralist or to give no more weight to moralism than to the many other problems with which they are faced.

Since the most immediately obvious characteristic of the leader's performance is his silent detachment, it is not surprising that his aloofness should elicit a variety of anxieties and defensive strategies. Any particular reaction is, of course, dependent on the member's unique apperception of the leader's motives. There are as many interpretations of and responses to the instructor's unwillingness to "become a part of the group" as there are individual members. Yet there is one member whose troubled response to the leader seems to arouse and reflect much of this anxiety. More often than not, the paranoid spokesman sounds the first alarm, and he then repeats his Cassandra-like warnings in the sessions that follow. He tends to equate the leader's silence, withdrawal, and "objectivity" with the most impressive and sophisticated presentation imaginable. He marvels at the leader's self-control, his imperturbability, and his knack for inducing panic in others. In this construction of the situation, the group is nothing more than a test of one's self-composure under stress, and for him the leader represents the exemplar of competence in such a situation.

The paranoid spokesman feels, nevertheless, that he is at a disadvantage. He cannot hope to equal the leader's insight into human behavior or appropriate the charisma which makes him so threatening. Unlike the leader, he has no official status or title; the leader alone has access to the experimental and academic skills and procedures from which much of his charisma is derived. The paranoid spokesman feels that he must remain as "cool" as the leader and he dreams of the day when he can entice or trick the leader into losing control of himself, if only for a moment. If only this monstrously infallible creature were to commit some unmistakably "uncool" act, then the spell would be broken and the illusion of omniscience and omnipotence shattered. His principal strategy is aimed at the maintenance of his own self-control and the destruction of the leader's "facade." There are times, however, when such an undertaking seems too futile and exhausting, when he no longer points to how much the leader is doing to influence the group but calls attention to how little he is doing to lead the class. The paranoid spokesman alternates between Dependent and Resistant Complaining, but he always demands that the leader act decisively, for good or evil, so that his intentions can be clarified and his actions accepted or opposed. Consider the career of Don, a fairly representative example of the paranoid spokesman.

In the first four sessions, Don said nothing. He sat quietly in a far corner of the classroom and seemed to be so involved in private fantasies that he was unaware of the group's existence. But in session five, the day of Peter's dramatic return from his one-session absence, Don entered the group with a rambling criticism of other members' dependency and a long, flattering description of Peter's cynicism and cleverness. He noted that both Peter and the leader were able to maintain a certain "psychic distance" from the group and expressed his admiration of Peter's early establishment of himself as a central figure.

"Dr. Dawes askes questions because he can point out things to the group without becoming involved . . . He reveals nothing of himself. . . . He keeps a certain distance away to study us for his own purposes. . . . If Peter's smart enough to stay away from class to experiment, I think that's neat."

Don continued to define work as shrewd, silent observation. Yet he frequently praised Peter's manipulative tactics and observed that both Peter and he, in their different ways, were making some effort to combat the official authority in the group. Peter's attitude toward Don was much less generous.

In the following session, Don was showered with criticism from all sides and was obliged to reiterate all that he had said before and to offer an additional explanation of his motives.

"At first I wanted to work and talk in here, but I saw that I had to repress these feelings. I need to stay up here in the grandstand, to do the minimum for the group and get the most out of it for myself. . . . It's like hiding behind a fortress. As long as you don't say anything, then nobody will have any material to use against you. If you don't stick your neck out, then you can keep a certain developed sense of maturity. I think the group brings out the worst . . . the tritest parts of people . . . I have always been fascinated by the difference between men like St. Francis and Pope John and murderers and other extreme types."

The root of Don's anxiety was his suspicion that the leader was masterminding the creation of an elaborate experimental trap in which to ensnare the trusting, gullible, and defenseless member. He delighted in calling attention to the leader's every move and in enumerating its implications for "the experiment" which was being conducted. Still, Don's early performances were characterized by repeated denials of anxiety. Although he never ceased to impress upon others the seriousness of their plight, he explicitly identified himself with the leader and argued that by imitating the leader's style he could protect himself from him. When attacked for not remembering the names of other members and for having no emotional investment in the group, he retorted that he was only following the example set by the leader, who "calls everybody 'you.'" He sometimes mocked the sensitive ones who insisted on displaying their distress for all to see and was summarily charged with being "cruel" and "indifferent." Peter, Carol, and Pamela vowed that Don would sooner or later be forced to "participate like the rest of us," and Peter needled him relentlessly for the rest of the summer.

In the eighth session Don's stand on several major issues appeared to change quite radically. After Naomi had reaffirmed her decision to leave the group, he suggested that the group be converted, by popular vote if necessary, to a lecture course. He described the leader as "a real pro . . . he spots our neurotic complexes immediately with that all-seeing eye of his." Hoping to find some escape from this menace, he demanded that, if his original request were not honored, the group renounce its official leader and withdraw into a full-scale "constitutional convention." He nominated Arnold as the person whom he would like to install as the "central foundation of this class." He accused the leader of taking sadistic pleasure in the helplessness of the group and of trying to appear more "profound" than he was. In the following meeting Don again asked for more active leadership. "Focus and direction," he stated, "are human needs. Government is part of our human nature." He identified the leader as the primary source of tension and described the group's feeble efforts to come to grips with this uneasiness as "a groping method of relieving the anxiety we feel because Dr. Dawes is not leading us." He then withdrew from the discussion and concluded that he, like the leader, was interested in learning "not about people, but scientific trends." His closing rejection of those who were attempting to effect some change in the situation was quite dramatic.

"This class is like a group of ants in a pot, trying to get out . . . a bunch of little ants running around in circles, frantically trying to solve their problems. They can't solve their problems, because they have blindfolds on."

In the next few sessions Don refused to enter into active participation. When approached he admitted that he felt "hamstrung" and "psyched out," but he defended his reticence as a "personal matter" not to be questioned or even mentioned by other members. When asked about his "responsibility to the group," he replied with "What group? We don't have any discipline here, and there is no group at this time." He preferred an impersonal atmosphere. "All of these confessions," he said, "embarrass me. I don't really like to hear about other people's problems."

After the cocktail party Don embarked on a feverish effort to seduce the leader into acting out his own impulses. He angrily described him as a "calculating enemy" and "an impenetrable fortress." He grew even more hostile, demanding lectures and "therapeutic support," labeling the leader a "stupid damn fool" for failing to provide "guidelines." Finally sensing that the leader would never acknowledge his complaints as valid, he concluded that so self-disciplined was the leader that he could even "fake acting out." He ended this session with a further explication of the strategy which he had been employing and in which he still had faith, despite his failure to elicit the "reaction" which he desired.

"This reminds me of the story of this experimenter who shut a monkey in a room and turned around to look through the keyhole and see what the monkey was doing. He found that the monkey was looking through the keyhole to see what he was doing. That's my reaction to you and the graduate student up there. Let's put you on the hook and see how you react when we play with you a little. Let's see with all of your knowledge of people and what you've learned in psychology whether you can still maintain yourself under control in that situation."

Don never found the crucial flaw in the leader's facade, and near the end of the summer he admitted that he had been foolish even to consider such a possibility. He was bitter and withdrawn throughout the last half of the group and at one point referred to the group as "a rudderless boat" and refused to "cast pearls before you swine." He would not commit himself to such an "uncontrolled organism" and continued to insist that progress was possible only if the group returned to a more regimented classroom format. In the final session, he proudly announced that he had survived the experience and was no more willing to accept the leader's definition of work than he had been in the first session. He criticized the group and the leader for "trying to change people. You can't do it if they won't help you. So forget it."

The paranoid spokesman is clearly in no position to win a popularity contest. Indeed, he usually grows increasingly hostile toward the group as the summer progresses and the enactment subgroup threatens to encroach upon his cherished privacy and ensnare him in its interpretive nets. Yet he remains an important figure in the resistance subgroup and can be counted upon to contribute his full share of Dependent and Resistant Complaining. He is the most articulate and dogged observer of what he sees as the leader's devious, malevolent influence on the group and is always among the first to reveal and explore the hypothesized bond between the leader and the hero. The paranoid spokesman summarizes, both for himself and for many less active members, the sense of manipulation, exploitation, and helplessness which the self-analytic group often evokes. He serves to define what the dangers are in such an ambiguous situation, and there are many members who, though they may not accept every detail of his definition of the situation, are drawn into the anxious, vigilant mood which he attempts to induce.

The paranoid resister is, as we have seen, intensely preoccupied with both nurturance and control issues. At one point we see him beseeching the leader to play a more active role in the group, at another we find him charging that the leader controls almost everything that happens. As a rule, he tends to favor the second perception of the leader and characteristically describes him as a powerful, cunning scientist who is not only capable of understanding what is taking place in the group but is also able to predict and even alter the future course of events. The paranoid spokesman thus makes little or no distinction between control and competence and tends to resent both as malevolent interference in the lives of passive, innocent victims.

He makes use of two major strategies and often employs them simultaneously. First, he strives diligently to force the leader to become more open in his dealings with the group. He asks not simply for structure and direction, but for more explicit and understandable guidance. When he feels that the leader is unwilling to provide the necessary support, he pleads that he at least confirm the group's accusation that he has been narcissistic and manipulative. In his more desperate and direct personal attacks on the leader, he tries to demonstrate that the leader too is human—weak, frightened, and sometimes even uncontrolled. But the leader seems to stand firm in his refusal to compromise with the forces of dependent and resistant complaint; even when he seems almost human, the cues are too ambiguous to be trusted.

The paranoid spokesman relies principally on his identification with the leader's silent, detached, observational stance, though he never abandons the fantasy of capturing the leader's self-control and reducing him to the status of a bewildered experimental subject. This second strategy is equally unsuccessful. Silence, he learns, is frequently as revealing as expression, and the leader seldom seems bewildered. Still it is striking how quickly other members notice and begin to respond to this identification and how often other members stress not the inadequacy of this strategy but their own fear of what they imagine to be a "strong, silent individual."

The paranoid resister fears and respects the hero, though the bases of this admiration vary from group to group. In group four, for example, Don welcomed Peter as a fellow manipulator and praised his cynicism and cleverness. He responded quite positively to Peter's rebellion, since for him the leader's charisma was derived less from his libidinal hold on the females than from his ability to influence the behavior and feelings of group members. Don was much too involved in his own battle with a malign, controlling authority to oppose Peter's efforts to overthrow the leader and sexualize member-member relationships. Though Peter scoffed at Don's fear of sexuality and his refusal to become involved and expressive, the major threat to the hero's strategy was posed not by Don but by Paul, the moralistic spokesman. A somewhat different situation prevailed in group one, in which both Frank, the paranoid spokesman, and Alvin, the moralistic spokesman, offered their sensitivity and succor as alternatives to the hero's charisma. In group one, both spokesmen competed with the hero for the affection of the females, and for Frank in particular the rivalry had clear sexual implications.

The Distressed Females and the Sexual Scapegoat

When one compares the factor profiles of the female members with those of the males, one is immediately struck by the relatively less consistent picture presented by the females. There were, to cite a single example, a total of nine males who were higher than the group on Enactment in every phase, whereas only two female members were equally consistent. The heroes' performances over time are remarkably similar and the resisters' profiles only slightly less so, but the female enactors, as we shall see, constitute a rather amorphous, inconsistent member type. Yet even their moderate degree of correspondence distinguishes them from the vast majority of other female members. How are we to account for the fact that, in general, female factor patterns are much more variable than are male performances over time?

On the whole, males are much more likely than females to be among the most active and central group members. Although this generalization may not hold for groups in which there are significantly more females than males or in which the males are unusually passive or intimidated, we found that a male member is more likely to become a key figure in the group, either by enacting the leader's interpretive role or by heading the resistance to enactment. A female member, however, is often destined for relative obscurity unless she happens to gain prominence by crystallizing the major issue in a single session or a single phase. One easily overlooked consequence of this lack of centrality is that it allows the member more freedom to change, or to alternate between strategies, than is permitted a figure such as the hero. The hero is motivated to maintain his position in the group, and the group also has a vested interest in his continuing to hold to a course which is deviant. This is not to say that a member such as the hero is not put under a great deal of pressure to "join the group" but only that the often less obvious demand that he maintain his deviant role, coupled with his desire to do so, tends to lock him in a role position from which it is difficult to escape. Similarly, many members rely on the spokesman to carry on the resistance for them, and this kind of reinforcement makes it extremely difficult for them to overcome their misgivings about work. The group is much less concerned with a member, male or female, who has achieved no such centrality.

In addition, we find that when female members fail to endorse the fivefold definition of work, they are more likely than males to deviate in the direction of too much dependency and too little enactment, though they may be more sensitive and more expressive than the males. Expression, and particularly the expression of distress, is not without its rewards, for it arouses both the aggressive interest of the hero and the sympathy and nurturance of the spokesmen. Participation in the loosely structured subculture of distressed individuals appears to offer many more possibilities for idiosyncratic self-expression than does commitment to either the enactment or the resistance subgroup, both of which must establish and enforce their own norms and maintain the appearance of intragroup harmony. It is thus not surprising that we find a variety of alternatives to work among the female members and the less forceful, nonheroic males and that this variety is reflected in their more variable factor profiles. Three brief vignettes will serve to illustrate this point.

Faith, the anxiety specialist in group four, frequently described the group as an extremely threatening and untrustworthy milieu, an atmosphere in which, said she:

"You might describe all relationships as taking place between a cutter and a cuttee. It's very painful and unnerving. That's why I'm so tense and shaky. Thank goodness Nature placed all of our valuable organs on the inside, where they can't be cut and mutilated. It seems to me that this group is a very dangerous place to come every day. It scares me to death."

This captures well the flavor of Faith's contributions throughout the summer. Her most persistent self-presentation is summarized by her comment that "I feel naked in here. I'm just the baby here." She described herself as immature, fragile, and unprotected. She seemed terrified by the "immense reservoir of hostility and potential for destruction in this group."

Toward the leader, Faith was openly flirtatious. She invited him to the cocktail party, coyly brought him beer and cookies the day after the party, and was very involved in a premature attempt to identify "teacher's pets" and other "favorites." In a discussion of the case of "Amy Bishop," which deals symbolically with a young girl's oedipal rivalry with her mother, she responded to one of the leader's interpretations with the excited interjection that "what he's saying is that the king is wearing nothing." She rejected both the leader and the hero as cruel and intrusive, but asked whether Peter was actually "as tough as he pretends to be." At one point, she suggested that he might be "afraid to take his towel off . . . to stand naked before the group . . . even though all of this brave talk about sex has been Peter's baby." Many of her contributions were cast in sexual terms, though for the most part this sexual imagery reflected a plea for nurturance. Her references to nakedness were in fact one way of demanding that the leader acknowledge her distress and call a halt to the psychological "uncovering" which she experienced almost as a physical threat. Faith hoped to alert the leader to the possibility that the further pursuit of knowledge might prove "harmful" to some members and hoped to make him understand how stressful the experience was for them. Faith's anxiety in the face of an unreliable leader and an abrasive hero, although not at all atypical, was sufficiently dramatic to make her a prominent target of Peter's interpretive assaults and a principal beneficiary of Paul's protective efforts.

Faith's model of work, if indeed she had one at all, was thoroughly passive. She hoped that the leader would supply "the answers," that on the last day he would renounce mysticism and say "OK, boys and girls, now this is what has been going on." She contrasted this ideal with what she perceived as the unpleasant reality of the actual situation. "It's like being in a dentist's chair. All of this probing is too personal, and the pain is destroying whatever beauty there is here." During one of the most intense battles between those who wanted to "get personal" and those who resisted or withdrew from such a program, she asked whether it would be appropriate to bring her father to the next session. Later in the same meeting, she criticized several members for dissecting the relationship which had developed between Charles and Lucy. Faith felt that "this relationship is the nicest thing that has happened here so far" and argued that "nice things shouldn't be analyzed to pieces." After the session, she revealed that Charles had previously expressed concern about her obvious anxiety in the group and had tried to reassure and support her through several minor crises in her life. For her, Charles was an ideal model of a leader—a fatherly figure who shielded her from danger. She found the official leader almost the polar opposite of this ideal, fled from his interpretive advances, and maintained an anxious, helpless stance throughout the summer.

Just as Faith specialized in the expression of anxiety, so Dolores was much given to moaning and sighs of loneliness and helplessness. One of her more positive assertions was a strong defense of apathy as "an honest reaction." The vast majority of her remarks about parental figures in general and the leader in particular were either quite depressed or blatantly manic. When unhappy, she would either withdraw completely or complain morosely that:

"Nobody here cares about anyone else's personal feelings. We should have closer contact, but how can you expect them to understand, say, that your mother killed herself and your father loved someone else? Nobody gives a damn, but they can't help it."

Much of this depression expressed Dolores' perception of the group as a setting in which "the individual must spread himself too thin. You can't really care." She often reminded the leader of her "uniqueness and individuality," often pleading with him to become "more personal." Once, when the leader seemed fascinated by Peter's heroics, she countered with, "Don't forget the rest of us; we are here too." She was preoccupied with the silent members and took their silence as a personal affront. When they failed to respond to her overtures, she sunk into an even deeper depression. For Dolores, membership in a self-analytic group was equivalent to being submerged and lost in a crowd.

At other moments, she would exclaim that ". . . things will be better. All of this will pass." Near the end of the group, she became involved in a discussion of rebirth and revelation, taking the position that "the sun will rise again; it always does." One of her most poignant denials occurred when she described the leader as a perfect father in whom she had placed her "complete faith and trust." This affectionate display contrasted sharply with her hostility toward the silent members, to whom she often turned in an attempt to gain from them some sign of involvement and understanding.

Faith and Dolores voiced hopes and fears which were shared by many other members, and particularly by their female peers. Their major performances came, naturally enough, at points in the group's history when anxiety or depression was most in evidence. They were almost exclusively concerned with being nurtured and protected. The disasters which they felt to be almost unavoidable were for Faith, exposure and for Dolores, rejection. Their fear of being abandoned by the leader was so intense that independence was simply inconceivable. Competence was for them hardly a relevant issue. Not only were they uneasy and defenseless, surely unprepared for enactment, but they showed no interest in moving toward enactment, which they dismissed as the negation of all that was kind, generous, and helpful.

This sketchy overview of the career of the distressed female suggests that the hero's deviance is only the most successful of many attempts to achieve uniqueness in the eyes of the group and of the leader. The distressed female's absorption in the state of her own troubled ego is in part an accurate reflection of what she feels. In addition, however, her expression of distress is only one facet of a larger strategy, which includes dependent loyalty and flirtation as well, designed to coax the leader into assuming what she sees as his proper role in the group: to care for the faithful and protect them from the hero and his minions. Her anguished cries for recognition betray the failure of this strategy, as well as the impossibility of realizing the deeper fantasy of a unique and exclusive relationship with the leader.

In Chapter 6 we pointed out that the principal deviant during the internalization phase is the sexual scapegoat. To some extent all of the resisters are scapegoated, but in three of the groups a hitherto inconspicuous member emerged and gained temporary centrality during this phase. The moralistic resister is reproached for his self-righteous suppression of interpretation. The paranoid resister is belittled for his inhibited, suspicious view of the leader. Both spokesmen are disparaged for assuming the role of self-appointed public defender. In its analysis of the sexual scapegoat, however, the enactment subgroup specifically addresses itself to his somewhat ambiguous sex role identity. The sexual scapegoat in these groups is invariably a male member who presents himself as very uncertain of his own masculinity. Whether through frank confessions or transparent denials, he offers himself to the group as an interesting case study.

The factor profiles presented in Table 7-4 point to a striking change over time. All three developmental summaries are characterized by a pronounced shift away from initially high scores on the Loyalty, Counterdependent Flight, and Colleague factor patterns in the direction of increased Rebellion, Resistant Complaining, and Distress in the later phases. The scapegoats appear to assume, at the beginning of the summer, a dependent, loyal, and somewhat distant stance toward the

Table 7-4
The Sexual Scapegoat

Phase	Member	Group	I	II	III	IV	V	VI
Initial	Lloyd	1	---	+++	++	---	+	++
Complaining	Hank	3	+	---	++	+	-	+++
	Charles	4	---	+++	---	++	--	-
Premature	Lloyd	1	---	+	++	++	+++	---
Enactment	Hank	3	-	+	+	-	+	+++
	Charles	4	0	++	++	++	--	-
Confrontation	Lloyd	1	--	+++	+++	---	+++	---
	Hank	3	--	+	--	++	0	+++
	Charles	4	-	++	-	+	-	--
Internal-	Lloyd	1	--	---	+	---	+++	---
ization	Hank	3	-	0	-	-	--	++
	Charles	4	--	-	--	---	++	---
Separation	Hank	3	0	++	+	--	-	-
	Charles	4	++	0	--	--	--	-
All	Lloyd	1	--	-	++	---	+++	---
	Hank	3	-	-	-	+	-	++
	Charles	4	-	+	-	-	-	--

Note: Individual factor scores for a phase are not computed unless the individual has twenty or more acts in that phase. Lloyd failed to meet this criterion for the last phase.

Factor Titles

I+: Enactment
I−: Dependent Complaining
II+: Loyalty
II−: Rebellion
III+: Counterdependent Flight
III−: Resistant Complaining
IV+: Colleague
IV−: Distress
V+: Anxiety
V−: Depression
VI+: Involvement
VI−: Neutrality

Symbol Key

0: Member's factor score = group mean.

+ or −: Member's factor score less than .5 standard deviations from group mean.

+ + or − −: Member's factor score less than 1 standard deviation from group mean.

+ + + or − − −: Member's factor score more than 1 standard deviation from group mean.

leader. They are consistently low on Enactment, and only Hank pulls the group toward Involvement. As the group develops and they become increasingly dissatisfied with the group and with their own positions in it, they become increasingly hostile and troubled and express some feeling that they are being abused or exploited. These generalizations are particularly true of the internalization phase, when they come under the interpretive fire of the enactors.

As we reviewed the career of the sexual scapegoat we found that prior to the internalization phase it is unremarkable. In most respects he is no different from many other minor members. There is, on the other hand, one distinctive preoccupation which seems to precede his ultimate deviance. The sexual scapegoat is likely to express an extraordinarily intense ambivalence toward the hero. He is impressed by and attracted to the hero but finds him too frightening and primitive to be tolerated. He often seeks the companionship of the most distressed and withdrawn females in the group, occasionally appearing as their spokesman, most often presenting himself as a fellow sufferer. He oscillates between attempting to dominate and speak for the distressed females and describing himself as even more forlorn and put upon than they. Consider, for example, the career of Charles.

In the first few minutes of the opening session, Charles suggested that the group choose a chairman "to keep things running smoothly." He mentioned his own experience with groups and described his occupational role as the supervisor of an office staffed primarily by young women. He was appalled when Peter took charge of the meeting without waiting for a formal vote. At the end of the session, he glanced toward Peter and announced rather ominously that "this man is going to be an important person in the group." Two days later, Charles became involved in a symbolic struggle with Peter for leadership of the group. Peter commented that "the real leader" in *Lord of the Flies* was Jack, who headed the most aggressive faction on the island. Charles nominated Piggy, "the genuine intellectual in the group," as "the one who actually deserved to become leader." Peter dealt quickly with this challenge, labeling Piggy "a weakling and a phony." Charles, astonished that no one came to his defense, found this discussion of leadership "disorganized and unproductive" and withdrew from the conversation.

Charles was anxious throughout the confrontation, frequently expressing the opinion that the rebellion was "getting out of hand." He sympathized with Naomi's discontent, seconded Faith's apprehensions about the level of hostility in the group, and allied himself with Lucy, an older member who said very little. His relationships with the female members were carried on largely outside of the class meetings, in the form of private conferences and mutual commiserations. While most members looked upon these tête-à-têtes, which they agreed were entirely platonic, with some bemusement, they were mentioned only infrequently in the early sessions. Near the end of the confrontation, however, Peter and Ross asked Charles to serve as chaperone for the upcoming cocktail party. While most members took this request as a joke, Charles responded with profound indignation and agreed with Arnold's refusal "to join the old men on the side lines." Charles shared Arnold's ambivalence about participating in the cocktail party. They were tempted to present themselves as spokesmen yet expressed a desire to be accepted as peers by the younger members and to play a part in the budding rebellion and the sexual liberation that might follow. Charles' reaction to the chaperone proposal touched off a wave of slightly mocking speculation as to whether Charles was beginning "to make a play for the women."

Early in the phase of internalization, Charles admitted that he had previously been jealous of Arnold and that he envied Peter's "attractiveness and intellectuality." At the close of session twenty-two, Charles again stated that he did not feel that Peter was trustworthy and moved his chair onto "the pedestal—the only safe place in the room." At the next meeting Charles continued to sit outside of the group circle and was soundly attacked by Peter, who accused Charles of placing himself "above the group."

In session twenty-five, Charles appeared with a guest, whom he introduced as "an eminently sexual gentleman who has come to select and seduce the most beautiful woman in the group." Peter suggested that the visitor leave and threatened to "tear off his mask." A little later in the session, Charles wondered aloud whether "working means uncovering personal complexes." He then described his relationship to his mother, considered the possibility that his wife resembled his mother, and came closer to relating homosexual feelings toward Arnold and Peter. The group's response to these revelations was chaotic. Several members wanted the guest to leave, but Peter now countered with the notion that he should be awarded the title of "Queen for a Day." Charles expressed a fear of "Peter's insight" and was certain that "he could just destroy me if he wanted to." Don, Roger, and Angus felt that the group was becoming "too therapeutic." The leader commented that the group was avoiding coming to grips with its dependency feelings. Roger agreed and Angus started to discuss the reading. Meanwhile Carol, Ross, and Pamela were seeking more information from Charles, but Charles could scarcely be heard, so great was the tumult which he had set in motion. Finally, Charles climbed onto the table and asked for silence. Faith asked only that Charles' relationship with Lucy be spared, but Pamela took the position that while this relationship was "the most beautiful thing that has happened here" it was, nevertheless, an appropriate subject for analysis. Near the end of the hour, the group calmed down, and the remainder of the session was devoted to a comparison of Charles' relationship with his mother and his attitude toward the females in the group. Charles thanked the group for its attention and interpretive efforts.

This discussion was not continued in the next session, and Charles did not request such a continuation. Instead, the group passed on to other, less disturbing topics, and Charles faded into the background. In the final meeting, he again expressed his appreciation for the one-session analysis and said that the group experience had been "enjoyable and worthwhile."

The sexual scapegoat, despite his own inability or unwillingness to join the enactment subgroup, makes an important contribution to the rise of that subgroup by urging the group to interpret his interpersonal difficulties. This encouragement is not always as obvious as was the case in group four, however. In group one Lloyd resisted quite strenuously an attempt on the part of several female members to demonstrate that women as well as men can be castrating. He did not, as did Charles, overrule the resisters' protest that those who express distress should be granted immunity from interpretation. Yet in the end the result was much the same, for Lloyd forced himself on the group no less than Charles.

The sexual scapegoat arises as a representative of the distressed, non-heroic individuals in the group, and the group's analysis of the scapegoat both reflects and promotes the dominance of the enactors and the demise of the spokesmen. The analysis of the scapegoat is in part an indication of the group's increasing capacity for applying what it has learned to what is taking place in the group. It also points, however, to the enactment subgroup's need to repudiate and distance itself from the dependent, inhibited, and incompetent members and to assert its own independence, potency, and competence. To the extent that other members, including those who now support enactment, cannot acknowledge their own fears of inadequacy, the analysis of the scapegoat remains symbolic and incomplete. Yet even when the scapegoating phenomenon is not thoroughly examined and understood and remains somewhat isolated from other events in the group, it signifies that an important step has been taken and that the integration of interpretation and sensitivity is now possible.

The Independent Enactors and the Collapsing Colleague

We turn now to a consideration of some key figures in the subgroup which emerges and dominates the group during the phase of internalization. It is at this point that sex role differences become particularly relevant, for male and female enactors serve equally crucial, though not altogether identical, functions during this phase. The male enactors, though often overshadowed by the hero, make an important contribution to the formation of the work group by presenting a more balanced and less alarming image of male enactment than does the hero. They often begin by supporting the hero's assaults on the distressed females and their protectors but then move toward greater sensitivity, just as the female enactors are beginning to endorse enactment in addition to sensitivity and expression. The female enactors are primarily responsible for synthesizing enactment and sensitivity. They prove that sensitivity can be employed in the service of work, but at the same time they argue that sensitivity need not be equated with abject helplessness or with a defensive refusal to permit any but the most innocuous interpretation. By remaining compassionate and expressive even while they interpret, they do much to undercut the spokesmen. By forging a more or less viable compromise with the hero, they make possible a work culture which is neither sadistic nor superficial. We shall discuss the performances over time of the male and female enactors, then pass on to a more intensive analysis of the independent enactors in group four.

In at least three of the groups there was one very active male whose factor profile, although notably high on the Enactment factor pattern, was on the whole unlike that of the hero. As the factor profiles of Malcolm and William, the two heroes in group three, are in many ways similar to those of the male enactors presented in Table 7-5, we might well have placed them in this section rather than in the summary table for the heroes. Our decision to classify them as heroes, though somewhat arbitrary from a purely statistical point of view, was based on our impressions of their performances in the group, which were more heroic than otherwise. The most significant point to be made here is

Table 7-5
The Male Enactor

Phase	Member	Group	I	II	III	IV	V	VI
Initial	Bob	1	+++	−	++	+	−−−	+++
Complaining	George	2	++	−−	−−−	+	0	−−
	Ross	4	+	−	++	++	++	−−−
Premature	Bob	1	+++	+++	+	+++	++	+++
Enactment	George	2	−	++	−−	+	++	−−−
	Ross	4	+	−−−	−	0	++	−−−
Confrontation	Bob	1	+++	+++	+	+++	−	+
	George	2	+++	+++	−−	−	−	−
	Ross	4	+	−−	++	−−	0	−−
Internal-	Bob	1	++	++	+	+++	++	+
ization	George	2	+++	+++	−−	+++	++	+
	Ross	4	++	++	++	+++	+	−
Separation	Bob	1	+++	+	+++	++	0	++
	George	2	+++	+	−	0	+++	−−−
	Ross	4	+++	−−	−	−	+	−
All	Bob	1	+++	+++	+	+++	+	++
	George	2	+++	++	−−	+	++	−−−
	Ross	4	+	−	++	++	+	−−

Factor Titles

  I+:   Enactment
  I−:   Dependent Complaining
  II+:   Loyalty
  II−:   Rebellion
  III+: Counterdependent Flight
  III−: Resistant Complaining
  IV+: Colleague
  IV−: Distress
  V+:   Anxiety
  V−:   Depression
  VI+: Involvement
  VI−: Neutrality

Symbol Key

0:	Member's factor score = group mean.
+ or −:	Member's factor score less than .5 standard deviations from group mean.
++ or −−:	Member's factor score less than 1 standard deviation from group mean.
+++ or −−−:	Member's factor score more than 1 standard deviation from group mean.

that in the one group in which a clearly distinguishable hero did not emerge, the factor profiles of the two most active enacting males fell somewhere between the typical profiles of the hero and the male enactor.

The male enactors begin by pulling the group toward Rebellion but then, unlike the hero, change in the direction of Loyalty. Only Ross' overall score is on the Rebellion end of the continuum, and even he is loyal during the internalization phase. The male enactors are lower on Counterdependent Flight than are the heroes, and one individual, George, is high on Resistant Complaining in every phase. The male enactors are all above the group mean on the Colleague and Anxiety factor patterns, especially during the internalization period when they are also most committed to Enactment and Loyalty. Finally, two of the three male enactors are well above the group on the Neutrality factor pattern, whereas all but one of the heroes is high on Involvement.

The male enactor is thus less rebellious and less counterdependent than is the hero. He is more likely than is the hero to maintain an anxious though neutral stance which does not include the expression of distress. The male enactor is less involved in a fantasied fusion with the leader than is the hero and less intent upon establishing a deviant role for himself. Such a member was Ross. While Ross was not among the two or three most influential males in group four, a study of his career demonstrates how a few males are able to preserve some sense of participation in the heroic style without renouncing collaboration with the female enactors.

In selecting the female enactors we first chose the members who appeared to make the most significant contributions to the development of the enactment subgroups, providing that each had enough acts to be factor scored for no fewer than four phases. We found two female enactors in groups one and four; group three, the group with no unique hero figure, produced three individuals. No female member in group two seemed to play an important role in the formation of the enactment subgroup. We then decided that since all but one of the members already chosen was above her group's mean score on the Enactment factor pattern for the entire summer, as indicated by the row labeled "All," any such member from group two would also be classified as a female enactor, as well as any additional such members from the other groups. But no female members of group two qualified for selection, and we found that all of the female members in the other groups had already been selected.

As has been noted, the performances over time of the female enactors are quite variegated. It would be useful, if one wished to pursue the matter further, to undertake further analyses of the data in order to differentiate two or more subtypes. This would, however, take us too far afield, and it seems more fruitful to restrict our attention to the general trends and salient exceptions reflected in the data summarized in Table 7-6.

Though two individuals, Judith and Pearl, are higher on the Enactment factor pattern in every phase, for the most part the female enactors shift from high scores on Dependent Complaining in the first two or three phases to high levels of Enactment during the internalization phase. They are staunchly loyal throughout the summer, with the partial exception of Marie, who is moderately rebellious in two phases. The most important trend on factor three is a gradual attenuation of their initial emphasis on Resistant Complaining. The female enactors move from extremely high scores on the Resistant Complaining factor pattern during the phase of premature enactment through a highly counterdependent stance during the confrontation period and end by deviating only slightly from the group mean in the last two phases. Although the female enactors alternate between the Colleague and Distress factor patterns, they tend to pull the group toward Distress. Only Carol and Pamela, both members of group four, are strongly committed to the Colleague pattern over all phases. The female enactors begin with a great deal of Anxiety, but later they begin to move higher on the Depression factor pattern and are especially depressed during the internalization period. Finally, they fluctuate between intense Involvement and extreme Neutrality in the first two phases, are clearly in favor of Neutrality during the confrontation, and swing back to strong Involvement during the phase of internalization. In the end they return to a more neutral position. Thus it is difficult to offer an adequate summary of the factor profiles of all of these female enactors, but we can discern a general tendency to move toward higher scores on the Enactment, Depression, and Involvement factor patterns, a moderate recovery from initial Resistant Complaining, and consistently high scores on the Loyalty factor pattern.

Janice's appearance in this table certainly deserves some further comment, for she is the only female enactor who is actually higher on the Dependent Complaining factor pattern than is the group for all phases. Janice, despite her increasingly high scores on the Dependent Complaining and Distress patterns and her extreme Neutrality in the last phase, was a key member of the work group in group one. Her disenchantment with the leader's definition of work was only partial; she provided eloquent endorsements of involvement and expression throughout the summer and helped to make sensitivity acceptable even to the hero in the group. She was, in addition, a strong supporter of enactment and independence in the first phase, but later, for a variety of reasons, she fell into depressed, dependent complaint. Most of her complaints in the last three phases of the group were directed not at the leader's insistence on enactment and independence but at what she

Table 7-6
The Female Enactor

Phase	Member	Group	I	II	III	IV	V	VI
Initial	Janice	1	++	+++	+	+	+++	++
Complaining	Marie	1	+	−	+++	−	+	−−
	Judith	3	++	+++	++	+	−−	−
	Molly	3	−	+	−−−	−	++	+
	Pearl	3	+	++	−−	+	++	−−
	Carol	4	−−	++	−	−	−−	++
	Pamela	4	−−	+++	−	+	+++	+
Premature	Janice	1	++	++	−−	−−	+	++
Enactment	Marie	1	−	++	−−−	+	0	−
	Judith	3	+++	++	+	++	+++	−−−
	Molly	3	−−	+++	−−−	++	+	+++
	Pearl	3	+++	−−	++	−−−	+++	−−−
	Carol	4	−	++	−−	−−	−	+
	Pamela	4	0	+++	−−	+++	−	+++
Confrontation	Janice	1	−	+++	−−	+	−	++
	Marie	1	−	+	++	−	−	−
	Judith	3	++	+++	++	−−	0	++
	Molly	3	+++	+++	+++	−	0	−
	Pearl	3	+++	+++	+++	+	++	−
	Carol	4	−	+	−	+	+	−
	Pamela	4	++	++	−	−	−−	−
Internal-	Janice	1	−	+	−−	0	−	+++
ization	Marie	1	+	+	++	−	−−	−
	Judith	3	++	++	+	+	−	0
	Molly	3	+	+++	−	−	++	+
	Pearl	3	+	++	−	−−	−	+++
	Carol	4	+++	++	+	+++	−	++
	Pamela	4	+++	++	−	+++	+	++
Separation	Janice	1	−−−	+	−−	−−−	0	−−−
	Marie	1	+	−−−	++	++	−−	−
	Judith	3	++	−−	+	−−	+++	−−−
	Molly	3	−	+++	+	+++	−−	+
	Pearl	3	+	++	−−	−−−	−	−
	Carol	4	+	+++	0	++	−	+
	Pamela	4	+++	++	−	+	+++	+++
All	Janice	1	−	+++	−−	−	−	++
	Marie	1	+	+	+	−	−	−
	Judith	3	++	++	++	−	0	−

Molly	3	+	+ + +	– –		+	+ +	+
Pearl	3	+ +	+ +	+		– –	+	+
Carol	4	+	+ +	0		+ +	–	+
Pamela	4	+ +	+ +	–		+ +	0	+ +

ctor Titles		Symbol Key	
+:	Enactment	0:	Member's factor score = group mean.
–:	Dependent Complaining		
I+:	Loyalty	+ or –:	Member's factor score less than .5 standard deviations from group mean.
I–:	Rebellion		
II+:	Counterdependent Flight	+ + or – –:	Member's factor score less than 1 standard deviation from group mean.
II–:	Resistant Complaining		
V+:	Colleague		
V–:	Distress	+ + + or – – –:	Member's factor score more than 1 standard deviation from group mean.
ʹ+:	Anxiety		
ʹ–:	Depression		
ʹI+:	Involvement		
ʹI–:	Neutrality		

saw as his efforts to form a personal relationship with the hero to the exclusion of the other members, including herself. Her collapse was not, however, as complete as Arnold's, which will be described in the next section. Janice continued to offer many helpful contributions throughout the summer, and one of her major performances is discussed in some detail near the end of Chapter 8 since it provides an excellent illustration of the integration of the five aspects of work.

Turning now to the career of Carol, the most active female enactor in group four, we find that her development in the group was characterized by an evolving commitment to work. Carol was, from the very beginning of the group, very involved in a mutually ambivalent relationship with Arnold, an older member whose career can be described as that of a collapsing colleague vis-à-vis the leader. Arnold's career was in many ways a mirror image of Carol's. Though he initially pulled the group toward Enactment and Rebellion, he shifted radically around the middle of the group and ultimately joined forces with the resistance subgroup. Extreme Loyalty replaced extreme Rebellion, and the high scores on Enactment in the first two phases gave way to equally high scores on Dependent Complaining. Taken together, these intersecting careers offer us an opportunity to explore further the dynamic constellations which enable some to work while others choose or drift into various alternatives to work.

In the introductory session, Carol's principal contribution was an angry demand that the leader push aside his desk and join the members in sitting around the large, circular table. The leader failed to respond to her demand. Arnold attempted to take charge of the opening discussion of anxiety, which began in the second session. He introduced himself as a "family man," a competent Rogerian therapist, an expert at handling such moments of interpersonal uneasiness. He assured the other members that their anxiety could be understood and mastered. Ross insisted that the group's anxiety was minimal, joined Paul in quibbling over the reading assignments, and supported Carol's concern over the pervasiveness of sibling rivalry. Carol replied that Ross was excessively competitive, but Don and Peter pointed out that Carol was equally competitive. Ross, however, defended Carol, arguing that she was "thinking only of the group's welfare." After Carol had expressed a fear of parental punishment for verbal misbehavior, Arnold described his own competence as a father. He contrasted his warm, permissive attitude toward his children with the stern, aloof father in the case which the group was discussing. Carol was ambivalent about the father's "passivity," for she admitted that it allowed the children in the case more "individual freedom" even though it deprived them of "a warm, communicative father."

Turning her attention more explicitly to the group situation, she rejected the notion that a group cannot be successful without a "strong" leader and suggested that the group nominate a member to assume the role of "group mother." She repeated this suggestion in the next session, explaining very patiently that "there is no leader here in the traditional sense of the term." She concluded that the group would have to become more "self-sufficient." She speculated at some length on the meaning of free will and determinism, then proposed that the group examine its reactions to the lack of structure in the situation. Toward the end of the third session she became hopelessly entangled in an attempt to specify how one might "express hostility without hurting others." She and Arnold encouraged the group to move toward more "open" discussion, though she was uncertain about how this might be done "without offending people." When in the fourth session several members began to express their anger at Peter, she persuaded most of them to postpone the attack until Peter returned. Ross was among those most interested in discussing Peter. Although for the most part he echoed Peter's counterdependency, if not his assaultiveness, Ross had objected to Peter's assertion that only the beggar is "truly independent." He felt that Peter had "gone too far" and was eager to confront him. When Peter did return, however, Ross entered no protest, but instead described Peter's contributions as "thought-provoking."

At the beginning of session five, Arnold apologized to Carol for his previous efforts to "set myself above you and the group." Arnold added that he also sought "an approachable kind of authority" but feared that the leader would continue to be passive and inaccessible. He then turned away from this brief lapse into dependent complaint and began to flirt with several female members. He established his age and educational background and emphasized his fear of "being put on the shelf with the old men." He encouraged the females to call him by his first name and denied any "paternal ambitions." Meanwhile, Carol fluctuated between extremely dependent and highly rebellious behavior toward both Arnold and the leader. She attempted again to prevent a confrontation with Peter, arguing that hostility might destroy the "harmony and cohesiveness" of the group. She welcomed Peter back to the group and suggested that if he would apologize for his unannounced absence, all would be forgiven. When it became clear that Peter was, in fact, "manipulating" the group, Carol called for the leader's assistance in controlling his "insincere and irresponsible" behavior. She turned to Arnold and Paul, asking that they take a "stronger stand" on the matter. When she discovered that the leader was interested only in questioning her motives, she replied with, "I know I'm being dependent, but I can't get fat on questions." Toward the end of the session, she made a partial recovery from her original dismay, and commented:

"More important than the way Peter's acting is the way we're reacting to him. Why are we reacting to him in this way? . . . Peter is an unknown element. We're not sure about him, and we're not sure about Dr. Dawes."

This moment of enactment, which occurred in the midst of an excited interchange between Peter and the rest of the group, proved to be somewhat premature. In the next session, Carol was again expressing her antipathy for the kind of group atmosphere for which she saw Peter asking, a situation in which "nothing is personal . . . I think some things aren't relevant, or at least that they're too personal and intimate to be brought into the group." Carol and Ross joined forces to defend against the leader's criticism of the formation of the "informal" group. They praised the "new group" for its "warmth," which they contrasted with the "tension" and "mistrust" in the formal group. Carol pleaded with Don to join the informal group, and Arnold provided a long summation of a *Reader's Digest* article on the virtues of self-control and a "more studied reaction" to situational pressures.

At the next meeting Carol apologized to Arnold for having "overreacted" to his "protectiveness" but concluded her remarks by casting doubt on his emotional stability and his "maleness." She castigated Don for having called her a "misguided fool" and for having described her as "competitive" and resentful of Arnold's position of leadership. This attack had driven her to tears at the end of the previous hour. She retaliated by pointing to Don's "insensitivity" and his cruel indifference to the inadequacies of others. Ross reaffirmed his admiration of and support for Carol. Carol ended the session by calling out to Arnold: "Arnold, Arnold, I can't get in touch with you . . . I can't seem to make you understand what I feel." After this session, Arnold withdrew from the group, and said very little until session twelve.

In the eighth session, Carol stated quite forcefully that the leader should "let us have the freedom to sit wherever we choose." She refused to allow Lucy, who was making her first effort to participate, to finish what she had to say. She continued to defend the informal group, then sided with Peter in attacking Angus and Roger for "wanting to take over the group." When Don observed that the leader was a psychiatrist whose services might be of some value in time of need, she retorted that "Freud analyzed himself."

Carol's behavior throughout the first two phases of the group was, as we have seen, characterized by an intensely ambivalent attitude toward male authority. Most of her contributions early in the summer reflected her attraction to and mistrust of both "active" and "passive" older men. Her remark, somewhat later in the group, that although she resented her "dominant" mother's "interference" in her life she was "never able to get along with my father either" sheds some light on the bases of her complex interactions with the males in the group. Her sporadic bursts of counterdependency were at times genuine efforts to escape from paternalistic overprotection, at times veiled complaints that the leader was too distant and unconcerned. When she urged him to surrender his official role and "join the group," she was asking not just for "freedom" but for a warm, personal relationship and for unconditional acceptance. For Carol, however, ambivalence toward authority was further complicated by a desire to become as central a figure in the group as was any male. It was difficult for her to proceed directly toward this goal without feeling guilty about being too competitive or assertive. It was necessary for her to devise less obvious strategies in order to become a key figure in the group.

Whereas she realized that she could not gain a great deal from the group experience if she did not defend her opinions and voice her grievances, Carol was at first unable to deal with the accusation that she was overly aggressive. It was this negative image of herself which Don played upon by pointing out that her rejection of Arnold's support was not entirely counterdependent; he suggested that it was also an attempt to undermine Arnold's bid for leadership. Don accurately assessed the significance of her suggestion that a group mother be nominated, though he did not anticipate the intensity of her latent guilt over the "unfeminine" tactics which she feared might be required. Her brief flight into tears, however, served to demonstrate how fragile and feminine she really was. Only Don and Peter remained unconvinced.

Carol's frantic attempt at reparation with Peter was only partly due to her desire to avoid the eruption of hostility. She also foresaw the development of his heroic centrality and hoped that he could be persuaded to abandon his deviant stance. Her move toward Arnold in search of a protector was in part genuine but also helped to pit male against male in order to attenuate the salience of any individual male. Toward the end of the premature enactment phase, she alternated between pleading for Arnold's understanding and allying herself with Peter in his fight against Arnold, Paul, and their nonheroic supporters.

Carol thus experienced many of the difficulties which were encountered by Faith and Dolores. She was disturbed to find that the leader intended to maintain his distance, withhold his advice, and ignore the members' requests for more direction and support. She was uneasy about Peter's demand for freer expression of hostile feelings and was tempted to accept the sanctuary offered by Paul and Arnold.

She was, on the other hand, much more ambivalent about settling into a dependent, distressed role than were Faith and Dolores. She was more counterdependent and more ambitious than were most of the other female members. Even more important, she did not simply flee from the hero but sought instead to come to terms with him, first by attempting to minimize his influence in the group, then by joining with him to overrule the nonheroic males. Even by the end of the premature enactment phase she had clearly spurned the nurturant attention of Arnold, though she had by no means resolved her disagreements with the leader or with Peter.

As for Arnold, Carol's ambivalent response to his protectiveness, coupled with his indecision, vitiated his initial efforts to present himself as a trustworthy spokesman. After Carol's counterdependency had triggered declarations of self-sufficiency by Pamela and Doris, Arnold tried to "come down off the pedestal," a move which only intensified his dilemma. Carol's alternately seductive and emasculating response proved to be the blow from which he never recovered. He withdrew from active participation in the group and never again presented himself as a strong paternal figure.

In session twelve Arnold again spoke freely. He admitted that the group's unmistakable lack of enthusiasm for his observations and suggestions had made him feel "ignored and hurt, and so I withdrew." Two meetings later, he asked that he be "allowed" to alter his role and "to be just myself" without fear of "punishment or rejection." He was encouraged by the leader's support for expression and asked, "Should this group be a kind of individual soul-baring which ultimately leads to therapy and catharsis?" After explaining his anxious withdrawal following Carol's questioning of his masculinity, he announced that he had concluded the first of many "confessions." Although this pronounced transition from seeming self-sufficiency and enactment in the first two phases to a dramatic collapse into dependent complaining is unusual, it is understandable when viewed in the context of Arnold's changing perception of the situation. In the beginning he had introduced himself as a professional counselor, a pillar of strength, a man who helped others and kept his own difficulties to himself. Later, however, the group's rejection of his services and the leader's refusal to reward him forced him to abandon this strategy. He came to espouse a diametrically opposed conception of a good member—needy, dependent, loyal, fully and honestly self-expressive. He saw rather quickly, however, that the leader's response to such expressiveness was ambiguous. Though he obviously supported expression, the leader was not prepared to guarantee individual attention or group acceptance. Arnold then concluded that the leader was "too calm and cold to be a real person. . . . He's too neutral and overpowering."

In one of the group's last sessions Arnold was able to make an explicit comparison between his father and the leader. He spoke at some length, emphasizing his desire for a relationship with a warm, loving paternal figure. He had at first tried to present himself as such a figure but had been unable to sustain his nurturant attitude toward others when the leader failed to reciprocate. He remained a more or less consistent member of the resistance faction throughout the summer. Near the end of the group he was almost totally absorbed in an angry attack on Peter, whom he charged with insincerity and blatant indifference to "the progress of the group." He fluctuated between assailing the leader with numerous complaints and making reparation for those complaints.

Much of Arnold's behavior was guided by the implicit assumption that the purpose of the group was to demonstrate concern for others and to assist those who felt unable to endure the stresses of group life.

This equation of nurturance and competence, although common to many members, is particularly characteristic of the spokesmen and of other aspirants to that role. Arnold's career, and especially the striking role reversal midway through the group, illustrates this equation and its consequences with exceptional clarity.

Returning for a moment to Ross, we see that in the first two phases he remained on the periphery of the group and did not become involved in most of the battles which were raging around him. He chose to avoid any direct confrontation with the leader by withdrawing into the informal group, with its relaxed and "noncompetitive" atmosphere. He came close to challenging Peter on several occasions but preferred for the most part to support rather than to take exception to his heroics. It is worth noting, however, that Ross did begin to move toward Carol, even though she began to undercut him as part of a broader plan to eliminate all of her male rivals.

While the group moved into the phase of confrontation Carol was finding it difficult to contend with the mixed feelings which Naomi's departure had aroused. She felt guilty for having taken up so much of the group's time with her own problems and concluded that she had been primarily responsible for "forcing Naomi out of the group." The realization that her need to stake out a central position in the group had made some members feel overwhelmed or out of place was only reinforced by Don's reminder that she was "just as dominating as Peter." Still, she did not fail to contribute to the growing hostility of the phase. She delighted in the whispering withdrawal initiated by Peter and joined with him in denouncing Naomi as "too sensitive and shy . . . she was just afraid of people." She hailed Peter as "the big man" in the group and conceded that her attempt to draw a distinction between "personal hostility" and "getting mad at people's behavior" had been futile. Several members pointed out that she had virtually abandoned her earlier insistence on tact and consideration. Now, however, she became concerned with the difference between "sex" and "affection," while Peter argued that this distinction was equally absurd.

Carol criticized the leader for mumbling and for not explaining the purpose of the tape recordings, then apologized and invited him to the cocktail party. After observing that he would probably be unable to attend because of "his duty to avoid one-to-one relationships," she decided that she had "put too much pressure on him by calling attention to his special role." After the party, she teamed up with Don to "get Dr. Dawes shook up." She reprimanded him for "not sharing your feelings with us as we share ours with you." She denied that the group had behaved "childishly" at the party. When the leader asserted that nothing particularly exciting had taken place at the party, she began to flirt with Arnold and suggested that there had been a great deal more than flirting at the party. She agreed with Peter's comment that "all we need is to get rid of Dr. Dawes."

Ross was active in planning for the party but was uneasy about the possibility that "something might get started." When Peter asked what dance music would be available, he offered only the "Nutcracker Suite" and suggested that Charles come as a chaperone. On the day of the party, he brought a young female guest to the group and introduced her as his date for the party. He accused Peter of being "too rebellious" but admitted that his attempt to start a second informal group, in addition to what had by now become "Peter's group," had been unsuccessful. Still he denied that he was in any way competing with Peter and said that he agreed with "most of what he says in here."

Early in the internalization period, however, Ross admitted that he "worshipped" Peter and praised him for his interpretive contributions. He discussed at great length the intense envy which had prompted him to organize his own informal group in opposition to Peter's daily gathering. At the same time, he described his ambivalent attitude toward the leader and considered the possibility that, unable to defeat either the leader or Peter "at his own game," he had tried to channel all of his energy into the activities of the informal group, in an attempt to avoid a more open confrontation with the leader and with his peer rivals. Ross was now able to urge others not to disregard everything that Peter said but to evaluate it as dispassionately as possible. Even Arnold was moved to confess that "I envied Peter for seeing things I didn't see. It's not that they weren't there."

All during the confrontation Carol worked to reconcile the polarities and inconsistencies which troubled her as much as they did anyone in the group. Eventually she was able to express and to permit others to express feelings which had at first seemed too personal or destructive even to be mentioned. After swinging back and forth between dependent complaints and counterdependent denials of distress, she became more confident of her capacity to work without overt, tangible rewards from the leader. She found that she could hold her own ground without the assistance of Arnold or Paul, yet no longer found it necessary to interrupt or ridicule them. Most important, she moved beyond her initial oedipal preoccupation with the leader, joined Pamela in asserting that the group had overcome its "authority problems" and had entered the stage of "member-member relationships," and clearly shifted her allegiance to Peter and Ross. The last moments of flirtation with the leader occurred late in the confrontation phase, and were accompanied by a rather defiant decision to address the leader by his first name. The leader of group four was, despite his uneasiness about his continuing influence in the group, unwilling to acknowledge the changes that were taking place in the libidinal economy of the group. The hostile, counterdependent, and defensive quality of the female enactors' assertion of independence was in part due to their need to overcome their own dependency and sexualized submissiveness, but it also served to counterbalance the leader's rather overdetermined insistence on interpreting only dependency feelings whenever the increasing sexualization of member-member ties became especially apparent.

In session twenty-three Peter demanded an explanation of the relationship which had developed, largely outside of the group, between Carol and Ross. For a while it looked as if Carol and Ross might side with Arnold and Paul in citing this demand as another instance of Peter's "too personal" approach. Instead, they related some of their feelings for one another, indicated how their relationship had affected their performance in the group, and argued that the group would lose a great deal if it continued to deny the relevance of such pairing activity. Two days later Charles became the center of attention, and shortly thereafter Peter's role in the group received intensive, insightful, and sympathetic scrutiny.

It should by now be clear that the independent enactors encounter all of the interpersonal conflicts that tend to block other members, though they somehow come closer to solving their own variants of these common problems than do the hero, the resisters, or the more intransigent distressed members. We have, however, no independent measures of "ego strength" or "tolerance for ambiguity," no indexes of "adjustment" or "interpersonal competence." Nor are we in a position to present any detailed information on the childhood histories or concurrent extragroup functioning of these members. We thus have no intention of, or justification for, relating their performance in the group to any such traits, attributes, or characteristics. We have not, of course, refrained from sharing with the reader some of our own clinical impressions and inferences, but we do feel that it would be premature and even misleading to cast them in the form of absolute, unconditional statements or general principles.

Implicit in all of this is our awareness of the fact that membership in a self-analytic group does not mean the same thing to every individual, and there is no reason why it should. For some members the group experience provides an opportunity to move in directions which we tend to think of as mature and beneficial for the group. In studying the careers of the independent enactors we arrived at the conclusion that not only did they work for and achieve some degree of personal growth, but that their growth contributed greatly to the progress of the group as well. Yet it is in some sense true that a group needs heroes and resisters just as much as it requires members who can integrate disparate and conflicting conceptions of work and reconcile the polarities which split the group. Moreover, it may well be that the personal growth which we observed was only illusory or too isolated to be more than ephemeral. We have, in addition, some reason to believe that the collapsing colleague, Arnold, gained at least as much from the group as did Carol and Ross. The summer's experience seemed to make him more aware of the disruptive patterns in his life, less afraid of expressing his feelings, and more willing to seek professional assistance in the future. Most of the older members, in fact, found the self-analytic group a particularly threatening and stressful experience. More committed to their professional identities and more concerned with maintaining their status and personal dignity, they were less adaptable in the new situation than were the younger, less constricted and self-conscious members. Despite the fact that the group met every day, the total time period was still quite short. It is possible that the older members need more time to open up, to examine their own assumptions and rigidities, and to enter into the long process of personal change. Without belaboring the obvious, then, it is clear that the self-analytic group is sufficiently unstructured to allow different members to make different uses of it. For some, it is simply the wrong group at the wrong time and under the wrong conditions.

✿   ✿   ✿   ✿   ✿

Thus far our discussion of the various individual careers has proceeded in a somewhat segmented fashion. It may be useful now to compare six of the member types examined in the earlier sections of this chapter to determine which factor patterns characterize each and, more specifically, which differentiate it from the others. We propose to contrast the performances of the hero, the moralistic resister, the paranoid resister, the sexual scapegoat, the male enactor, and the female enactor.

Our analysis of the six member types was based on a pooling of the comparable members from the four groups, those whose factor profiles were presented in Tables 7-1 through 7-6, and an examination of the differences between member types over all phases, together with the significant changes over time. The association between the six types to be discussed and the six factors on which they may be compared is shown in Table 7-7, which shows the mean deviations in terms of

Table 7-7
Mean Factor Scores by Member Type

Member Type	Factor					
	I	II	III	IV	V	VI
Hero	.75	−.72	.95	.00	−.32	.49
Female Enactor	.34	.80	−.23	.14	.10	.15
Male Enactor	.94	.33	.00	.66	.26	−.29
Paranoid Resister	−.39	−.56	−.50	.06	.42	−.57
Moralistic Resister	−.32	−.11	−.80	−.12	.20	−.62
Sexual Scapegoat	−.54	.32	.10	−.29	.27	−.32
ω^2	41%	34%	36%	7%	5%	14%
p	<.001	<.001	<.001	<.05	<.05	<.01

Factor Titles

I+: Enactment
I−: Dependent Complaining
II+: Loyalty
II−: Rebellion
III+: Counterdependent Flight
III−: Resistant Complaining
IV+: Colleague
IV−: Distress
V+: Anxiety
V−: Depression
VI+: Involvement
VI−: Neutrality

standard deviation values for each factor by member type over all sessions. The statistic ω^2 (cf. Hays, 1963), which appears at the bottom of the table, is a rough estimate of the percentage of the total variance of each set of factor scores accounted for by the sixfold typology. This statistic and the significance levels shown in the table are based upon one-way analyses of variance.

It is not at all remarkable that the six member types are statistically different from each other. What would have been remarkable, and most discouraging, would have been to find no reliable differences among these sets of members who played such dissimilar roles in their respective groups. What we learn from these results is that the differences among the member types on all six factors may be discussed with reasonable confidence that we are not straining to make sense out of random numbers, and, further, that factors one, two, and three are the main factors which differentiate among the various types of members. We shall now attempt to summarize what these data suggest about each class of members, how these portraits distinguish among the member types, and we shall add, whenever appropriate, some indication of the important time trends which are masked by these data over all phases.

The now familiar picture of the hero emerges as we find him the most rebellious, the highest on Counterdependent Flight, and, at the same time, second only to the male enactor in assuming the leader's interpretive role vis-à-vis other members. In addition, the hero is the highest of all six types on Involvement and the only type which, on the whole, is more depressed than anxious. The hero's rebelliousness contrasts sharply with the female enactor's loyalty, although it should be noted that the cleavage is marked only in the first three phases and that both types shift toward the group mean during the internalization and separation phases. The additional polarization between the hero's strident counterdependency and the female enactor's resistance and mistrust is also an early phenomenon that ends with the confrontation. In contrast to the male enactor, the hero is not only more rebellious and involved, but he is also considerably lower on the Colleague factor pattern. It is especially during the internalization phase that the male enactor is likely to be higher on the Enactment, Loyalty, and Colleague factor patterns than is the hero.

The male and female enactors, whose importance in creating the work group during the internalization period has been stressed repeatedly in this chapter, approach this phase from rather different directions. The male enactors tend to begin on the rebellious end of the continuum, but becomes more loyal, whereas the female enactors become slightly less loyal as time passes. The female enactors, as they move toward centrality in the postconfrontation work group, become less anxious and more depressed; it is this trend, together with their higher scores on Involvement and generally lower scores on the Enactment and the Colleague factor patterns, which differentiate the female enactors from their male counterparts.

The contrast between the hero and the two types of resisters is informative; despite the fact that all three types are more rebellious than loyal, in addition to their rebellious tone the resisters are the principal advocates of dependent and resistant complaint. Furthermore, the resisters are generally anxious and neutral, whereas the hero is depressed and involved with the leader.

Looking simply at the two types of resisters, several differences are evident. The paranoid resister, who is more likely than the moralistic resister to lead the full scale attack on the leader during the confrontation phase, is characterized during this phase by extreme values on Dependent Complaining, Rebellion, and Resistant Complaining. The moralistic resister picks up the refrain during the internalization period, although both resisters are extremely anxious and distant in this phase. The moralistic resister moves in exactly the opposite direction from the female enactor, beginning with a more intrapunitive, depressed stance and ending with an anxious, extrapunitive attitude toward the leader and the enactment subgroup.

The career of the sexual scapegoat even prior to the internalization phase in which he and the moralist become the objects of the group's not altogether benign attention is rather different from any other member type. His hallmark in the early phases is Dependent Complaining, but this is paired with the Loyalty rather than the Rebellion factor pattern. During and after the period in which the scapegoating occurs his performance shifts away from Loyalty and Involvement with the leader and toward an understandable expression of Distress.

In summary, then, we have attempted to describe from several perspectives the member types who join together to form the principal subgroups first presented in Chapter 6. We have pointed to the early fragmentation of the group along several dimensions, explored the forces which polarize or unite the various member types and subgroups, and, hopefully, shed some light on the antecedents and consequences of work in a self-analytic group.

Some Relevant Literature on Interpersonal Styles, Role Differentiation, and Typologies

The vast majority of theoretical and empirical studies of role differentiation and interpersonal styles in the small group field have not focused as closely as has this analysis on the member-leader relationship. However, we have found that an individual performance cannot be properly scored or completely comprehended unless one has some knowledge of the member-member relationships operating simultaneously and some notion of the ways in which member-leader and member-member dynamics are interwoven. As this chapter has demonstrated, we have related individual performances over time to changing thematic concerns, subgroup affiliations, and attitudes toward the several aspects of work. Only by viewing the member-leader interaction in the broader context of group development could we come to some understanding of the various members' careers. It is our contention that this and other studies are comparable in many respects, and we shall consider some of the correspondences and disagreements which have impressed us.

Many early analyses of role differentiation in small groups sought to identify the personality traits or interpersonal orientations of the peer "leaders" who seemed to emerge in such settings. Gradually, however, researchers became somewhat disenchanted with this approach to the problem and turned their attention to more complex conceptions of leadership and more sophisticated techniques for evaluating the interrelationships among personality, situation, and performance (Gibb, 1954; Mann, 1959; Couch, 1960). In recent years leadership has often been equated with a constellation of functions, essentially invariant from group to group, which may be performed by several members, or by different members at different moments in the group's history. Arsenian, Semrad, and Shapiro (1962), for example, point to "cohesion" and "dispersion" as the two "integral functions" in small groups and argue that any number of more or less interchangeable "billets" or roles may discharge these functions.

Perhaps the most comprehensive and systematic theoretical position yet advanced is that derived from the basic distinction between "instrumental" and "expressive" goals. Benne and Sheats (1948), Bales (1953), Slater (1955), Parsons and Bales (1956), and many others have noted the importance of the instrumental-expressive role differentiation in a variety of groups and have described the roots of this differentiation in the family. Benne and Sheats were among the first to draw a distinction between "group task roles" and "group building and maintenance roles;" this fundamental dualistic typology, which is at the heart of Bales' (1950, 1953, 1956) contributions, is by now quite familiar. There has always been some question, however, about the status of various "individual" and/or "deviant" roles which have been observed in small groups. Slater (1958) is one of several writers who have commented that increasing group size and high levels of frustration and intragroup conflict are frequently accompanied by further role differentiation. But it is not clear what course this further differentiation is expected to follow, and there is some uncertainty as to whether the newly differentiated roles can be considered "functional" in the same sense as the "task" and "social-emotional" leaders originally described.

Dunphy (1964), in a study of two Social Relations 120 groups which ran for a full academic year, employed the General Inquirer (cf. Stone et. al., 1962) to analyze the group members' perceptions of central figures in the group, including the leader. He discovered five principal roles or "role images" common to both groups and found that they were differentiated early in the group and persisted in a relatively stable fashion throughout the group's development. He came to the conclusion that two of these role images corresponded fairly closely to those of the instrumental and expressive leaders. The instructor was identified as the task leader, and a loyal female occupied the position of social-emotional leader (sociocenter). The other three roles—"aggressor," "scapegoat," and "seducer"—appeared to reflect the partial breakthrough of the sexual and aggressive drives which the "normative structure" of the group was at times unable to suppress.

Though we do not wish to overstate the parallels between Dunphy's findings and our own, several similarities are apparent. As in our study, the role differentiation which he documents was for the most part discernible even in the first phases of the group, though there were some important changes over time. Dunphy raises the possibility that there are major roles other than those of the task and social-emotional leaders which are worthy of study and argues that these roles are not necessarily the result of further differentiation of the initially amorphous roles of the task and social-emotional leaders. Most important, he views the entire constellation of roles as mirroring the group's attempt to establish an acceptable level of impulse expression. The role specialists are described as "actors" whom the group encourages to play out the central conflicts and polarities within the individual members. Some members press for more "personal" involvement or freer expression of hostile feelings; others demand a minimum of involvement and a maximum of impulse control. One salient difference between the two studies is that we found the male and female enactors to be agents of compromise and resolution, whereas none of Dunphy's role types seemed to serve this function in any consistent way. Thus, although Dunphy's types are not identical to ours, we do conceptualize in much the same manner the basic issues in the group and the major conflicts between the various role types.

Equally stimulating though less empirically grounded contributions have been offered by writers more identified with the group psychotherapy and sensitivity-training traditions than with academic psychology. Redl (1942) introduced the concept of the "central person" who serves as a "crystallization point" for other members. Redl expanded upon Freud's (1955b) model of leadership and delineated a number of paths to centrality. Some years later Redl (1959) questioned the assumption that performance can be effectively predicted from a knowledge of personality characteristics and argued that the phenomenon of "role suction" is frequently the prime determinant of performance. A more explicitly interactional point of view has been put forth by Stock, Whitman, and Lieberman (1958), Whitman and Stock (1958), and Whitaker and Lieberman (1964). These authors have developed a theoretical framework based in part on French's concept of "focal conflict." They have presented numerous illustrations of the interrelationships between individual "nuclear conflicts" and "group focal conflicts." Their treatment of deviant members is particularly helpful, for they show how the deviant threatens existing group "solutions" to focal conflicts and necessitates further compromise measures in order to maintain the group's sense of consensus and solidarity.

A few authors (e.g., Frank et. al., 1952; Kaplan and Roman, 1963) have described salient member types in psychotherapy groups. Bion (1961) makes some mention of "flight-flight" leaders who seem similar to the moralistic and paranoid resisters we have described. On the whole, however, the group psychotherapy tradition does not seem to have generated much interest in typologies. This generalization, is almost equally applicable, however, to the other traditions. Most typologies of small group members tend either to deal with only two or three types or to offer skeletal catalogues without much attempt to describe the various types in any detail or to explore the interrelationships among them. Dunphy's study of two self-analytic groups is one important exception, as is the work of Bennis and Shepard (1956) and Stock and Thelen and their co-workers (Stock and Thelen, 1958).

Bennis and Shepard's (1956) discussion of group development notes the early split between the "dependent" and "counterdependent" members, with each dominating a subphase of the group. Similarly, the group later polarizes around the intimacy issue, and the most conspicuous members in this phase are the "overpersonals" and the "counterpersonals." Although the authors do not trace the subgroup affiliations of these members over time, it is clear that in each stage the central polarity in the group is between the two "conflicted" subgroups who cannot tolerate one another's efforts to find a solution to the problem. It is the "unconflicted" members who emerge at each stage and encourage other members to forge a viable compromise between the two extreme positions. We have described the role of the independent enactors during the internalization phase as similar to that of the unconflicted members, but we have found that their careers are far more varied, and more conflictful, than Bennis and Shepard have suggested.

The work of Stock and Thelen and their associates is too complex to be reviewed in much detail here. They begin by operationalizing Bion's (1961) concepts and then apply them to the analysis of interpersonal styles, subgroup formation, group problem solving, and patterns of individual and group change. One aspect of their research is particularly relevant. Stock and Hill asked members of two training groups to sort descriptive statements in order to obtain a self-descriptive Q-sort from every member. The Q-sort data from each group were factor analyzed, and these factor analytic data were used to determine the structure of "self-perceptual subtypes" in each group. At least one of the groups was characterized by a subgroup structure similar to the one which we have described. This group was dominated by a struggle between several members who expressed "a strong need for intimacy and clash" and who worked to establish "very wide limits on the expression of emotionality in the group" and an opposing subgroup which demanded more controlled, impersonal interaction (1958, p. 215). The other, more homogeneous group demonstrated a greater capacity to resolve conflicts. Although Stock and Hill did not study the developmental histories of these groups in great detail, they do note several of the same polarizing tendencies and subgroup splits which we have observed.

Many workers in the academic, sensitivity-training, and group psychotherapy traditions appear to share our conviction that we must move beyond earlier conceptions of leadership and begin to identify and study a variety of central figures in the group as well as the principal subgroup formations which occur at different phases in the group's development. We do feel, however, that it is important to maintain some distinction between the analysis of the relative positions of major members or member types and the examination of shifts in subgroup structures. Several of the member types which we have discussed were at one point or another either allied with no particular subculture or not clearly involved in the central conflict with which the group as a whole was preoccupied. Yet these periods of deviance or disengagement are certainly crucial for our understanding of the individual career. Even more important, we have been constantly reminded of just how necessary it is to look closely at change over time if one wishes to understand either subgroup formation or individual careers. The hero and the resisters, for example, can be identified early in the group; the independent enactors emerge more slowly; and the sexual scapegoat's centrality is limited to a single phase or even to a single session. Without a careful study of such phase-by-phase developmental trends, we could not have made much headway in our analysis of the changing subgroup structure, the most salient member types, or the subtle interrelationships among subgroups and central figures.

Chapter 8

The Determinants of
the Member-Leader Relationship

Our discussion thus far has demonstrated the usefulness of an act-by-act scoring system for examining various aspects of the member-leader relationship. It is now time to put together the pieces of this intricate puzzle. The central question of this chapter is: What determinants of an individual's behavior need to be considered if one is to approximate a full analysis of the member's behavior? We shall, as before, concentrate on the issue of why individuals and groups differ in their capacity and willingness to work. To the limited extent that new data will be introduced into this chapter, it will entail presenting some of the differences between groups which have thus far been ignored in favor of showing the uniformities across the four groups under study.

We propose to look at ten sources of variation in the member-leader relationship, each of which, if altered, can produce major changes in the observed behavior of the member. Figure 8-1 is a sketch of this analytic scheme, and there is at least some temporal or causal progression implied by the location of each component. The figure suggests that we should look at the individual as he enters the group to determine what needs, experiences, and expectations will affect his behavior in the group. However, given the actual nature of the new situation and the member's apperception of this reality, the initial behavior of the new member reflects both the transfer of his habitual style and his decision regarding how he should present himself in the new situation. Any full analysis of the member-leader relationship should involve a consideration of the leader, his conception of the professional role, and his definition of work. As the group moves along, cliques develop, a history is molded, and the groups all seem to arrive at a point of maximum frustration, polarization, and impasse. The

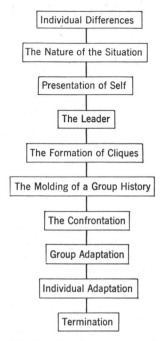

Individual Differences

The Nature of the Situation

Presentation of Self

The Leader

The Formation of Cliques

The Molding of a Group History

The Confrontation

Group Adaptation

Individual Adaptation

Termination

Fig. 8-1. The determinants of the member-leader relationship.

analysis of the confrontation and its consequences for individual and group adaptation is a central concern of this study. Finally, we note the importance of the approaching end of the group in determining individual behavior in the final phases of group development. In discussing these ten components of the member-leader relationship we shall attempt to demonstrate how the determinants represent a set of conceptually distinct but causally interrelated aspects of the total situation.

Individual Differences

What initial differences between the members would one wish to note if one wished to explain in these terms the interindividual variation that is apparent across the many member-leader relationships? This is no time for an exhaustive list, even if one could be made; we shall discuss only a few of the individual differences that have been found relevant. For example, we might begin by noting the sex of the member. Without ignoring altogether the notable exceptions among each sex, it could be pointed out that the males are more rebellious, the females more loyal and trusting in their dealings with the leader. But what kind of variable is gender? This simple varible leads into a tangle of possible determinants: early socialization, oedipal residues, sex roles and expectations, needs, tensions, etc. There are so many interconnected ways of conceptualizing the relevant prehistory and entering state of the member that one must simply take a plunge in some direction or another. In this study two closely related ways of describing the individual have been employed: themes and strategies. We have asked how a particular performance reflects the theme or themes in terms of which the situation is made sensible to the member and, given a particular theme, what strategies are employed to arrive at certain goals while simultaneously avoiding certain disasters. It must be apparent that we could just as easily ask about each new member which themes are most active, which most conflict-laden, or which are quiescent. We could also ask what characteristic strategies are employed by the member across all themes or within single and uniquely salient themes.

Our analysis in Chapter 4 of the single performance in terms of themes and strategies represents our best thinking on how the pregroup history of the individual can affect his behavior in the group. By extension, it might seem reasonable to infer that to the degree that a person persists in one or a combination of factor patterns throughout the group, we might look, postdictively, into the individual's past and hope to find reasons why certain themes absorbed him or certain strategies seemed useful in the new situation. For example, there is some reason to hope, on the basis of these data, that intensive scrutiny of the heroes might yield richer evidence than we could produce regarding why the heroes tend to view the leader as someone to fuse with, why they tend to mask their underlying depression with a strident, rebellious style, or why the alternative strategies that betray a sense of separation and anxiety need to be opposed so vigorously by the heroes. The phenomenon of transference in therapy is closely akin to the process needed to explain, if only partially, the continuities in theme and strategy that connect the individual before and the individual during the group sessions.

Rather than pursue the impact of individual differences upon the eventual member-leader relationship in terms of each factor pattern, let us turn to the issue of work. It would not seem unreasonable to expect that individuals enter the new situation with differential amounts of experience and self-satisfaction in being expressive, independent, involved, and sensitive. One might wish to extrapolate not only from prior authority relations but from prior peer group relations as well, since the willingness of a member to be any of these things depends in part upon the kinds of needs, successes, and expectations that have come to be associated with a group of peers. To be more specific, our observation of these four groups leads us to believe that some individuals enter the situation quite prepared to be open about their feelings. Prior therapy may be the relevant factor, or exhibitionism, or any of a number of qualities of the person's experience or resultant personality. Other members are more repressed or more concealed, and their ability to work is curtailed by their inability or reluctance to make public what they are feeling. Older members and individuals who feel they are of higher status than most other members are particularly able, at least in the early sessions, to carry on in the absence of explicit directions from the leader. Some members, especially those who are apprehensive or mistrustful of what others might think of the inner world they know all too well, avoid involvement with the leader for the same reason they have avoided many other close relationships. It appears that some individuals enter the situation particularly capable of representing each aspect of work, whereas others enter with a handicap that may have been with them for quite a while.

The relevance of individual differences is not confined to the separate aspects of work; on the contrary, we find it is the pressure to combine independence with involvement, enactment with expression, or any other combination of work aspects that brings to the fore the importance of prior experiences and expectations the members bring with them into the new group. For very few members would one be able to say that they walked in the door ready to work, ready to sustain the many activities and attitudes that comprise work in its fullest sense. Looked at in its obverse form, we find that some members' partial definitions of work—partial, that is, relative to the leader's and increasingly the group's definition of work—are at least as difficult to alter as other members' total opposition to all forms of work. In more than one case the man whose whole notion of enactment and independence placed these activities in the service of preserving a lofty, invulnerable position found himself more and more alienated from the group as the pressure for expression and involvement increased. In such cases, as with the others whose partial definition is rigidly maintained, might it not be said that these individuals enter with a somewhat lower chance of shaping and being part of the eventual work phase of the group? There is a limit to how far we can press the issue of individual difference since we carried out no prior assessments of individual personalities. These speculations are intended simply to indicate how important it may be in a given case to consider the particular history and personality of the new member.

At this point we would propose quite a different line of analysis, although it stays with the confines of individual differences. We refer to the dual problem of the biased sample and the missing member. Obviously, groups will differ according to their special allotment of individuals. Beyond noting who was in the group, we would suggest that if one group has, for example, double the number of certain kinds of individuals found in the second group, the first group is more than twice as likely to develop along certain lines, given the possibilities of coalition formation and monopoly over group issues. On the other hand, if one group is "missing" certain key members, there may be limited opportunity for the group to recruit any member to serve certain key functions in the group.

Some of the most prominent differences between the four groups may be traced to these two consequences of the individual differences component. Each group contained individuals who were so unique that various developments and entanglements might not have occurred in their absence. To cite one example, the two groups containing young, articulate clergymen were so affected by their contributions and/or by the projections these members occasioned that one could not safely consider the various member-leader relations that evolved without noting this factor. Turning to the multiplicative effect of oversampling certain kinds of members, we might note that the early development of group two was much affected by the mutual support generated among the pseudo-mature, but basically concealed and distant, members of the group. The expression of distress and resentment was made rather difficult by the fact that these members acted as though all would be well if the younger members simply suppressed these feelings as quickly as possible and moved toward a highly structured, affectless group for which they would willingly and competently serve as leaders.

The case of the missing members is not as easy to document. Who can say for sure that a given group had no potential hero? Who can rule out the capacity of one leader or one setting to discourage what another will permit? Somehow, despite the uncertainty of it all, it often seems that the full cast of characters has not appeared. In group two we are struck by the absence of any consistently active females who could provide the group with a model of sensitivity and involvement; in the absence of such a female, work seemed to be an activity relegated either to the overly assaultive hero or to an underexpressive male. In group three, there were two members, William and Malcolm, who were the group's closest approximations to what we have called the hero. Was it the fact that Hank and Alfred talked so much that deterred either or both of these other members from asserting themselves more? Did the leader move in too early, preempting the hero role as a result of his own annoyance with the group's sluggish beginning? We will never know for sure, but it could also be true that William and Malcolm, on the basis of their prior experiences and resultant personalities, were so different from the heroes found in the other three groups that they could not sustain activities which came naturally to the other three heroes.

It remains to state our estimate of the magnitude of the association between this individual differences component and the resultant variations among member-leader relations. Despite our assertions that the differences between members and between groups may be traced to variations in the individual pregroup histories and personalities, we would not wish to overstate how *directly* the link may be traced. In a way, our explanation of all the remaining components of the member-leader relationship is a treatise on why consideration of personality factors alone will not yield substantial correlations with observed behavior. It is an examination of how many nonrandom effects play upon the resultant behavior, and to treat these effects as "error" is to tolerate a very large estimate of error indeed.

Before turning to these other factors, we might pause for a moment and consider what complexity of statements about individual differences are needed if one is not to add still another source of error: intra-individual variation. To put it quite simply, if one knows that an individual's feelings toward the leader change over time, what hope is there to predict his feelings on the basis of a single antecedent measure of personality? It is like trying to hit a moving target with a fixed battery position. One solution is to average all the data points for a given individual over time. This might increase the correlation somewhat but one would not be very proud of describing a person who shifts from being very high on anxiety to being very high on depression as somewhat average on factor five. In such a case, what would an accurate prediction of a position never occupied by the member add to one's knowledge? A second solution, and here we leave the realm of most quantified personality assessment techniques, would be to predict an individual's feelings and behavior on the basis not of a single score but a series of conditional statements that would fit the range of possibilities open to the individual across a range of conditions. In this manner we can state the conditions under which the member might be expected to be anxious or depressed, and the various conditions could be matched to the actual leader's style and the developing history of that member in that group. In the absence of such a predictive statement, with only the unconditional assessment of personality to fall back on, the odds are that the actual continuities between the pregroup history of the member and his feelings in the group will be hopelessly swamped by the other determinants of his behavior to which we may now turn.

The Nature of the Situation

As the new member walks in the door, what does he find? What are the differences in the nature of the situation that must be considered?

One might think first of the official definition of the group's purpose: Why have the members come and why has some institution set aside time and space for this group? On the other side of a not terribly soundproof wall another group is meeting to learn elementary Greek. Somewhere else in town some patients have just assembed to be cured by "the group." These are extreme differences, but they highlight how important it is to know what kind of a group one is talking about. We have discussed the leader's definition of work and the member's definition of work, but few other kinds of groups would come to such definitions. These leaders and, increasingly, these members are creating a culture not out of a void but out of the larger cultural milieu in which these goals and behaviors are legitimate.

The situation, then, is comprised of the various givens, and only some are as visible as the room, the locale, and the particular array of members and leaders. Perhaps we should include the reputation of the course as well as the catalog description. Groups three and four were conducted during the same summer, one a floor above the other at the same time of day. Members were allotted to one or the other group. This arrangement probably affected the members even before the groups started. One member felt rejected not to be in with the leader she already knew. In addition, an undercurrent of rivalry made each leader perhaps a bit more impatient than usual for his group to "get going," a bit less willing to let things happen.

Returning to the members, we would emphasize the initial expectations and impressions aroused by the new situation. We could focus upon the orientation session, the list of assigned readings, or even that ear-splitting silence that no one seems able or willing to prevent in the first few minutes of the first session. A major source of variation in much that follows can be identified as the member's initial perception of what kind of enterprise it looks like the group will turn out to be. On the basis of her personality alone, one could not explain Jane's first session agitation. But to know the resemblance between the activities of this group and her own father's livelihood is a helpful bit of information. For one member it is like being back in group therapy; for another it is the weirdest damn course he has ever seen; for a third it is a testing ground in which he can determine whether his talents lie in the direction of social psychology. Other groups in other settings provide their members with distinctively different promises, threats, and opportunities. The effect of all this upon work is almost as diverse as the number of members, but several effects have some generality. For some members the group is forever "too big," and they retreat into silence or denials of most of the feelings being expressed. Whether the partial cause is size, the presence of observers, or the mixed sex composition of the group, the one aspect of work most affected by various structural factors is expression. The group activates in some members a variant of the control and sexuality themes, the fear of being exposed, judged, and rejected. At what seems like the opposite extreme, we find the girl who stated she wished to join the group so she could participate in "genuine communication" with "*honesty* and *no* barriers." Unfortunately, this conception of the situation seems to have so terrified her that she spent much more time imploring others to be open than managing to do so herself. The net effect of various rumors about how "great" the group is because you "really get down to the naked truth" seems quite similar in its effect, which is mainly to suppress any affect except that of the most dramatic and stylized form.

Presentation of Self

If we combine the first two components, we find we have placed a person with a given history, personality, and set of expectations within a situation he does his best to apprehend in meaningful terms. What does he do? Shall we imagine him reacting to the new situation as he did to earlier situations of this type? Yes. Shall we tease out the connection between his image of the situation and his initial behavior? By all means. But where might we go wrong if this were all that we did? To consider the presentation of self (cf., Goffman, 1959) in the earlier sessions is to move in on the errors of prediction based on only the first two components, and the first point to be made is that people seem to have rather special feelings about new situations. True, they make everyone somewhat or even considerably anxious. But the new group is also a new chance for everyone, and this implies not only a chance to transform oneself but also a chance to let one's public behavior reflect more accurately than before the changes that one senses internally but cannot put into action yet in old relationships. The new group is a chance to be what one has become.

We are arguing here that especially in the earlier sessions the individual not only reacts as he "must" but as he "chooses" to react. In their first few communications with the leader and the group the members are completing the sentence stem which reads, "I am the kind of person who—." Whether they portray themselves as cool, outraged, pathetic, or helpful, they are beginning the adjustment of their public identity to the particular setting and audience. We may suggest several reasons why prior assessment of the individual personalities involved would not lead to an accurate prediction of this process. First, to the extent that the member views the new group as insulated from his prior or concurrent relationships, he may use the new situation as an opportunity to make adjustments in his habitual way of behaving, and not all of these adjustments will be in the direction of evident maturity. Some members loosen their control over feelings of distress or anger, and the fact that these individuals appear more upset or agitated may reflect not a difference in personalities so much as a difference in the use they are making of the new situation. Second, the early presentation of self may constitute a test for others, including the leader. Certain aspects of oneself are revealed, and the reactions of others are checked to determine how free or judgmental, how hostile or accepting the new group will be. Some members want their initial performances to be taken seriously; others want them to be ignored. The overly dramatic female does not want her expressions of terror to be used against her; the protective male may not wish to be seen as feminine or without problems himself. Many early presentations of self are efforts to establish the context for later behaviors; for example, "Please view my soon-to-be-revealed anger and vindictiveness in the light of my earlier demonstration of feminine helplessness," or, "Please view my soon-to-be-revealed wobbly self-esteem in the light of my earlier demonstration of self-assurance and helpfulness." The third aspect of self presentation involves the member's assessment of the particular audience. In terms of the member-leader interaction, the member is acting upon his assessment of what aspect of himself will appeal to or engage the leader. The hero behaves as if the leader is annoyed by expressions of dependency; the sensitive ones behave as if the leader is bored by the hero's posturing and would prefer to hear their expressions of distress and vulnerability. In short, we are maintaining that the early presentations of self are affected by the opportunities available in a new situation, by the member's inclination to zig before he zags, and by his reading of what parts of himself will be accepted and validated by the leader and the other group members.

Any notion that the presentation of self is carried on in isolation from the other members is quickly dispelled by noticing the rapid rise of central figures in the group, members whose intensity, doggedness, or narcissism causes other members to begin defining themselves more and more in terms of their similarity with or differences from these pivotal individuals. The net effect of this crystallization is severalfold.

Members whose major concerns are not engaged by the preoccupations of the most vivid and challenging members may drift to the periphery of the group, preferring to wait until a more propitious moment to speak. Quite commonly, the females feel alienated by some male members' endless and obsessional rituals of challenging and placating the leader. It is not their issue, they maintain.

The second important consequence of the crystallization is that other members find their territory preempted by the member who arrives there first. The early sessions are not unlike a game of musical chairs. Two or more members, given similar personalities and the need to present themselves in similar ways, may eye the same chair. In the mad scramble, the one bumped out of his preferred location may pull himself together and capture quite an unlikely position. In group one, we were struck by the similarity of Frank and Harry in the opening session. When Harry preempted the hero chair, Frank did not take the adjacent chair. Instead, he ended up as the spokesman for the distressed members in opposition to Harry and the leader. We suspect that any prediction on the basis of personality factors alone would have missed by a mile the effect which Harry's presence in the group had upon Frank's eventual role.

If we turn for a moment to the issue of work, it is clear that some members will determine far more than others what the content of the group's work is likely to be. The early polarization around sensitivity, the mounting hostility toward the hero and against the leader for ignoring the hero's rudeness, the eventual efforts to tame the hero and broaden the range of acceptable styles—all these processes are set in motion by the initially unequal impact of the various members upon the agenda and climate of the group. Furthermore, there is a subtle but important connection between the leader's style, the hero's initial style, and the direction in which most members must move in order to work. Among the most envied and resented aspects of the leader's total performance is his evident capacity to control his actions, to be silent and to think while others are reacting wildly to the "blooming, buzzing confusion."

Although his behavior differs from the leader's in many respects, the hero also appears to other members to be "playing a game," and his detachment and seeming deliberateness are often as irritating as the jibes he aims at his fellow group members. The very act of interpreting what another member is doing, especially if the interpretation appears both uncomplimentary and dispassionate to its recipient, tends to be seen as calculated. The notion soon develops that the hero wishes to remain above the melee, the better to manipulate the image he puts before other people. On the other side of the group, we find the members who feel out of control, whose initial reactions, they fear, are casting them in a bad light. Who, in such a situation, is more likely to be resented than the ones who seem able to manage an effective front?

The point to be made here is that the path to work is effectively blocked by a number of misconceptions and misperceptions of the situation. Many members underestimate the viability and effectiveness of their own egos, assuming more than is true that they are helpless pawns rather than free agents in the process of self-presentation. They also misconstrue any evidence that another human being is able to remember what happened yesterday or to make sense out of what is happening today as evidence that the person is unfeeling and uninvolved. Given such a view of the situation, how possible is work? Expression is the least difficult aspect to manage, and the process of presenting onself as pathetic and distressed quickly becomes instrumental to the formation of a clique made up of fellow-sufferers. Independence is difficult when the leader is seen as both a threat and as one's legitimate source of support. The momentum of involvement is constantly checked by the impulse to flee or to deny one's vulnerability. In addition, the member's ability to take on the leader's role is curtailed by the member's equation of interpretation with detachment to the point of indifference and perceptiveness to the point of omniscience. We shall return to the fate of these and other members in our discussion of individual adaptation, a process that begins early in the group but accelerates only after certain crucial group developments have occurred.

If the path to work is blocked in part by the misconception of those who present themselves as weak and fragile, so too is it blocked by the heroes, although in a different manner. The equation of dependency and anxiety with weakness and immaturity also rests on some misperceptions. In part they take some members too literally, in which case everyone is misled; in part they are reacting to the threat posed by such members and such feelings. Their scorn for the anxious, dependent members is not unrelated to their own inability to accept these feelings in themselves. The hero and many other early expressers do much to convey the impression that only certain feelings are "real," while other feelings are "weak." If, then, interpretation is a weapon to be used against weak feelings and weak members, many feelings will remain unexpressed, at least until the confrontation, when a number of members will have their chance to modify the hero's belittling style.

In summary, analysis of the presentation of self enables the investigator of interpersonal relations to ask about, rather than assume, the particular continuity between the individual entering the group and the individual's initial behavior. It permits one to explore what uses the member is making of the new situation either to consolidate old changes or to explore new avenues of interaction. Moreover, it points the way to a dimension of early group life, the extent to which the member feels that he or others are capable of choosing the parts of one's self that should be presented. From the individual variation along this continuum derives much of the envy and scorn so characteristic of new groups.

The Leader

Although we have not emphasized this fact thus far, it should come as no surprise that the leaders of the four groups were not identical in personality or style. Even the two groups which had the same person for their leader did not have identical leaders; in fact, the two profiles of leader acts scored for this leader in two different groups are neither the most nor the least similar of the six possible pairings. In his second group this leader seemed much more impatient with expressions of dependency and guilt inducing. Perhaps he was hoping for the kind of fireworks he found in his first group; perhaps he was confronted by such a different array of individuals that even reversing the order of the two groups would have made no difference. The point to be made is that leader differences represent a vital link in the analysis of variations among member-leader relationships.

Some differences stand out immediately. The leaders in groups one and two were on the elliptical side, but one accomplished this by rather long, analogic interpretations, the other by rhetorical questions that added a quality of distance to his performance. The leaders in groups three and four were more argumentative, with one directing most of his attention to guilt inducing, the other to evidence of withdrawal. How do these and the additional differences between the leaders relate to differences between the groups? To take the simplest example, the group with the most distant leader seemed almost to mirror its leader's evident sense of uneasiness that things might go too far. The whole structure of the group, instituted from the start by the leader, seemed to hold down the intensity and directness of the interaction. Each session was begun by having a member summarize the preceding session, and the resultant impetus toward observation and interpretation seemed also to interrupt the continuity of feelings across sessions. When one member departed from the reportorial style to express a personal grudge against the hero, he was attacked for misusing the summary function for his own needs. We are jumping ahead, but it must also be noted that this group's most rebellious act, a party, served mainly to arouse depressive feelings; the group could not decide whether to be depressed because its leader was too uncaring to attend the party or because the leader seemed to be offended by their defiance. This group had the briefest period of internalization of the four groups, and we would maintain that one part of any full explanation of this fact would involve a look at the particular leader. If the leader is apprehensive about the consequences of expression, if expression is hampered by the structure of the sessions, or if the members are uncertain about the durability of the leader under attack, then the fusion of expression and enactment will be a difficult business.

A second example of how the leader can affect the group's ability to work comes from the group with the longest initial complaining phase. Here the independence aspect of work was difficult to achieve because the group and the leader battled over the correctness of the leader's inactive, nondirective role. Not unlike the child thrust too forcefully from the dependent position, the most active members clung to their sense of deprivation, which only made the leader more insistent that it was their group to do with as they saw fit. Quite a similar sequence of events took place in the group whose leader seemed most unnerved by manifestations of withdrawal. In this group the confrontation was prolonged by the attractiveness to the members of rebelling by withdrawing rather than by direct encounter. The clash was delayed until various efforts to defy the leader by withdrawal were found to be inappropriate for transmitting all the messages, hostile and otherwise, they were meant to convey.

On the more general level, a question can be asked regarding how the leader facilitates or impedes the group's ability to manage the separate aspects of work and their fusion into one full definition. All four leaders were found to be impeding the members' expression of their view of the leader as manipulative, devious, and narcissistic—the content of factor three, Counterdependent Flight versus Resistant Complaining. To the extent that the leader becomes quarrelsome or leads the group down blind alleys of interpretation that fail to validate their feelings, the group may become blocked and begin to abandon the goal of expression altogether. In general, however, the behavior of these leaders seems more to have facilitated expression. Most of the responses by the leaders indicate their acceptance of expression, and their rejection is aimed primarily at the members' denials and evasions.

The analysis of the leader's role in Chapter 5 is our answer to the general question of how the leader's behavior bears upon the formation of work goals. We would add to this picture not only the evidence regarding leader differences but also our awareness that the leaders commit serious tactical errors. Most of these errors involve shaming of the member, personal denials, or, the biggest category of all, inaccurate and misleading interpretations. There is no use in stopping at the leader's behavior to all members; what he does, over and over, to a given member is, for that member, the relevant aspect of the leader. In other words, when we find a leader shaming a member by ridiculing his contribution or by causing the group to laugh at him, it matters little that for most members the leader seems accepting and fair. Similarly, consider the member who presses in on the leader with a perfectly valid interpretation of what the leader has been up to, only to find the leader dodging and squirming with all kinds of denials. For that member, the leader is a fraud, urging others to openness he cannot manage himself. Our empirical analysis breaks down at this point, since we kept no record of whom the leader was responding to, but the transcript and tape recordings are full of member-leader relationships that could be more fully understood simply by tracing what the leader was doing to this or that individual member. Sometimes the effect is inhibitory, sometimes most encouraging and helpful.

It would not do to overemphasize the unique ways in which the leader affects the members. There are uniformities in the leader's role in relation to all members and across groups, and these uniformities constitute a major factor in determining the member-leader relationships. Beyond his purported function as blank screen and recipient of the members' projections, the professional role of the leader has different effects upon different individuals, as a function of their personalities, expectations, and presented selves. Perhaps there are leaders, for example, who elicit no competitive behavior from any of the active males, but the phenomenon of rivalry seems so ubiquitous as to suggest that the mere fact that the leader is there, behaving in any of a number of ways, contributes directly to this and to many other commonly observed member-leader outcomes.

The Formation of Cliques

Thus far we have constructed an image consisting mainly of separate individuals as they enter and present themselves within a new situation, and one aspect of this situation upon which we have concentrated is the leader. Our next task is to demonstrate that out of these beginnings come developments which greatly alter the behavior of individuals. If one ignored the fact that cliques form, or if one blindly assumed that each clique was composed solely of people who would naturally have behaved in similar ways, there would be many surprises provided by the actual events.

Fairly typical was group one in which the members split into two factions, the hero with his camp followers and the distressed-resistant subgroup which united in common outrage at the hero for one set of reasons and at the leader for another. The first point to be made might be that the members of each clique have a tendency to overestimate the solidarity of other cliques and to underestimate the extent to which others share their annoyance that the group is becoming so polarized. We would do well to avoid this pitfall by stating from the outset that the boundaries and prescribed behaviors remain quite vague. But from the vantage point of the member, it usually seems that the group is about to be taken over, that a course is being set for the group which they had best oppose sooner rather than later. In the case of group one, it was the more dependent members who sparked the hero into strident disassociation from the prevailing mood, which in turn provoked "the sensitive ones" to band together to prevent the hero from forever setting the tone of their group.

The hero's clique contained the hero, at least one other member whose style was very similar, and a few individuals who tended to admire and defend the courage and autonomy demonstrated by the hero. The clique which contained the sensitive ones was headed by one and sometimes two spokesmen, and only the latter tended occasionally to deny that the distress they were expressing was actually felt by them. The reader may recognize that the height of this polarization corresponds, in each group, to the second phase, premature enactment, during which the heroic enactors cause the group to choose sides.

The net effect of this schism, and this is what makes a discussion of cliques a necessary component of any full analysis, is that each member comes to adjust what he says not solely to his own expressive needs, nor to the probable response of the leader and all members, but to his reference group, to his "team." At times this has some rather unexpected consequences. The spokesman in group one, who might well have become the hero had Harry not preempted that role rather forcefully, drifted for a while into the role of sounding-board for the distressed members whom he hardly resembled at all on personality grounds. Given his tolerance of slightly paranoid constructions of reality and their actual distress, they made a potent combination. Each member who wished to be associated explicitly with one or the other clique, and this would cover one-half to three-quarters of the group during any session, acted as if he were both relieved and constricted by the existing polarization. Members seemed to suppress certain feelings lest they be tagged as members of the other clique, and when two of the heroes tried to broaden how much of themselves they had made public, they were told, in effect, to stay in character, that feelings of conscience or inadequacy were appropriate only for members of the opposing camp.

If we look at how this development affects work, we find that at least until the internalization phase each subgroup exposes no more than several aspects of the definition of work at which the group finally arrives. Thus the tug-of-war between cliques is in part a tug-of-war between opposing partial definitions of work. Many of the misconceptions described under the section on presentation of self become incorporated into the self-congratulatory attitude which the clique maintains: "Well, at least we're trying to understand something instead of bleating like poor little lambs," or, "Well, at least we're willing to admit that we're not perfect and don't have to go around being crude and insensitive." Under these conditions, in which to interpret is to set oneself above his distressed peers and to express anxiety or dependency is to part company with the heroic elite, work in its fullest sense is very unlikely. This is more or less the state of affairs prior to the confrontation. What we are interested in documenting is that when one member emphasizes his feelings of anxiety and another makes insulting interpretations, these performances often could not be explained solely by the members' antecedent experiences or even their private reactions to the leader and to the entire situation. Only if one asked which cliques had formed and what feelings qualified an individual for membership in the clique, or excluded him from it, could one understand the observed behavior.

This brings us to another familiar aspect of cliques, their tendency to be exclusive. In group three, and to a lesser extent in all groups, the males dominated much of the early discussion. In group three the members came to identify this process as the operation of a "boys' club" from which girls, with one partial exception, were barred. Whether it be the exclusion of girls or of the up-to-then silent members, it becomes harder and harder for some members to break into the conversation. It must be remembered that these are large groups, and one function of cliques is to crystallize the group around the active members who either speak for the less active members or satiate their need to speak. One often hears a member say, "In other groups I really speak a lot more," and this statement may indicate that the member is unable to attract as much attention as the more vocal members of his own clique. It is worth considering how well one could predict this fact on the basis of a priori measures of personality.

The Molding of a Group History

Just as one might be misled if his view of individuals ignored their tendency to cluster into cliques, so too one's view of the events prior to any given time period might be misleading if he did not understand how the groups mold their own history. We refer here to the dual processes of myth-making and collective amnesia. The past that affects the group is not only the past captured by the tape recorder but is, in addition, a purposefully distorted and partial view of what has happened. One major weakness of the act-by-act scoring system as a research method is that it leads to a mechanical summation of acts, whereas the group is capable of assigning quite disparate weights to the events in the process of recording and retelling its own history. As a partial effort to mitigate this weakness of our chosen method, it is important now to speak of the group's past as the group tends to view it.

We might consider first some of the early events which are immortalized, if not in song and story, at least by the cryptic references whose meaning perhaps all members, or, certainly, all members of one's own clique, are supposed to understand. One class of such events deals with the leader, and the group may revive over and over again a particularly unhelpful, embarrassing, or foolish intervention. Whether it be an instance of silence in the face of "simple and necessary" questions or an early manifestation of the leader's chosen role, the clique most interested in legitimizing its distress and its resistance to the leader can remind itself of the outrage by referring to the events in question. In one group an early interpretation by the leader had the effect of exposing the latent hostility of the most dependent member and the latent submissiveness of the most rebellious member, and neither member enjoyed being told how much he resembled the other. The net effect of this intervention was that the two members moved closer together in common opposition to the leader, and this interpretation was used thereafter by each ("Did you hear what he said to you?") to goad the other into a spasm of resentment against the leader. Incidents suggesting that the leader is indifferent, incompetent, playing favorites, and so forth make useful pellets around which to crystallize the member's apprehensions regarding the leader. The image of the leader in one clique is often turned upside down by the opposing clique, one clique remembering the off-target interpretations, the other remembering the ones that seemed particularly insightful. Thus if one asks why two cliques differ in their willingness to take over the leader's interpretive role, the answer must often reflect the fact that the two cliques either remember different interventions or assimilate them into the images of the leader that they have already formed.

One class of pivotal events concerns the hero, and enough has been said already on this score to permit us merely to remark upon this aspect of the group's history-making. Evidence that the hero is not perfectly comfortable himself tends to be forgotten; outrageous and damaging remarks are inscribed in large script within the diary of the sensitive ones. Later, many events come out of amnesia, including the memories that modify somewhat the stereotyped views various cliques have developed regarding the hero.

A third and closely related set of events concerns the expression of distress. When a member leaves the group, fails to show up the day after an unkind word, or displays some tension or unhappiness, the history of the group gives these occurrences great weight, since they demonstrate to all but the most callous how pressing is the need for sensitivity. In retelling these events, the damage is often greatly exaggerated and the members seem to aggravate their fears and their guilts by overdramatizing the event in question. More is involved than simply the piling up of charges against the assaultive hero or against the leader. To some extent, the fact that dramatic exchanges do occur in one's group is taken as evidence of the group's value and potential. The group may seem as delighted as it is shaken by such proof that it has moved beyond the level of superficial pleasantries.

Finally, there are events which we would prefer to class under their specific heading, the events surrounding the confrontation and its resolution. We include here "the day of the big attack," the rebellious and exclusionist attacks that are at least partially directed to the leader. The above examples have sufficed, we hope, to demonstrate that as the various subgroups and cliques mold their separate histories, they add a new prize to the contest: the right to determine the effective past, the past to which new activities will be related. In this context, it becomes a major task for the leader to keep the recollection of the past as accurate as possible, and beneath this strategy lies the assumption that neither the reconstructed past nor the actual past is the sole determinant of current feelings and behavior. The leader's concern for accuracy reflects more than pedantry; it is based on a belief that at some level of consciousness the member is affected by his memories of the real events. To the extent that the reconstructions depart from the actual events, the member's understanding of what is going on will to that degree be obscured. But so will one's understanding be obscured if one underestimates the potency of the group's official history, however distorted it may be.

Confrontation

In arguing that a full analysis of the member-leader relationship demands that special attention be paid to the confrontation between the members and the leader we seek to look beyond the particular interchanges to the consequences of these events for the separate members and the group as a whole. Our thesis is that the confrontation represents more than the discharge of accumulated frustration; it is a test, an activist surge whose aim is to find out some things and to change some things. Much of the group's future course depends upon what is found out and what, if anything, is changed. The first question, then, is what processes differentiate between the confrontations which facilitate work and those with a more inhibitory effect.

To answer this question it might be helpful to reconsider the purpose of the confrontation. Groups may differ in both their original aims and how well they are realized, but some common elements can be extracted. Our discussion of this phase in Chapter 6 isolated many goals, some of which were: (1) to express the accumulated frustration of dependency needs; (2) to mount a successful rebellion against the leader, in the interest of redistributing his power more equitably; (3) to voice the member's growing fears of being manipulated; (4) to take revenge upon the hero and to break the hero's tie with the leader; (5) to "do something" that might alleviate the distress and declining self-esteem of the members; and (6) to either reduce the level of sexuality and aggression in the group or to add sensitivity to charisma as a way of becoming a valued and central person in the group. Not all these goals were shared by each participant, but through the concerted action of many members, these and other goals were pursued with considerable vigor and intensity.

There are many ways to approach the question of why one confrontation succeeds more than another. The aims listed above are complex and at times mutually contradictory. One approach to this issue is to raise three questions about the confrontation phases of any group in the belief that different answers will point to quite different consequences. The questions are: (1) Do the members know what they are doing? (2) Can they sustain the confrontation? (3) How does the leader react? To the extent that the members are aware of their hostility and express it directly, the odds go up that the confrontation will succeed in transforming the group. An unsuccessful case is found in group two; the opening round of the confrontation, a party held over the leader's muffled opposition, was ineffective partly because the latent purpose of the party was not discussable. A group's inability to discuss the hostility embedded in a collective act does not prevent the act from causing depression; it only dampens the expressive, cathartic effect which it might have had. Similarly, the group's awareness of what it is doing may be impeded by displacements of hostility from the leader onto some surrogate figure. One consequence of the displacement in group two was that few members could attack the hero as vigorously as they wished since, after the leader's interpretation of the displacement, an attack upon the hero seemed perilously close to an attack upon the leader, and most members were unwilling to face these feelings directly at that time. As a result, they turned on the individual who attacked the hero the day before, thereby venting their anger at quite a different aspect of the leader, his "intellectuality." Thus the first point to be made is that one needs to know not only whether the confrontation has occurred but how directly the hostility was expressed.

A closely related point deals with the member's ability to sustain the confrontation. We conceive of a continuum along which the expressed hostility varies; it goes from attack to resistance to whining to withdrawing. To the extent that the confrontation slides off toward withdrawal, the members stand a good chance either of not knowing what they are feeling or else of learning that they are not capable of expressing what they feel. We are suggesting that groups vary in the extent to which they pass what seems at the time like the point of no return. If hostility is constantly being expressed by guilt inducing or withdrawal, the confrontation is less likely to produce a major transformation simply because the members have not abandoned the relative safety of remaining impersonal, indirect, and uninvolved. In group three the confrontation was heavily laced with guilt inducing, in group four with withdrawal. We are not suggesting that these feelings were not active and did not also need to be expressed; all we are noting is that they tended to obscure the additional feelings of resentment and fury that were most clearly expressed in group one. Paradoxically, our conviction that these latter feelings needed to be expressed derives less from the notion that they were ferociously intense than from the notion that, seen in the light of day, they could have been accepted for the small part of the whole which they represented. Unexpressed or stifled by denials and other modes of expressing hostility, they remained more terrifying to their possessors than they needed to be.

This brings us to the leader's response. Here we find a vital link in the chain because one of the most important consequences of expressing hostility is the discovery that the world does not immediately collapse. The leaders under study here were not unthreatened but neither did they keel over upon hearing that their actions offended and angered some of the members. In general, it can be stated that the greater the leader's capacity to accept and absorb the hostility directed at him, especially if the members are aware of the feelings they are expressing, the greater the chance that the confrontation will alter the group's structure and the individual's capacity to work. If, on the other hand, the leader arouses an unmanageable amount of anxiety and/or depression in the members, the effect will be inhibitory. Retaliation, defensiveness, and hurt feelings on the part of the leader are not unknown in these groups. It would be accurate to say that each leader reacted in these ways to at least a few of the members in his group. We are not dealing here with all-or-none phenomena. The balance of all four leaders' responses was on the accepting side, and this point is as worthy of emphasis as is the fact that some members of each group were more apprehensive or more guilty after the confrontation than before it because of the leader's response.

The next two sections of this chapter deal more fully with the consequences of the confrontation. The purpose of this section has been to indicate that some of the group differences and variations among individuals will make little sense if one ignores the existence and the particular qualities of the confrontation. If this phase is in part a test, it matters whether one group finds itself and the leader capable of surviving it. If this phase is in part a vital source of new data for the group, it matters whether the data suggest that some of the members' earlier perceptions of themselves and the leader now seem inaccurate. The major facilitating effect of the confrontation involves: (1) a growth in the sense of self-sufficiency among members together with a lessened conviction that they need to present themselves as helpless and pathetic or superhuman and scornful; (2) a revision in the image of the leader in the direction of being more human and more trustworthy; and (3) an altered view of the relationship with the hero. The successful revolt tends to bring the hero and at least some of the other group members closer together. The hero may become more willing to be sensitive and to admit weakness; the spokesman has himself expressed feelings, not all of which can be passed off as righteous indignation; and many of the other members now find that their image of the hero seems exaggerated either because it always was or because the hero has begun to change. In short, from any of a number of perspectives the observer of group life will understand the feelings expressed by members only if he knows if the confrontation has or has not occurred and knows, in addition, what changes have been set in motion by this key event.

Group Adaptation

There are three aspects of the group which are properties of no single individual but whose role in determining individual behavior should not be ignored: norms, structure, and climate. Our interest in these properties does not begin with the postrevolt period, but, to the extent that the confrontation has been successful, it is particularly appropriate to inquire how these collective properties are developed and altered in the final phases of the group. Once again we are interested less in going over the events of the work phase than in demonstrating how the members, having constructed the norms, structure, and climate of their group, are then singly and collectively influenced by their own creation. An outside observer might not immediately sense the changes brought about by the confrontation. He might occasionally hear an explicit verbalization of norms; more often he would find that for one member to interpret what another member was doing no longer caused a flurry of indignant or sulky resistance. As in most groups, the existence of norms can be inferred most easily when someone is accused of violating the as yet unverbalized standards of behavior. During the work phase, the major transgressions involve behaviors which inhibit work: denials, moralizing, remaining inaccessible, etc. From the reactions to the still resistant subgroup and from the decrease in sniping between the hero and the sensitive ones, we infer that a new norm has been constructed. Sometimes one of the more independent members will successfully verbalize the implicit norms, thus emphasizing that a member's acceptance into the group is conditional upon new and in many ways broader standards of behavior. We have pointed to some of the components of this new normative structure by listing five aspects of work: enactment, expression, independence, involvement, and sensitivity, the last of these being added primarily by the members. To cite but a single example of how this determinant might add to the analysis of an individual's behavior in a given situation, we might consider Frank, one of group one's spokesmen. We find him, during the period after the confrontation, becoming less rebellious, less mistrustful, and more willing to join in the interpretive analysis of group events. We could make little headway in understanding his performances by considering only his personality, his early presentation of self, or his role in leading the attack upon the leader, although all these components are relevant. One would need to know what norms were then active and the extent to which Frank felt he had helped to create these norms. At the point when interpretation was seen neither in terms of compliance with the leader nor as precluding sensitivity, Frank grew more willing to take over various aspects of the formerly resented leader. The difference between reacting to the leader's pressure and reacting to group norms is a major one, especially for the more rebellious males, and the growing sense of autonomy and satisfaction which often accompanies the work phase is directly attributable to this difference.

Along with changes in the normative underpinning of the group come changes in the relevance of previously inactive or less combative members. Characteristically, the females enter the center ring in great number only after the confrontation, and many of the quieter males begin to assert themselves at this point. These developments are the result and the further cause of a shift in group structure. Only after the confrontation does "the group" take on a new meaning, and this meaning includes certain rights of all members to be seen and to contribute what they have to offer. We could easily overstate exactly how pervasive this expansive, inclusive mood seems to be. Scapegoating seems to belie its total hold on the group, even though it could be argued that from the members' point of view, hazing feels like a more rather than a less united activity. Viewed in this light, the increase in flirting and pairing indicates the extent to which the members feel freed from their absorption with the leader and the previously central figures; almost anyone might get involved if all that was needed was the capacity to be interested in a fellow group member. The depolarization of the group and the decline of explicit focusing upon the leader make possible various feelings and behaviors which would be hard to understand if removed from their group context. Within the revised group structure the leader is more likely to be relevant to issues of intimacy and pairing, a shift which causes anxiety on the part of some which could not be understood except in this light. Similarly, the undertone of depression, caused by the fact that failure is a meaningful word if the group is responsible for its own fate, is a unique product of this structural change.

Lest we seem, like many writers on group processes, to view the group as one big success story, it should be noted that some changes which follow the confrontation can hardly be called creative adaptations. In group two the attack upon the leader was only partially successful; lingering resentments and unresolved conflicts erupted and then were quickly covered over. In most groups the moralist remained trapped in his resister role, and the remainder of the group seemed less and less able to consider the moral issues of interpersonal life in other than the "group language" with which they felt comfortable. In other words, the group's access to the symbol system employed by "the outside world" tends to decline and this raises the question of transfer of learning. There is a distinct possibility that as the group constructs its own culture it simultaneously makes more difficult the application of what members learn inside the group to the postgroup experience. To the extent that the moralist's references to the world beyond are rejected out of hand, it may indicate that just such a "special" but inapplicable experience is being developed.

The plights of the moralist and the sexual scapegoat suggest that the new structure is not without its drawbacks. Although it is less true than during the period when interpretation seemed to be the private preserve of the hero, the members still seem to assume that bravery and the ability to "take it" are desirable attributes of anyone subjected to the scrutiny of the group. On the grounds that "enough is enough," there is a tendency to enforce a certain time limit on a member's stay upon "the examining table," and the group turns away in search of "the next volunteer." The process of work, even after the confrontation, is often ungainly or unsatisfying to all concerned, and this may lead the group back to an idealized image of the leader. The mounting sense of inadequacy in the face of a most difficult task may cause members to forget the leader's blunders and inaccuracies and to remember only the ease with which he seemed to make sense of the chaos.

This brings us to the third group property, its climate. Not only does the group have a range of predominant moods, but it develops as well its "official" mood. In one official version of group one's climate, it was important for the group to see itself as no longer anxious; the group atmosphere was described as energetic and free. In the period following the confrontation a certain giddiness may prevail, almost as if the right to regress and be silly were part of the prize won by means of the confrontation. Our purpose in discussing group climate is to illustrate that the task of explaining one member's sudden switch from expressing anxiety to denying depression is made much easier by remembering how contagious a manic surge can be and how likely it is that more and more members will turn from their primary personal concerns to enter into the gaiety and laughter.

One final note on the nature of group level determinants might be in order. When we observe that Frank in group one and Carol in group four shift from Dependent Complaining toward Enactment right after the confrontation, what conclusions do we draw? The answer, we suggest, depends upon their position relative to the group. Frank did move toward Enactment, but he remained on the same end of the distribution of such factor scores throughout the group, the Dependent Complaining end. That is, his individual contribution to the group did not shift from pulling in one direction to pulling in the opposite direction. He abandoned his leadership of those on the Dependent Complaining end, and he moved more toward the middle of the distribution, but his role in the group was not reversed. In contrast, Carol started on the Dependent Complaining end and shifted to such an extent that she became one of the group's major enactors. As a result, we are in a position to infer greater personal change on her part than on the part of Frank. The question to be asked is not simply whether the individual has moved but whether his position relative to the group has changed. As the group climate changes, nearly all members are affected by the shift. Thus a person may appear less anxious than before but become even more deviant in that direction if the group shifts faster than the individual. Any full explanation of this change would take account of both the changes in climate of the whole group and the member's reasons for becoming even more out of tune with the prevailing affective tone of the members around him.

Individual Adaptation

If personal change within the member-leader relationship involved only a gradual shift in the member's perceptions of and responses to the leader, our presentation of the individual adaptation component would be simple and to a large extent unnecessary. We could note some of the most important positive consequences of any exchange between the member and the leader, but especially the consequences of the confrontation. We could note the greater accuracy with which the members assess the leader's motives and actions, the decreasing number of projections which clutter up the member-leader relationship, and the rise in the members' acceptance of the leader's preferred role. Although there are variations among members, the main trend after the confrontation is in these directions. However, most of these changes could be analyzed within the context of our previous discussion of the successful confrontation. The change which forces us to include a separate component in our analytic scheme is of a different order. It concerns the ego implications of the confrontation or any other re-orienting exchange with the leader.

One of the many ways to approach the personal transformation to which we refer would be to go back in time to the member's initial set toward the leader and the group to ask, "What guarantees does this member ask of the situation before he can work?" The sensitive ones, for example, seem to demand a guarantee that they will not be hurt, that they will be protected and honored for their honesty rather than scorned—a reasonable, and very human, demand. One of the hero's demands seems to entail a guarantee that he not be seen as the teacher's pet or as a "fink," to cite one hero's initial attempt to differentiate himself from a case figure. More important than that demand is the hero's need to have his feelings validated by others. The hero's fury at the more repressive or conventional members indicates some inner uncertainty about how real the feelings he expresses actually are. When a person experiences his impulses as rather alien to himself, he is not in a very good position to know when he is pretending and when he is being honest. The denier who fails to see the validity or the logic behind the hero's affect sounds rather like a voice within the hero, a voice which constantly wonders how much the hero's own expressions are pure nonsense and froth. In such a state, the hero asks for a guarantee that he be allowed to say whatever he likes without censure, that others immediately reassure him that a profound and "gut-level" feeling has just been verbalized, and that others are experiencing the same feelings.

The list of other guarantees which members demand from each other is limitless: "Don't remember my moments of distress"; "Tell me I'm not as bad as I present myself as being"; "Know when I'm unhappy and come to my rescue"; etc. Behind each demand for a guarantee is a conception of oneself as unable to bear any disappointment or frustration of one's demands. To the extent that the leader or any other person is relevant to the member's demands, the member is turning over to others the task of maintaining his self-esteem and equilibrium; beyond a certain point, this is a demand which no other mortal can meet. The transformation which follows the confrontation is often the result of a member's dual realization that others cannot serve this function and that the guarantees were not necessary in the first place. For a person to modify or abandon his demands on others, it usually takes more than failure to find someone who will satisfy them. It usually takes a revision in one's conception of how much humiliation, harshness, and isolation one can endure. For this reason, we see the personal growth that follows the confrontation as reflecting an inner or ego process, an altered estimate of how devastating it would be to find that the leader was not enchanted by one's every word, to find that some members resented one's centrality, or that some others might well be expected to be insensitive given their different backgrounds and value systems. The disaster which each strategy is an effort to avoid comes to appear more bearable than one had originally maintained.

Thus the changes observed in members who previously were distressed and blocked can be ascribed not only to the actual decline in abusiveness around them, not only to increased evidence that some other members share their feelings, but also to an altered sense of just how safe and protected they need to be. Of course, all these factors are intertwined, and each person still would maintain that he has his limits. But what is the origin of this altered self-image? To some extent, the answer to this question would take us back to the beginning of the group, to the propensity of individuals to treat this new experience as others treat new encounters with a fortune teller. The extent to which individuals place in temporary storage their already accumulated self-conceptions and treat new data from strangers as sacred pronouncements is both amazing and at the same time a tribute to these members' openness and eagerness to learn more about themselves. It is part of the magic of the new group that these recent acquaintances are endowed with greater objectivity, perceptiveness, and willingness to be honest than one's oldest friends or even oneself. It soon becomes apparent that the process of forming valid self perceptions can be aided by but not entirely turned over to one's fellow group members and the leader. It becomes increasingly possible and even necessary for the member to recall insights already in storage, and not uncommonly one finds that these compare rather well in terms of accuracy with the inferences and interpretations that are coming in from the outside. Not only does the member discover what insight into himself he has contained all along, he discovers some of the strengths he had previously underestimated.

Since it is our purpose to demonstrate that these alterations in self-esteem and self-image are themselves determinants of what feelings the member is expressing, we might consider the female member in group three who shifted dramatically from a constant refrain of anxious concern about the leader to a far more self-reflective and expressive style. Among the other reasons one might offer for this shift, one would wish to note how differently she conceived of her own strength and resilience. Her need to feel feminine was no longer to be satisfied by having others view her as weak and helpless; it could now be satisfied by her own view of herself, a view that was not even contradicted by her increasingly central role in the work group. In such members we sense a gradual decline in the use of the leader and other members as validators, as mirrors designed to cast one's reflected image. To the extent that this happens, the member can work more effectively on the issues that are of genuine concern to him, more secure in the knowledge that there is some inner stability and reserve supply of self-esteem that make the exploration less a gambling of one's total resources. One's differences from others testify simply to the diversity of the human animal, not to the urgent need to copy this or that other person, and this is especially true in relation to the leader whose role casts him in a unique relationship to the group.

It must be clear that this transition is intimately related to the individual's capacity and willingness to work, since so much of work entails a tolerance of the inevitable risks. To be able to take on the leader's role and know within oneself that the accusations of "grade grubbing" describe only a small part of one's motives or to know that another member's conviction that interpretation is sadistic is partly *his* problem makes enactment much more possible and much less a furtive or frenzied activity. To know that the reality of the leader's role does not permit an unambiguous relationship in the authority area, to express one's feelings without a guarantee of their total acceptance by others, to be involved with the leader and other members without an ironclad guarantee of reciprocity—all these adaptations to the reality of the situation and the reality of one's own self are at the heart of what we mean by work in its fullest sense. In the interest of completeness, we should mention that some members make less creative and liberating adaptations. For some work stops after the confrontation; for others it never really begins. But these cases can be accounted for without a separate analytic component. Only the internal restructuring of the self-percept and one's conception of reality causes the kind of shift that needs the special attention we have given it.

Termination

The approaching end of the group causes shifts in members' feelings that would surprise the observer who is unaware of the time dimension built into groups of this kind. The most characteristic effect of termination is that the members begin packing their bags, although a few members who find they have little to pack may begin frantically unloading the feelings and needs which they had concealed throughout the group's history. Equally familiar is the regressive move back to the belief that it was, after all, the leader's group, and he had better hurry up and tell all if the members are ever to know the true meaning of their experience.

Some unexpected and usually unresolvable issues have a way of arising in the last few days. One leader used the last session to reveal for the first time how inaccurate was the members' view of him as impersonal and distant. Various dramatic events, such as sitting in the leader's chair or tearful confessions of distress, may occur. The point to be emphasized is not simply that these things happen but that one needs to know whether the protection of having only 50 more minutes left is partially determining the behavior in question. If so, then this determinant becomes an essential ingredient of any full analysis of the feelings involved. As the members attempt to seal off their experience, or else to have their final fling without fear of the consequences, the group ends.

One Final Case

Our journey has carried us full circle, and we may now demonstrate by means of the transcript presented in Chapter 2 the usefulness of the descriptive and analytic system presented in the subsequent chapters. We propose to discuss one member, Janice, and in looking at her performance during session fourteen we can bring back into focus the two questions we raised initially: What is going on? What does it mean?

For our purposes here we can list rather briefly the five distinct but interrelated activities in which Janice was engaged during session fourteen: (1) in her opening remarks, Janice attempted without success to persuade Alvin to admit the dilemma posed by his inability to "disassociate himself" from his clerical role and reveal himself as "a kid," a man, or a person; (2) she differentiated at various times between honest expression and being intellectual and while at first she said how good it seemed that the group was intellectual, she later accused Harry, the already established hero, of being too intellectual, citing as evidence her presumption that Harry derived his insights from the readings rather than from his own "emotional experience"; (3) Janice's resentment and competition with Harry was a persistent theme in her performance, and it is clear that she would accept neither Harry's efforts at enactment nor the leader's interpretation that some members were reacting to Harry as they were to the leader; (4) she saw the leader as "equating" his attitude with Harry's attitude; and (5) Janice's remarks about the leader suggested the existence of positive, accepting feelings, especially in her effort to make personal contact with the leader, but they also demonstrated her capacity to acknowledge and tolerate the leader's ambiguous role, which, for her at least, included being teacher, leader, peer, and person.

How might we tackle the descriptive task if we wish to move beyond the summary given above? In this study we have employed an act-by-act scoring system designed to categorize and record how the member feels about the leader. The scoring system does not stop at the explicit references to the leader; it would ask, for example, whether Janice's comment that she "reveres Freud very greatly" might be expressing, among other things, her feelings toward the leader. In this case the answer is as definite a "yes" as we are ever able to manage. Her whole performance is an attempt to cast herself as the true believer, in contrast to Harry the rebel, and this reference to Freud would be scored on its appropriate level of inference, Level three. The scorer would also ask whether Janice was using Harry as an equivalent for the leader, something many members were doing at this time, but here the answer is negative. Far from equating Harry with the leader, she is Accepting and Showing Dependency vis-à-vis the leader by implying that she will not tolerate interpretations from a mere group member.

The results of an act-by-act scoring of Janice's performance reveal that although during much of her interchange with Harry she fits the factor pattern we have called Loyalty, we find evidence of Enactment when she tries to draw out Alvin, Independence when she leads the group into a reconciliation with the inevitable ambiguity of the leader's role, and Involvement when she attempts to break through the third person references to the leader with "Hello down there." Our discussion of work created a descriptive system that was derived from the 12 factor patterns, and it is helpful to note how precisely Janice's performance fits all the aspects of work which we isolated. If, then, we have before us an instance of work, how might the conceptual scheme developed in this chapter aid in the full analysis of this performance?

The first component suggests that we might wish to know about some aspects of Janice's personality, her previous contacts with groups of this kind, etc. Beyond noting that Loyalty is not unexpected from females, we might wish to know that Janice had been a group worker in a social work agency. It might help to record how important it was for her to succeed in the academic study of matters with which her time as a social worker had given her considerable experience. We know nothing of her early family history, and perhaps someone interested in individual differences might explore these or other avenues with profit. From what she says about Freud, we can infer that reverence is a feeling presumably not reserved only for one authority figure. A related clue might have been provided when, in the previous session, she imagined that the girl in the case under discussion would like nothing better than "a nice seductive father" since she had been "rejected by her father when she was very young." We do not pretend to know whether Janice is describing what she had had and assumed everyone else wanted or what she did not have and wished now to find, or even whether these would prove to be useful clues to her past. We do suspect that her acceptance of and involvement with the leader in session fourteen could probably be made more understandable if one asked what Janice was like before she entered the group.

The second component, the nature of the situation, is relevant to Janice's capacity for enactment. Her efforts to involve Alvin and her awareness of the difference between feeling and intellectualizing reflect both her previous experience and the perceived relevance of this new situation for those earlier learnings. But "the situation" was more than simply another group. For Janice, it was a group in which she was almost not included. The original list of group members posted by the leader did not contain her name, and the leader added her to the group only when she made it clear how important it was for her to take the course. The group, it may be assumed from her several allusions during group discussion to having been excluded, had become a place in which she needed to prove her value and the wisdom of the leader's special dispensation. Given Janice's comment about the case figure's need for love because she was rejected when young, we might as easily trace this feeling to her early experience with the group as to her early childhood. Janice announced once that she felt like the youngest member of the group, being the last to be added, and perhaps that lay behind her need to help Alvin to see himself as "a kid."

Out of the interaction of personality factors, initial expectations, and her unique experience of the new group came the determinants of Janice's self-presentation. One sees in session fourteen little of the early anxiety and inhibition which Janice reported to the group. Her initial presentation of self involved a clear portrait of herself as loyal but distressed, a conjunction of feelings that could be managed only by a highly intropunitive explanation of why she felt so constricted and fearful. In addition to casting herself as the expresser of feelings, especially feelings of inadequacy, she began quite early to demonstrate one use of interpretation that set her apart from the hero rather quickly, i.e., the interpretation of one's own distress. Thus although the expressive aspect of work was part of her initial self-presentation, there were intimations of self-awareness and sophistication. The major aspect of work which was missing in the early sessions was independence, and she was as far over on the dependent side as the hero was on the counterdependent side.

We come now to a consideration of the leader. As noted, the leader was responsible for an early sense of rejection; evidently her application had not aroused any special interest on the leader's part in having her as a member. In contrast to the more complaining members, Janice was neither surprised nor disappointed by the leader's inactive but interpretive style. It seems evident that she anticipated some pressure toward expression and perceived it in the leader's comments. This pressure she handled by expressing the distress she was feeling.

Some aspects of the leader's performance were less tolerable, however. Janice seemed increasingly irritated at the leader's support for the hero. In part it was an issue of jealousy, as we shall see, but another aspect of her irritation derived, as do many negative responses to the leader, from a feeling of being unseen. What she seemed to say from the start was, "How could the leader say that people are displacing their feelings toward him onto Harry; I'm not. Even if others are doing this, don't *I* count?" Thus the leader aggravated Janice's already acute sense of insignificance and irrelevance by his vague interpretations and his efforts to uncover the hostility felt toward him by discussing the hostility toward Harry.

As the group began to crystallize, with the hero on one side and the spokesman on the other, Janice maintained her distance from both sides of that battle. Her role in the second or premature enactment phase was that of the accepting enactor. She was angry at Harry, but she did not join the subgroup that refused to work at all until Harry was crushed, hopefully by the leader. Her position was becoming increasingly isolated in the group, in part because almost no one else in the group was trying to oppose Harry while remaining at the same time loyal and interesting to the leader. As a result, Janice was hardly visible when the confrontation began in session eleven, although her anger at Harry was as intense as anyone's. For many members the confrontation involved a broadside attack on the hero, the leader, and the course, and this did not fit Janice's feelings at the time.

How then do we explain Janice's performance in session fourteen? We see here an effort to have her own fight with the hero, with the prize being the leader's respect and attention. Her performance is designed to elbow this ersatz disciple right out of the picture by showing him up as unable to express feelings except when the book tells him what to feel, by reminding him that he is only a peer and not the leader, and by being the first to forge a more personal, but ambiguity-tolerating, relationship with the leader. The roots of this performance stretch back to Janice's earlier exclusion from the group and probably back into her pregroup personality and experience, but by session fourteen these early determinants had set in motion a presentation of self and a particular relationship to each member and to the leader which constitutes important additional determinants of the observed behavior. For reasons largely independent of what Janice did, Harry's heroic style made possible her performance by excluding, up to that point, the various aspects of work, expressions of distress and sensitivity especially, which Janice could emphasize in her own search for "a connection" with the leader, as she would soon thereafter describe her goal.

Janice's performance anticipates the future development of the group very well, especially in her synthesis of the various aspects of work. From this session to the end of the group there were a number of changes in Janice's performance. She was the most active female member of the emergent work group and received a torrent of praise from the leader, the hero, and most other group members for one delicate act of resolving the chronic fight between a male and a female member of the group. However, without going into the evidence and all the reasons why, it may serve as a final reminder of how intricate is the set of causal connections that determine a member's actions if we note that Janice did not sustain her work orientation throughout the final sessions. The outcome for Janice could not be explained fully without knowing how adroitly the hero shifted his style to make less and less applicable the substance of Janice's criticisms. Nonetheless, her performance in session fourteen fits well our notion that part of the successful confrontation often involves having a female rise up to challenge the hero, and many of the changes in the hero and in the group as well date from this session. This was the last session of the confrontation in group one, and Janice's performance laid the ground for many of the normative and structural changes which facilitated and sustained the group's ability to work.

This brief case study suggests how intertwined individual dynamics and group structure can become. Some of the determinants of Janice's performance can be traced to the unique person who arrived in the group on the first day, others depend on which of several options she decided to choose when confronted by a new situation with its particular leader and its particular array of fellow group members; still other determinants can be seen as residing in the kind of group she and all the others made of the resources and initial inclinations at their disposal. We have tried, given this complexity, to do our best at describing the four groups we observed.

Perhaps the clearest way to indicate how each of the components discussed in this chapter play a part in a performance such as Janice's would be to suppose that one could magically rearrange the personnel and events that go into these determinants. We would propose that Janice's performance would have been fundamentally different if the individual differences component had been altered; for example, if she had had no previous experience with groups of this kind, if someone with Harry's vitality and abusiveness had not been in the group, or if Janice had entered with less need for support or greater need for concealment. She might have been included on the initial group roster which we suspect would have changed her perception of the new situation and her subsequent behavior. It would not have been impossible or even unlikely for Janice to have presented a different aspect of herself to the new group; she could have emphasized much earlier than she did her considerable capacity for tolerating the ambiguity of the leader's role. Had she initially defined herself as an expert in understanding group process, it is unlikely that her performance in session fourteen would have been unaffected. We can wonder how differently Janice's career in the group would have been if she had found a different leader, one whose support was either less desired or more consistent. We may also wonder how she would have fared if she had been in group three, with its highly vocal and exclusive "boys' club"; she might have been silenced or else goaded into a far more direct and successful effort at enacting the leader's interpretive role.

Much of Janice's behavior was determined by the fact that Harry was in the same group, that he developed the relationships he did with the leader and the other group members, and that he rejected Janice along with a number of members whom she did not resemble very closely. What if she had been more accepted by the hero? What if there had been no other members willing to tolerate her move toward resolving the member-leader conflict by developing a more independent and personal relationship with the leader? There is no need to proliferate the alternative conditions beyond a certain point. It can be seen that each component of the member-leader relationship suggests antecedent conditions and events that might have been otherwise. If Janice in session fourteen differs from another member from her own or some other group, we can only point to a whole set of possible causes of the differences. Even the rudiments of a full analytic scheme make it less likely that one will fixate upon his favorite causal factor to the exclusion of additional and important determinants of the observed behavior.

Some Concluding Remarks

As we reflect upon the ground covered by this study, we feel impelled to remind ourselves and the reader that this has been, at its heart, an empirical study of four interesting but inevitably special groups. We are not unaware that things turn out differently in different settings, with different members and different leaders, etc. Beyond the justification of this effort on the grounds that one must start somewhere, we would wish to underscore the methodological and conceptual gains which others may find helpful in their roles as participants, professionals, or researchers within a group setting.

We have tried to indicate that the study of fairly long-term groups in their natural setting is both possible and fruitful. We have suggested that the combination of systematic observation techniques with more clinical or impressionistic methods may offer more than either method used singly. The statistically derived factors and the intersession or interindividual differences which they generated proved useful mainly in forcing us to ask questions, many of which would not have been raised if we had relied simply on our tape recordings and our memories. The questions could not have been answered, however, without reexamining the relevant transcripts. This circular process of consulting first one and then the other source of questions and answers prevented us from either being overwhelmed by the complexity of our raw data or being trapped into increasingly sterile and misleading preoccupations with our numbers.

We have employed the member-leader scoring system in the observation of introductory psychology classes with some interesting results. Other applications of this approach to the study of family interaction, therapy with one or more patients, and work teams seem worthy of consideration. However, we would prefer to emphasize how possible it is to construct a system that taps what one wishes in the end to think about and understand than to argue for the wholesale application of these 16 categories to situations where other feelings and issues appear more worthy of investigation. What we do hope is that other researchers will share our conviction that all claim to reliability and the capacity to generate interesting results is not abandoned when one turns to the study of feelings, even to the study of feelings that are expressed symbolically and indirectly.

Our results have prompted us to develop a number of crosscutting conceptual schemes. Our discussion of the various interpersonal themes and strategies may be more generally applicable than the particular set of factor patterns they were intended to clarify. We would not assert that all six factors would emerge with the same degree of independence of one another that we found here. However, some of these six factors or 12 factor patterns may suggest to some participant or leader of a group dimensions along which important variations may occur. In a similar manner, we would not be terribly surprised to hear that other groups develop via different phases or around different issues, nor will we be anything but pleased to have others delineate additional classes of members and their diverse careers. All that we can do in an empirical study of this kind is to describe what did occur, try to understand what we have found, and then hope that either the methods, the results, or the conceptual framework erected to make sense of the data will be useful in other settings.

It might be appropriate, in closing, to reemphasize our awareness that the member-leader relationship constitutes only one aspect of what takes place in any group. Although we have found, as have others before us, that in the self-analytic group this relationship becomes less central to the members under certain conditions, we have emphasized the continuities and transformations in this single aspect of group life, leaving for other investigations the closer study of member-member or more solitary and intrapsychic events with which such groups abound. Hopefully many will find, as we did, that the self-analytic group is a promising site for the investigation of individual and interpersonal dynamics. From our concerted efforts we may find our collective understanding of these processes becoming increasingly intricate, accurate, and relevant to effective and satisfying interaction in groups.

References

Arsenian, J., E. V. Semrad, and D. Shapiro. An analysis of integral functions in small groups. *International Journal of Group Psychotherapy*, 1962, **12**, 421–434.

Bach, G. R. *Intensive group psychotherapy*. New York: Ronald, 1954.

Bales, R. F. *Interaction process analysis: A method for the study of small groups*. Reading, Mass.: Addison-Wesley, 1950.

Bales, R. F. The equilibrium problem in small groups. In T. Parsons, R. F. Bales, and E. A. Shils, *Working papers in the theory of action*. New York: The Free Press, 1953, 111–161.

Bales, R. F. Task status and likeability as a function of talking and listening in decision-making groups. In L. D. White (Ed.), *The state of the social sciences*. Chicago, Ill.: University of Chicago Press, 1956, 148–161.

Balint, M. *Thrills and regressions*. London: Hogarth Press, 1959.

Barron, M. E., and G. K. Krulee. Case study of a basic skill training group. *Journal of Social Issues*, 1948, **4**, 10–30.

Benne, K. D. From polarization to paradox. In L. P. Bradford, J. R. Gibb, and K. D. Benne (Eds.), *T-group theory and laboratory method*. New York: John Wiley and Sons, 1964, 216–247.

Benne, K. D., and P. Sheats. Functional roles of group members. *Journal of Social Issues*, 1948, 4(2), 41–49.

Bennis, W. G. A genetic theory of group development. Unpublished manuscript. Massachusetts Institute of Technology, 1957.

Bennis, W. G. Defenses against "depressive anxiety" in groups: The case of the absent leader. *Merrill-Palmer Quarterly of Behavior and Development*, 1961, **7**, 3–30.

Bennis, W. G., and H. A. Shepard. A theory of group development. *Human Relations*, 1956, **9**, 415–437.

Beukenkamp, C. *Fortunate strangers*. New York: Holt, Rinehart, and Winston, 1958.

Bibring, E. The mechanisms of depression. In Phyllis Greenacre (Ed.), *Affective disorders*. New York: International Universities Press, 1953, 13–48.

Bion, W. R. *Experiences in groups*. New York: Basic Books, 1961.

Blake, R. R. Studying group action. In L. P. Bradford, J. R. Gibb, and K. D. Benne (Eds.), *T-group theory and laboratory method*. New York: John Wiley & Sons, 1964, 336–364.

Blake, R. R., and Jane S. Mouton. Personality factors associated with individual conduct in a training group situation. Human Relations Training Laboratory, *Research Monograph*, No. 1, Printing Division, University of Texas Press, 1956.

Borgatta, E. F. A systematic study of interaction process scores, peer and self-assessments, personality, and other variables. *Genetic Psychology Monographs*, 1962, **65**, 219–291.

Borgatta, E. F. A new systematic interaction observation system: Behavior scores system (BSs System). *Journal of Psychological Studies*, 1963, **14**, 24–44.

Borgatta, E. F., L. S. Cottrell, and J. H. Mann. The spectrum of individual interaction characteristics: An inter-dimensional analysis. *Psychological Reports*, 1958, **4**, 279–319.

Bradford, L. P. Membership and the learning process. In L. P. Bradford, J. R. Gibb, and K. D. Benne (Eds.), *T-group theory and laboratory method.* New York: John Wiley and Sons, 1964(a), 190–215.

Bradford, L. P. Trainer-intervention: Case episodes. In L. P. Bradford, J. R. Gibb, and K. D. Benne (Eds.), *T-group theory and laboratory method.* New York: John Wiley and Sons, 1964(b), 136–167.

Bradford, L. P., J. R. Gibb, and K. D. Benne (Eds.). *T-group theory and laboratory method: Innovation in re-education.* New York: John Wiley and Sons, 1964.

Cabot, H., and J. A. Kahl. *Human relations: Concepts and cases in concrete social science.* (2 vols.) Cambridge, Mass.: Harvard University Press, 1953.

Carter, L. F. Evaluating the performance of individuals as members of small groups. *Personnel Psychology*, 1954, **7**, 477–484.

Chin, R. The utility of system models and development models for practitioners. In W. G. Bennis, K. D. Benne, and R. Chin (Eds.), *The planning of change.* New York: Holt, Rinehart, and Winston, 1961, 201–204.

Coffey, H. S., M. Freedman, T. Leary, and A. Ossorio. A technique of group psychotherapy. *Journal of Social Issues*, 1950 **6**(1), 25–36.

Couch, A. S. Psychological determinants of interpersonal behavior. Unpublished doctoral dissertation, Harvard University, 1960.

Deutsch, M., A. Pepitone, and A. Zander. Leadership in the small group. *Journal of Social Issues*, 1948, **4**(2), 31–40.

Dunphy, D. C. Social change in self-analytic groups. Unpublished doctoral dissertation, Harvard University, 1964.

Durkin, Helen E. *The group in depth.* New York: International Universities Press, 1964.

Erikson, E. H. *Childhood and society.* New York: W. W. Norton, 1950.

Erikson, E. H. *Young man Luther.* New York: W. W. Norton, 1958.

Erikson, E. H. Identity and the life cycle. *Psychological Issues*, 1959, **1**(1), 1–171.

Erikson, E. H. Youth: Fidelity and diversity. *Daedelus,* 1962, **91,** 5–27.

Ezriel, H. Notes on psychoanalytical group therapy: II, Interpretation and research. *Psychiatry,* 1952, **15,** 119–126.

Fenichel, O. *The psychoanalytic theory of neurosis.* New York: W. W. Norton, 1945.

Foulkes, S. H., and E. J. Anthony. *Group psychotherapy: The psychoanalytic approach.* Baltimore, Md.: Penguin Books, 1957.

Frank, J. D. Training and therapy. In L. P. Bradford, J. R. Gibb, and K. D. Benne (Eds.), *T-group theory and laboratory method.* New York: John Wiley and Sons, 1964, 442–451.

Frank, J. D., J. Margolin, Helen T. Nash, A. R. Stone, Edith Varon, and E. Ascher. Two behavior patterns in therapeutic groups and their apparent motivation. *Human Relations,* 1952, **5,** 289–317.

Freud, S. Three essays on the theory of sexuality. In *Standard edition,* Vol. 7. London: Hogarth, 1953, 135–243.

Freud, S. Totem and taboo. In *Standard edition,* Vol. 13. London: Hogarth, 1955(a), 1–161.

Freud, S. Group psychology and the analysis of the ego. In *Standard edition,* Vol. 18. London: Hogarth, 1955(b), 69–143.

Freud, S. Instincts and their vicissitudes. In *Standard edition,* Vol. 14. London: Hogarth, 1957, 117–140.

Friedman, L. J., and N. E. Zinberg. Application of group methods in college teaching. *International Journal of Group Psychotherapy,* 1964, **14,** 344–359.

Gibb, C. A. Leadership. In G. Lindzey (Ed.), *Handbook of social psychology,* Vol. II. Reading, Mass.: Addison-Wesley, 1954, 877–920.

Gibb, J. R. Climate for trust formation. In L. P. Bradford, J. R. Gibb, and K. D. Benne (Eds.), *T-group theory and laboratory method.* New York: John Wiley and Sons, 1964, 279–309.

Goffman, E. *The presentation of self in everyday life.* New York: Anchor, 1959.

Harman, H. H. *Modern factor analysis.* Chicago, Ill.: University of Chicago Press, 1960.

Hays, W. L. *Statistics for psychologists.* New York: Holt, Rinehart, and Winston, 1963, 323–333.

Herbert, Eleonore L., and E. L. Trist. The institution of an absent leader by a students' discussion group. *Human Relations,* 1953, **6,** 215–248.

Heyns, R. W., and R. Lippitt. Systematic observational techniques. In G. Lindzey (Ed.), *Handbook of social psychology:* Vol. 1. Reading, Mass.: Addison-Wesley, 1954, 370–404.

Horwitz, L. Transference in training groups and therapy groups. Topeka, Kansas: Paper at the American Group Psychotherapy Association, New York City, 1964.

Horwitz, M. Training in conflict resolution. In L. P. Bradford, J. R. Gibb, and K. D. Benne (Eds.), *T-group theory and laboratory method.* New York: John Wiley and Sons, 1964, 365–378.

Jones, R. M. *An application of psychoanalysis to education.* Springfield, Ill.: Charles C. Thomas, 1960.

Kaplan, S. R., and M. Roman. Phases of development in an adult therapy group. *International Journal of Group Psychotherapy,* 1963, **13,** 10–26.

Kelman, H. C. The role of the group in the induction of therapeutic change. *The International Journal of Group Psychotherapy,* 1963, **13,** 399–432.

Kelman, H. C., and H. H. Lerner. Group therapy, group work, and adult education: The need for clarification. *Journal of Social Issues,* 1952, 8(2), 3–10.

Klein, Melanie. *The psychoanalysis of children.* London: Hogarth, 1932.

Klein, Melanie. *Contributions to psychoanalysis: 1921–1945.* London: Hogarth, 1948.

Klein, Melanie. A contribution to the psychogenesis of manic-depressive states. In *Contributions to psychoanalysis.* London: Hogarth, 1950, 282–310.

Klein, Melanie. *Envy and gratitude.* New York: Basic Books, 1957.

Klein, Melanie. Our adult world and its roots in infancy. In *Our adult world.* New York: Basic Books, 1963, 1–22.

Klein, Melanie, and Joan Riviere. *Love, hate and reparation.* London: Hogarth, 1937.

Leary, T. *Interpersonal diagnosis of personality.* New York: Ronald, 1957.

Lewin, B. D. *The psychoanalysis of elation.* New York: W. W. Norton 1950.

Mann, R. D. A review of the relationships between personality and performance in small groups. *Psychological Bulletin,* 1959, **56,** 241–270.

Mann, R. D. Dimensions of individual performance in small groups under task and social-emotional conditions. *Journal of Abnormal and Social Psychology,* 1961, **62,** 674–682.

Mann, R. D. The development of the member-trainer relationship in self-analytic groups. *Human Relations,* 1966, **19,** 85–115.

Medley, D. M., and H. E. Mitzel. Measuring classroom behavior by systematic observation. In N. L. Gage (Ed.), *Handbook of research on teaching.* Chicago, Ill.: Rand McNally, 1963, 247–328.

Meehl, Paul E. *Clinical versus statistical prediction.* Minneapolis, Minn.: University of Minnesota Press, 1954.

Miles, M. B. The T-group and the classroom. In L. P. Bradford, J. R. Gibb, and K. D. Benne (Eds.), *T-group theory and laboratory method.* New York: John Wiley and Sons, 1964, 452–476.

Mills, T. M. A sociological interpretation of Freud's "Group psychology and the analysis of the ego." Unpublished manuscript, 1959.

Mills, T. M. *Group transformation: An analysis of a learning group.* Englewood Cliffs, N.J.: Prentice-Hall, 1964.

Munroe, Ruth L. *Schools of psychoanalytic thought.* New York: Holt, Rinehart, and Winston, 1955.

Murray, H. A., et al. *Explorations in personality.* New York: Oxford University Press, 1938.

Parsons, T., and R. F. Bales. *Family, socialization, and interaction process.* London: Routledge & Kegan Paul, 1956.

Redl, F. Group emotion and leadership. *Psychiatry,* 1942, **5**, 573–596.

Redl, F. Implications for our current models of personality. In Bertram Schaffner (Ed.), *Group processes: Transactions of the fourth conference.* New York: Josiah Macy, Jr. Foundation, 1959, 83–131.

Schein, E. H., and W. G. Bennis. *Personal and organizational change through group methods: The laboratory approach.* New York: John Wiley and Sons, 1965.

Schutz, W. C. *FIRO: A three-dimensional theory of interpersonal behavior.* New York: Holt, Rinehart, and Winston, 1958.

Semrad, E. V., and J. Arsenian. The use of group processes in teaching group dynamics. *American Journal of Psychiatry,* 1951, **108**, 358–363.

Semrad, E. V., S. Kanter, D. Shapiro, and J. Arsenian. The field of group psychotherapy. *The International Journal of Group Psychotherapy,* 1963, **13**, 452–475.

Slater, P. E. Role differentiation in small groups. *American Sociological Review,* 1955, **20**, 300–310.

Slater, P. E. Contrasting correlates of group size. *Sociometry,* 1958, **21**, 129–139.

Slater, P. E. Displacement in groups. In W. G. Bennis, K. D. Benne, and R. Chin (Eds.), *The planning of change.* New York: Holt, Rinehart, and Winston, 1961(a), 725–736.

Slater, P. E. Toward a dualistic theory of identification. *Merrill-Palmer Quarterly of Behavior and Development,* 1961(b), **7**, 113–126.

Slater, P. E. *Microcosm: Structural, psychological, and religious evolution in groups.* New York: John Wiley and Sons, 1966.

Smith, M. B. Explorations in competence: A study of Peace Corps teachers in Ghana. *American Psychologist,* 1966, **21**, 555–566.

Stock, Dorothy, and W. F. Hill. Intersubgroup dynamics as a factor in group growth. In Dorothy Stock and H. A. Thelen, *Emotional dynamics and group culture.* New York: New York University Press, 1958, 207–221.

Stock, Dorothy, and H. A. Thelen. *Emotional dynamics and group culture.* New York: New York University Press, 1958.

Stock, Dorothy, R. M. Whitman, and M. A. Lieberman. The deviant member in therapy groups. *Human Relations,* 1958, **11**, 341–372.

Stone, P. J., R. F. Bales, J. Z. Namenwirth, and D. M. Ogilvie. The general inquirer: A computer system for content analysis and retrieval based on the sentence as a unit of information. *Behavioral Science,* 1962, **7**, 484–501.

Thelen, H. A. Methods for studying work and emotionality in group operation. Unpublished manuscript, Human Dynamics Laboratory, University of Chicago, 1954.

Thurstone, L. L. *Multiple Factor Analysis.* Chicago: University of Chicago Press, 1947.

Tuckman, B. W. Developmental sequence in small groups. *Psychological Bulletin*, 1965, **63**, 384–399.

Watson, Jeanne. Some social psychological correlates of personality: A study of the usefulness of psychoanalytic theory in predicting behavior. Unpublished doctoral dissertation. University of Michigan, 1952.

Wechsler, I. R., and J. Reisel. Inside a sensitivity training group. *Industrial Relations Monograph*, No. 4. Los Angeles: Institute of Industrial Relations, University of California, 1959.

Weick, K. E. Systematic observational methods. In G. Lindzey and E. Aronson (Eds.), *Handbook of Social Psychology*, Rev. Ed. Reading, Mass.: Addison-Wesley. In press, 1967.

Whitaker, Dorothy Stock, and M. A. Lieberman. *Psychotherapy through the group process*. New York: Atherton, 1964.

White, R. W. Motivation reconsidered: The concept of competence. *Psychological Review*, 1959, **66**, 297–333.

White, R. W. Ego and reality in psychoanalytic theory: A proposal regarding independent ego energies. *Psychological Issues*, 1963, 3(3), 1–210.

Whitman, R. M. Psychodynamic principles underlying T-group processes. In L. P. Bradford, J. R. Gibb, and K. D. Benne (Eds.), *T-group theory and laboratory method*. New York: John Wiley and Sons, 1964, 310–335.

Whitman, R. M., and Dorothy Stock. The group focal conflict. *Psychiatry*, 1958, **21**, 269–276.

Zinberg, N. E., and D. Shapiro. A group approach in the contexts of therapy and education. *Mental Hygiene*, 1963, **47**, 108–116.

Index